DAY HIKES AROUND

Sonoma County

95 GREAT HIKES

Robert Stone

Day Hike Books, Inc.

RED LODGE, MONTANA

Published by Day Hike Books, Inc.
P.O. Box 865
Red Lodge, Montana 59068

Distributed by The Globe Pequot Press
246 Goose Lane
P.O. Box 480
Guilford, CT 06437-0480
800-243-0495 (direct order) · 800-820-2329 (fax order)
www.globe-pequot.com

Photographs by Robert Stone
Design by Paula Doherty

The author has made every attempt to provide accurate information
in this book. However, trail routes and features may change—please
use common sense and forethought, and be mindful of your own
capabilities. Let this book guide you, but be aware that each hiker
assumes responsibility for their own safety. The author and publisher
do not assume any responsibility for loss, damage, or injury caused
through the use of this book.

Cover photo:
Stillwater Cove, Hike 21

Back cover photo:
View of Lake Sonoma from the South Lake Trail, Hike 46

LINDA STONE

hiking partner, Kofax Stone

Acknowledgements

*I wish to thank the following people who generously gave
of their time with enthusiasm, provided valuable information,
and whose assistance helped make this book a reality.
Your pride for Sonoma County is contagious.*

Mary Abbott, Laguna de Santa Rosa Foundation

Ranger D.J. "Deej" Beane, Jack London State Historic Park

Mark Belhumeur · Tim and Anna Cahill · George Carl

Mark Cleveland, Sonoma County Regional Parks

Scott Clyde · Catherine DePrima · Renata and Tom Dorn

June Douglas, Sonoma County Regional Parks

Joan Finkle and her 4-legged companions Ella and Honey

Scott and Juliana Galvin · Philip Hampton · Jan Harris · Keo Hornbostel

Joe Honton, Laguna de Santa Rosa Foundation

Nina Laramore, Laramore Communications · Lucy Lewand

Michele Luna, Stewards of the Coast and Redwoods

Rosemary McGinnis · Pamela Mendala · Kate Navarrette

Rosemary Pastore · Tyffani Peters, Wolf Communications

Wendy Peterson, Executive Director Sonoma Valley Visitor Bureau

Mo Renfro, Santa Rosa Visitor Bureau

Charlie Ristad, Sonoma County Regional Parks

Amie Rubenstein, Glodow Nead Communications

Silvia and Scott Simpson · James Soule · Leo Vrana

Barry and Kathryn Weiss

Susanne Woodrum, Sonoma County Economic Development Board

Table of Contents

THE HIKES

North Coast — Mendonoma:
North Sonoma Coast — South Mendocino Coast
Sea Ranch to Point Arena

Central Coast Sonoma County
Jenner to Sea Ranch

Southern Coast
Bodega Bay · Jenner

North Central Sonoma County
Guerneville • Forestville • Windsor • Lake Sonoma

Calistoga Area

Central Sonoma County
Santa Rosa • Sebastopol • Rohnert Park

Southern Sonoma County
Santa Rosa to Sonoma

Southern Sonoma County—Marin County line
Petaluma • Novato

Sonoma County and the Hikes

California's Sonoma County is known for its wineries and magnificent natural landscape—a picturesque mix of rugged coastline, steep cliffs, forested hillsides, and verdant agricultural valleys. The cities, towns, and villages are as diverse as the geography. In addition to the nearly 200 wineries, the county has thousands of acres of parkland, including 11 state parks and more than 40 regional parks.

Sonoma County is located 35 miles north of San Francisco via the Golden Gate Bridge. The county lies between the Pacific Ocean and the Mayacmas Mountains, the range that separates Sonoma and Napa counties. The wide variety of landscapes and microclimates can be attributed to Sonoma County's unique location between ocean and mountains.

This collection of 95 of the county's best day hikes provides access to both well known and out-of-the-way greenspace. Hikes are found along the Pacific, across the coastal ridges, into the wide valleys, and through thick forests. A third of the hikes are on the coastline, accessed by Highway 1. Many coastal access points that are not easily recognized from Highway 1 are clearly described. The remaining hikes explore the inland mountains, hillsides, and valleys through the many state parks and undeveloped land. Highlights include fog-shrouded redwood forests, creekside canyons, wildlife sanctuaries, lakes, tidal bays, wave-pounded coastline, and sweeping panoramic views.

The first 37 hikes are located along the coastline. The spectacular Sonoma coast stretches 58 miles from Bodega Bay to Gualala. Vertiginous Highway 1 connects the coastal towns as it snakes along the dramatic oceanfront cliffs and bluffs. There are breath-taking panoramas of the crashing surf, offshore rocks, and steep forested hills. The serpentine road passes old logging and fishing communities such as Bodega Bay, a historic fishing village with a marina; Jenner, at the mouth of the Russian River; Fort Ross, a Russian settlement dating back to 1812; Timber Cove, perched on the rugged cliffs; Stewarts Point, just north of Salt Point State Park; Sea Ranch, stretching over ten miles on a grassy marine terrace; and Gualala, just across the northern border in Mendocino County.

The rich inland valleys are perfectly suited for vineyards and farms, which stretch across the county's rolling hills. The Russian River basin nourishes the area, winding through the county from Cloverdale to the ocean at Jenner. The river's meandering course flows from valleys to forests to the dramatic coastline. Hikes 38—95 are located in inland Sonoma County along the Mayacmas. Less populated northern Sonoma County is home to Austin Creek and Lake Sonoma State Recreation Areas—Hikes 38 through 49. Traveling farther south leads to Santa Rosa, the largest city in Sonoma County. Its central location offers easy access to nearly every area in the county. On the east side of the city is a string of connecting parks covering thousands of acres. Hikes 50—76 are a short drive from the city and include the beautiful Annadel State Park and Sugarloaf Ridge State Park.

Between Santa Rosa and San Pablo Bay are the towns of Sonoma, Rohnert Park, Petaluma, and Novato. Several additional state and regional parks are scattered throughout the area, including Jack London State Historic Park and Mount Burdell Open Space Preserve. The entire region is part of the expansive San Pablo Bay watershed, giving rise to many migratory routes for birds. Hikes 77—95 are located in this area.

A quick glance at the hikes' summaries will allow you to choose a hike that is appropriate to your ability and desire. An overall map on the next page identifies the general locations of the hikes and major roads. Several other regional maps (underlined in the table of contents), as well as maps for each hike, provide the essential details. Relevant maps are listed under the hikes' statistics if you wish to explore more of the area.

The main driving routes are Highway 101 and Highway 1. Highway 101 is the major north-south freeway through the center of the county, connecting San Francisco to Mendocino County. Highway 1 follows along the coastline from Los Angeles to the northern end of the state. Other key routes within the county are Highway 12, through Sonoma Valley, and Highway 116, from Highway 101 to the coast.

A few basic necessities will make your hike more pleasurable. Wear supportive, comfortable hiking shoes and layered clothing. Take along hats, sunscreen, sunglasses, drinking water, snacks, and appropriate outerwear. Use good judgement about your capabilities—reference the hiking statistics for an approximation of difficulty, allowing extra time for exploration. Enjoy your hike!

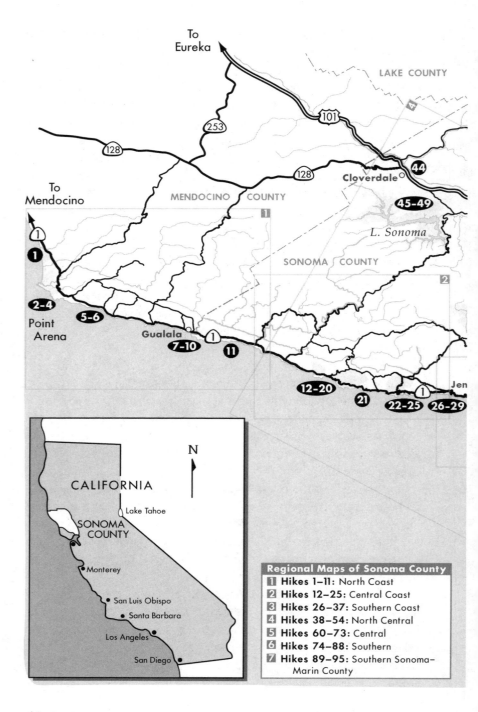

To
Eureka

LAKE COUNTY

253

101

128

To
Mendocino

MENDOCINO COUNTY

128 Cloverdale

44

45-49

L. Sonoma

1

1

SONOMA COUNTY

2

2-4

5-6

Point
Arena

Gualala

7-10

1

11

12-20

21

22-25 26-29

Jen

N

CALIFORNIA

Lake Tahoe

SONOMA
COUNTY

Monterey

San Luis Obispo

Santa Barbara

Los Angeles

San Diego

Regional Maps of Sonoma County
1 **Hikes 1–11:** North Coast
2 **Hikes 12–25:** Central Coast
3 **Hikes 26–37:** Southern Coast
4 **Hikes 38–54:** North Central
5 **Hikes 60–73:** Central
6 **Hikes 74–88:** Southern
7 **Hikes 89–95:** Southern Sonoma–
   Marin County

MAP of the HIKES
SONOMA COUNTY and VICINITY

Master Map

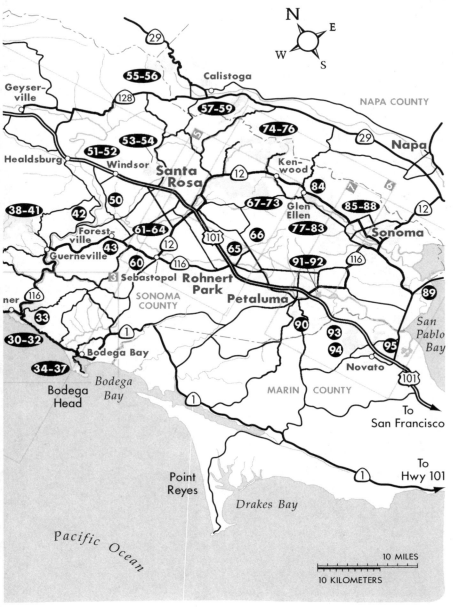

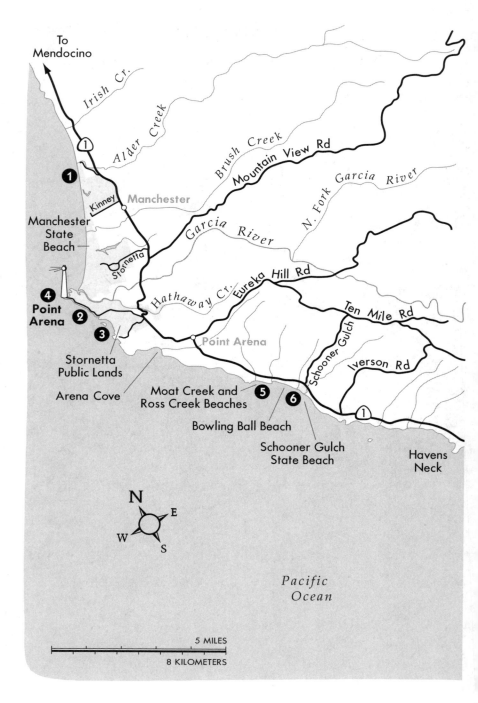

To
Mendocino

Irish Cr.

Alder Creek

1

❶

Kinney

Manchester

Brush Creek

Mountain View Rd

N. Fork Garcia River

Manchester
State
Beach

Stornetta

Garcia River

Hathaway Cr.

Eureka Hill Rd

Ten Mile Rd

❹

Point
Arena

❷

❸

Point Arena

Schooner Gulch

Iverson Rd

Stornetta
Public Lands

Arena Cove

Moat Creek and
Ross Creek Beaches

❺

❻

1

Bowling Ball Beach

Schooner Gulch
State Beach

Havens
Neck

N
E
W
S

Pacific
Ocean

5 MILES

8 KILOMETERS

North Coast: Mendonoma
NORTH SONOMA COAST– SOUTH MENDOCINO COAST

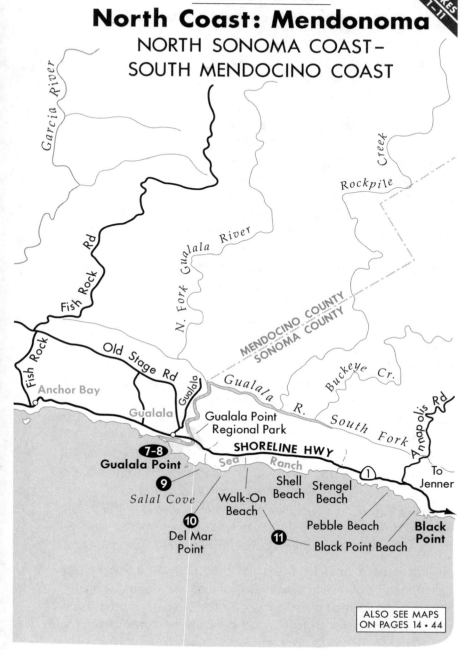

Garcia River

Rockpile Creek

Gualala River

N. Fork Gualala River

Fish Rock Rd

Fish Rock

Old Stage Rd

Fish Rock

Anchor Bay

Gualala

Gualala

MENDOCINO COUNTY
SONOMA COUNTY

Buckeye Cr.

Gualala R.

South Fork

Annapolis Rd

Gualala Point
Regional Park

SHORELINE HWY

Gualala Point

7-8

Sea Ranch

1

To Jenner

9

Salal Cove

Walk-On Beach

Shell Beach

Stengel Beach

10

Del Mar Point

Pebble Beach

Black Point

11

Black Point Beach

ALSO SEE MAPS
ON PAGES 14 • 44

1. Manchester State Beach
ALDER CREEK to KINNEY ROAD

Hiking distance: 2.5 miles round trip
Hiking time: 1.5 hours
Elevation gain: 50 feet
Maps: U.S.G.S. Point Arena and Mallo Pass Creek

Summary of hike: Manchester State Beach is between Point Arena and the town of Manchester in Mendocino County. The large beach encompasses 1,400 acres with ponds, bluffs, grass-covered dunes, and five miles of dramatic sandy coastline. It is the closest point to Hawaii on North America. Alder Creek borders the state beach to the north, where the San Andreas Fault runs into the Pacific Ocean. At the mouth of the creek is a fresh-water lagoon inhabited by migratory waterfowl. The Garcia River flows into the sea at the southern border. This hike begins at Alder Creek and strolls south along the isolated dune-backed beach scattered with giant driftwood logs. Horses and dogs are allowed.

Driving directions: From Gualala, just north of the Sonoma County line, drive 21 miles north on Highway 1 (the Shoreline Highway) to posted Alder Creek Road at mile marker 22.48. The turnoff is located 7 miles north of Point Arena and 2 miles north of Manchester. Turn left and drive 0.7 miles to the trailhead at the end of the road.

Two additional roads access the state beach. The southern access is on Stoneboro Road at mile marker 19.65. Turn left and drive 1.6 miles to the parking area at the end of the road.

The central access is on Kinney Road at mile marker 21.48. Turn left and drive 1.1 miles to the trailhead at the end of the road. En route, the road passes the Manchester Beach KOA on the right.

Hiking directions: From the north end of Manchester State Beach, head down the dunes and toward the ocean along the large lagoon formed by Alder Creek. Curve south on the sandy beach, passing piles of driftwood beneath the steep cliffs. The eroding cliffs begin to fade into low dunes along this isolated

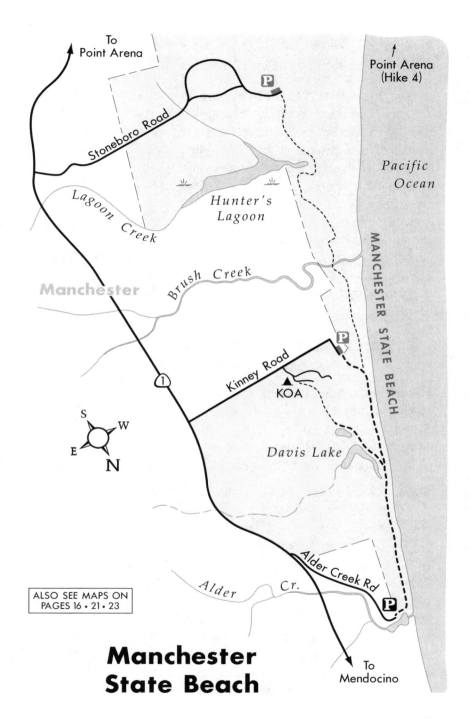

To
Point Arena

↑
Point Arena
(Hike 4)

P

Stoneboro Road

Pacific Ocean

Lagoon Creek

Hunter's Lagoon

MANCHESTER STATE BEACH

Brush Creek

Manchester

P

① Kinney Road

▲ KOA

Davis Lake

S W
E
N

Alder Creek Rd

Alder Cr.

P

ALSO SEE MAPS ON
PAGES 16 • 21 • 23

Manchester
State Beach

To
Mendocino

stretch of coastline. At 0.6 miles is a broad, open draw heading inland. Up the draw 150 yards is Davis Lake. A marked side trail follows the south side of the long and narrow lake, leading through the wetlands to the KOA campground. Back at the shoreline, continue south along the beach, with a view of Point Arena and the lighthouse. As the dunes begin to grow in size, watch for a distinct trail channel in the cliffs. Head up the channel to the bluffs. Walk through the tall grass overlooking the coast. Curve east to the trailhead parking lot at the end of Kinney Road. Return by retracing your steps.

To extend the hike, the trail continues south along the coastal dunes. The mouth of Brush Creek is in a half mile and Hunter's Lagoon, tucked into the dunes, is at just under a mile. Ascend the 80-foot dunes for a view of the narrow, mile-long lagoon. The trail leads to the parking area at the end of Stoneboro Road at 1.5 miles.■

2. Garcia River and the Northern Bluffs
STORNETTA PUBLIC LANDS

Hiking distance: 2.5 miles round trip
Hiking time: 1.5 hours
Elevation gain: 50 feet
Maps: U.S.G.S. Point Arena
        Bureau of Land Management Stornetta Public Lands map

**map
page 23**

Summary of hike: The Stornetta Public Lands encompass 1,132 acres on the southern Mendocino County coast, north of the town of Point Arena. The land, with two miles of jagged coastline, lies adjacent to the Point Arena Lighthouse (Hike 4) and Manchester State Beach (Hike 1). The Garcia River (named for Rafael Garcia who built a mill here in 1869) flows through the property and enters the ocean just north of the lighthouse peninsula. The river runs along the San Andreas Fault zone and forms an estuary in the valley. It is a wintering habitat for tundra swans and also supports silver salmon and steelhead trout. This hike follows the bluffs between the river and the lighthouse to the oceanfront. At the turbulent sea, the weather-carved bluffs form a

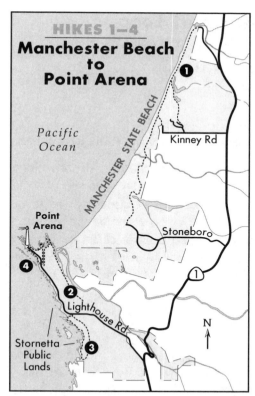

HIKES 1—4
Manchester Beach to Point Arena

series of narrow finger-like peninsulas and pocket coves. Dogs are allowed.

Driving directions:
From Gualala, just north of the Sonoma County line, drive 16 miles north on Highway 1 (the Shoreline Highway) to Lighthouse Road on the left at mile marker 17.00. Lighthouse Road is located 2 miles north of Point Arena and 3.5 miles south of Manchester. Turn left and drive 1.4 miles to the posted pull-out on the left at the far end of the grove of cypress trees.

Hiking directions: Walk a quarter mile back up the Lighthouse Road to the gated dirt road on the left (north). Pass through the trailhead gate, and head north on the two-track road. Stroll through the old corral and loading chute site. Veer left, crossing the pastureland to the west end of a cypress grove. Continue past the grove to the bluffs above the Garcia River. Follow the edge of the bluffs, overlooking the river basin. Near the ocean, the Garcia River forms a huge lagoon bounded by a sandbar covered in downfall logs. A channel on the southwest side of the arroyo is open to the sea. Follow the bluffs to the dramatic oceanfront cliffs. Pass the narrow finger-like peninsulas and pocket coves toward the Point Arena Lighthouse. Weave along the chiseled terrain, dotted with offshore rocks, while marveling at the seascape. Return by retracing your route or by following Lighthouse Road 0.8 miles to the trailhead.■

3. Southern Bluff Loop
STORNETTA PUBLIC LANDS

Hiking distance: 1.6 miles round trip
Hiking time: 1 hour
Elevation gain: Level
Maps: U.S.G.S. Point Arena
Bureau of Land Management Stornetta Public Lands map

Summary of hike: The Stornetta Public Lands stretch along two miles of awesome, weathered coastline surrounding the Point Arena Lighthouse. The bucolic land includes riparian corridors, extensive wetlands, ponds, cypress and pine groves, sand dunes, and meadows. The crenulated coastal cliffs are riddled with sea caves, endless sea stacks, natural rock arches, embayments, a blow-hole, the Sea Lion Rocks, and the historic lighthouse. This hike follows the coastline south of the lighthouse, overlooking the crashing surf from 80-foot bluffs. Dogs are allowed.

Driving directions: From Gualala, just north of the Sonoma County line, drive 16 miles north on Highway 1 (the Shoreline Highway) to Lighthouse Road on the left at mile marker 17.00. Lighthouse Road is located 2 miles north of Point Arena and 3.5 miles south of Manchester. Turn left and drive 1.4 miles to the posted pullout on the left at the far end of the grove of cypress trees.

Hiking directions: Pass through the entrance gate to the south-facing oceanfront cliffs. Walk out on the peninsula to the west, and cross over a natural arch, passing tidepools below. Curve along the bluffs, overlooking the caves and the flat, grassy plateau of Sea Lion Rocks. Pass old pier pilings and follow the vertical cliffs to stunning sea stacks and a natural bridge spanning the ocean. The public land ends a short distance ahead by a fenceline and a group of homes. Return along the bluffs or follow one of the inland routes, forming a loop. ■

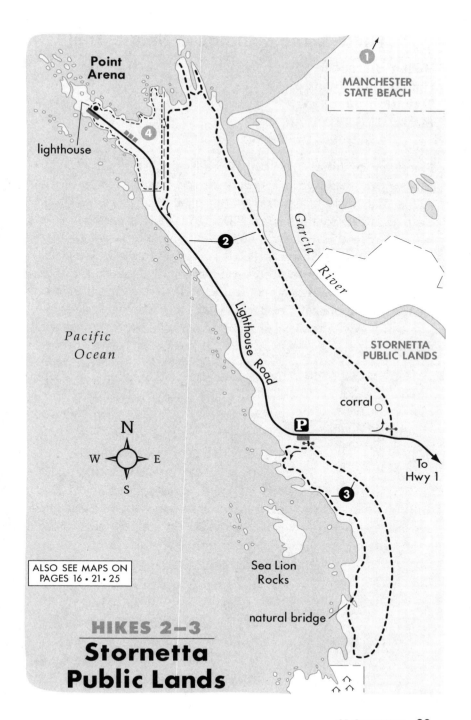

Point
Arena

lighthouse

④

MANCHESTER
STATE BEACH

①

②

Garcia River

*Pacific
Ocean*

Lighthouse Road

STORNETTA
PUBLIC LANDS

corral

P

To
Hwy 1

③

N
W · E
S

ALSO SEE MAPS ON
PAGES 16 · 21 · 25

Sea Lion
Rocks

natural bridge

HIKES 2–3
Stornetta
Public Lands

4. Point Arena Lighthouse Nature Trail

Hiking distance: 0.7-mile loop
Hiking time: 30 minutes
Elevation gain: Level
Maps: U.S.G.S. Point Arena
　　　　Point Arena Lighthouse map

Summary of hike: The Point Arena Lighthouse sits on a long, narrow peninsula two miles north of the quaint town of Point Arena. The original brick and mortar lighthouse from 1870 was destroyed in the catastrophic 1906 San Francisco earthquake. It was rebuilt and now stands at 115 feet. The site is completely surrounded by the Stornetta Public Lands (Hikes 2 & 3). The lighthouse offers docent-led tours and has a small museum. The tour climbs 145 stairs, an equivalent to six stories. From the top of the lighthouse is a dramatic bird's-eye view of the amazing geography and a view into Devil's Punchbowl, a huge sinkhole near the

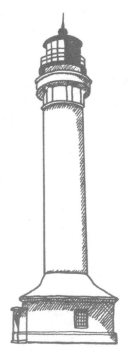

end of the peninsula. The movie *Forever Young* with Mel Gibson was filmed here in 1992. The producers built a gazebo on the bluffs, which still remains. This hike circles the perimeter of the property atop the coastal terrace surrounding the point. Cormorants, sea lions, and harbor seals can be seen on the coast and offshore rocks just south of the point. This is also a great place to observe migrating gray whales from December through April.

Driving directions: From Gualala, just north of the Sonoma County line, drive 16 miles north on Highway 1 (the Shoreline Highway) to Lighthouse Road on the left at mile marker 17.00. Lighthouse Road is located 2 miles north of Point Arena and 3.5

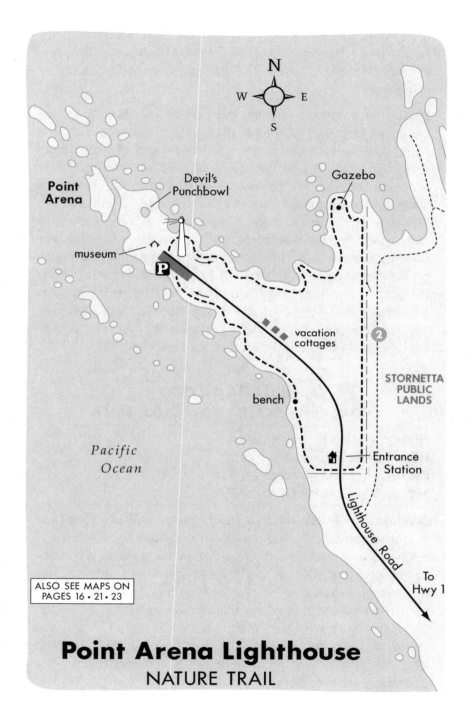

Point Arena

Devil's Punchbowl

Gazebo

museum

P

vacation cottages

bench

Pacific Ocean

STORNETTA PUBLIC LANDS

Entrance Station

Lighthouse Road

To Hwy 1

ALSO SEE MAPS ON
PAGES 16 • 21 • 23

Point Arena Lighthouse
NATURE TRAIL

miles south of Manchester. Turn left and drive 2.2 miles to the Point Arena Lighthouse entrance. Continue 0.2 miles to the parking area on the left, adjacent to the lighthouse. An entrance fee is required.

Hiking directions: Take the path on the north edge of the peninsula, following the white fence on the edge of the eroding cliffs. Continue past deep coves and overlooks of the offshore rocks to the gazebo at the northeast corner of the lighthouse property. Loop around the finger of land, with great views of the lighthouse and northern coastal vistas. Follow the edge of the Stornetta Public Lands (Hike 2). Pass a gated entrance to the open space, and continue across the flat grasslands to Lighthouse Road by the entrance station. Cross the road to the south edge of the peninsula, with endless offshore formations and the Sea Lion Rocks. Bear right and follow the scalloped bluffs. Benches are interspersed along the trail to enjoy the steadily changing vistas. Look for sea lions on the offshore rocks. Pass the vacation cottages and complete the loop at the lighthouse. ■

5. Bluff Top Loop
MOAT CREEK BEACH • ROSS CREEK BEACH

Hiking distance: 1.2-mile loop
Hiking time: 45 minutes
Elevation gain: 90 feet
Maps: U.S.G.S. Point Arena

Summary of hike: Perennial Moat Creek and Ross Creek flow from the coastal hills into the ocean between Point Arena and Anchor Bay. Oceanfront bluffs separate the two sandy beach coves. Atop the 90-foot bluffs is a little known community trail that is maintained by volunteers. The loop trail circles the perimeter of the bluffs, connecting the two sheltered beach coves. En route, the trail passes a cormorant rookery. The blufftop meadow is also the site of the defunct Whiskey Shoals subdivision. This hike begins at Moat Creek Beach and follows the oceanfront cliffs to Ross Creek Beach.

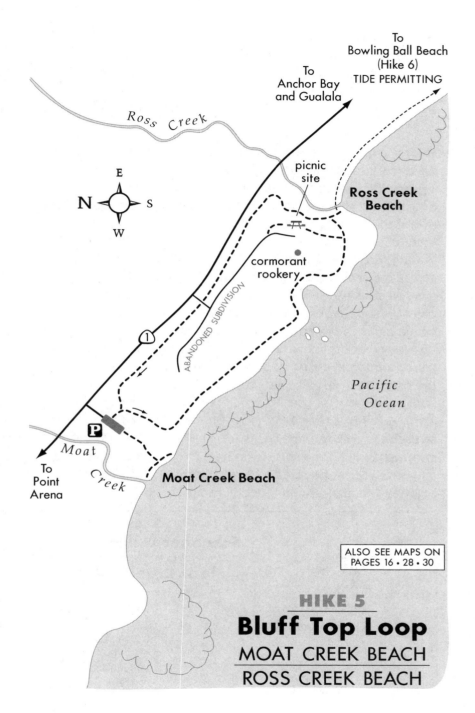

To
Bowling Ball Beach
(Hike 6)
TIDE PERMITTING

To
Anchor Bay
and Gualala

Ross Creek

picnic
site

**Ross Creek
Beach**

N ⊕ S
E
W

cormorant
rookery

ABANDONED SUBDIVISION

①

*Pacific
Ocean*

P

Moat

To
Point
Arena

Creek

Moat Creek Beach

ALSO SEE MAPS ON
PAGES 16 • 28 • 30

HIKE 5

Bluff Top Loop
MOAT CREEK BEACH
ROSS CREEK BEACH

Driving directions: From Gualala, just north of the Sonoma County line, drive 12 miles north on Highway 1 (the Shoreline Highway) to the posted Moat Creek turnoff on the left at mile marker 12.88. The turnoff is located 8.5 miles north of Anchor Bay and 2 miles south of Point Arena. Turn left and park in the large dirt lot.

Hiking directions: The trail at the far southwest end of the parking lot leads 200 yards to Moat Creek Beach, a popular surfing and tidepooling beach in a sheltered cove. From the east side of the parking lot, take the posted trail and begin the loop on the right fork, hiking counter-clockwise. Climb the hillside to the grass-covered bluffs and the edge of the 90-foot bluff overlooking Moat Creek Beach. Head southeast, with amazing vistas across the scalloped coastline, the grassy coastal terraces, and the forested hills. Curve around a deep, vertical-walled cove, passing the cormorant rookery on the left. At the southeast end of the bluffs is a junction overlooking Ross Creek Beach. The left fork stays atop the bluffs to a picnic site in a pine forest and a paved road from the abandoned subdivision. Continue straight on the right fork, and descend steps into the gulch and a junction. Detour on the right fork to Ross Creek Beach. (During low tide, Bowling Ball Beach—Hike 6—can be reached by following the sandy beach beneath the bluffs for a half mile south.) Return and continue on the north fork, weaving through a pine grove on the spongy needle-covered path. Curve north and parallel Highway 1, completing the loop at Moat Creek. ■

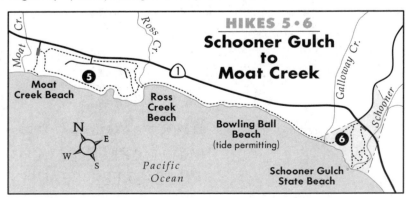

6. Schooner Gulch State Beach and Bowling Ball Beach

Hiking distance: 1 mile round trip
Hiking time: 40 minutes
Elevation gain: 80 feet
Maps: U.S.G.S. Saunders Reef and Point Arena

map
page 30

Summary of hike: Schooner Gulch State Beach covers 53 acres of undeveloped state park land between Point Arena and Anchor Bay. The state beach is a protected cove tucked between towering cliffs with a small creek, tidepools, wave-carved formations, and driftwood. A quarter-mile trail descends through a redwood-filled ravine to Schooner Gulch Beach. To the north, another trail crosses the 80-foot windswept bluffs to overlooks of Schooner Gulch and continues north along the beach to Bowling Ball Beach. The beach was named for its smooth spherical boulders. The embedded sedimentary rocks, called concretions, formed in concentric layers along the exposed cliffs. Eventually they fell from the eroding cliffs to the beach below. This garden of finely ground geological formations sits at the base of the cliffs but can only be seen during low, minus tides. There is no direct access to Bowling Ball Beach from the bluffs. However, the beach can be accessed from Moat Creek along the base of the cliffs, located 1.4 miles north (Hike 5), or from Schooner Gulch, a half mile south. Dogs are allowed.

Driving directions: From Gualala, just north of the Sonoma County line, drive 10.6 miles north on Highway 1 (the Shoreline Highway) to Schooner Gulch, directly opposite Schooner Gulch Road at mile marker 11.41. The parking pullout is on the west (ocean) side of the road just north of the concrete bridge crossing over the gulch. The pullout is located 7 miles north of Anchor Bay and 3.4 miles south of Point Arena.

Hiking directions: Begin the loop on the north trail atop the pine-dotted bluffs just north of Schooner Gulch. At the Y-fork, take the right fork to the oceanfront cliffs. Descend to the right on a wooden staircase to a jumble of rocks and driftwood at the

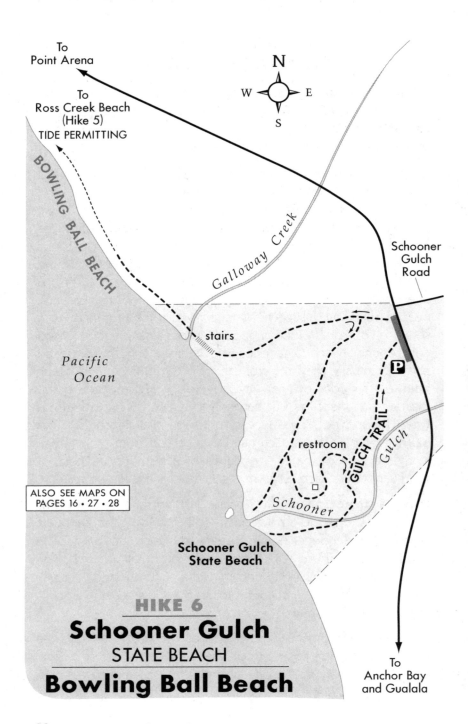

To
Point Arena

To
Ross Creek Beach
(Hike 5)
TIDE PERMITTING

N
W E
S

BOWLING BALL BEACH

Pacific
Ocean

Galloway Creek

Schooner
Gulch
Road

stairs

P

GULCH TRAIL

Gulch

restroom

Schooner

ALSO SEE MAPS ON
PAGES 16 • 27 • 28

Schooner Gulch
State Beach

To
Anchor Bay
and Gualala

HIKE 6

Schooner Gulch
STATE BEACH

Bowling Ball Beach

mouth of Galloway Creek. Cross the rocks to the sandy beach, and head north along the base of the 80-foot striated cliffs. Bowling Ball Beach, with the prehistoric spherical boulders, resides a quarter mile ahead, but the boulders are only visible during minus tides. After exploring the orb-like rocks in the parallel grooves and ridges along the cliffs, return to the first junction near the trailhead. Take the right fork and cross the grassy bluffs to a Y-fork overlooking Schooner Gulch Beach. The right fork stays atop the grassy bluffs to the headland that protects the beach. Descend on the left fork, and weave down to the Gulch Trail. Bear right and descend to the mouth of the creek and the sandy beach cove. The creek spills onto the beach strand and enters the sea at the base of the northern cliffs. Return a quarter mile up the Gulch Trail in a shaded redwood forest with an understory of ferns, completing the loop at Highway 1. ■

7. Gualala River Trail
GUALALA POINT REGIONAL PARK

Hiking distance: 2.4 miles round trip
Hiking time: 1 hour
Elevation gain: 80 feet
Maps: U.S.G.S. Gualala
　　　　 Gualala Point Regional Park map

map
page 33

Summary of hike: The mouth of the Gualala River lies on the Mendocino-Sonoma county line. The river flows north and south, parallel to the coast, along the San Andreas fault line. Just to the north of the river is the town of Gualala, a former logging town. On the south side of the river mouth is Gualala Point Regional Park. Gualala (pronounced *wa-LA-la*) is the Pomo Indian word for where the waters meet. This hike follows the elbow of the river on the Sonoma County side. The trail begins in the Gualala Point Campground and weaves through a shady forest with redwoods, bay laurels, alders, rhododendrons, and sword ferns. The path skirts the protected estuary, a prime bird habitat, as it leads to overlooks of Gualala, the mountains, and the river. The hike ends on the extensive driftwood-strewn sandy beach and sandspit, where the river empties into the ocean.

Driving directions: From Gualala, just north of the Sonoma County line, drive one mile south on Highway 1, crossing over the Gualala River, to the posted Gualala Point Regional Park turnoff on the right at mile marker 58.20. Turn left (inland)—directly across from the park entrance—and drive 0.7 miles to the Gualala Point Campground. Park in the day use parking spaces on the right by the map kiosk. A parking fee is required.

The turnoff is located 7.6 miles north of the Sea Ranch Lodge.

Hiking directions: Walk to the south end of the campground road under a dense redwood forest to the signed trail. Skirt the edge of the Gualala River through the lush forest with gnarled bay laurel. Cross a bridge over a water channel, and emerge in a grassy clearing with tall brush. Walk under Highway 1, following the course of the river in an open meadow. Leave the grassy river flat and traverse the hillside, climbing to the blufftop and over-look. Savor the picture-perfect view of the river flowing out of the forested mountains and along the town of Gualala. The trail soon joins the park road at a picnic area. Continue along the road a short distance to the park visitor center. To extend the hike to the beach and oceanfront bluffs, continue with Hike 8.■

8. Whale Watch Point Loop
GUALALA POINT REGIONAL PARK

Hiking distance: 2-mile loop
Hiking time: 1 hour
Elevation gain: Level
Maps: U.S.G.S. Gualala
Gualala Point Regional Park map

Summary of hike: Gualala Point Regional Park is located at the northwest corner of Sonoma County between the town of Gualala and the Sea Ranch residential community. The oceanfront park encompasses 103 acres along the southern banks of the

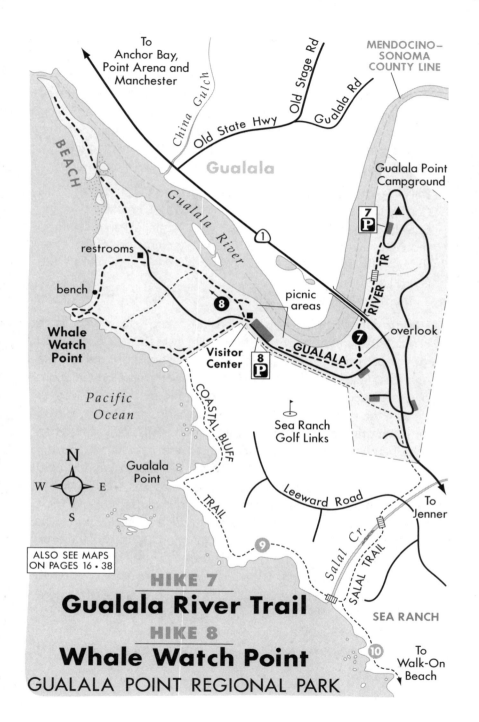

To Anchor Bay, Point Arena and Manchester

MENDOCINO–SONOMA COUNTY LINE

China Gulch

Old Stage Rd

Gualala Rd

Old State Hwy

Gualala

Gualala River

BEACH

(1)

Gualala Point Campground

7 P

RIVER TR

restrooms

bench

picnic areas

8

Whale Watch Point

Visitor Center

8 P

GUALALA

7

overlook

Pacific Ocean

COASTAL BLUFF TRAIL

Sea Ranch Golf Links

N

W E

S

Gualala Point

Leeward Road

To Jenner

Salal Cr.

SALAL TRAIL

ALSO SEE MAPS ON PAGES 16 • 38

9

SEA RANCH

HIKE 7

Gualala River Trail

HIKE 8

Whale Watch Point

GUALALA POINT REGIONAL PARK

10

To Walk-On Beach

Gualala River. Within the park's boundary are a variety of habitats, including redwood forests, a protected estuary, oceanfront bluffs, a marine terrace with old Monterey cypress groves, a freshwater marsh, sand dunes, and a sandy beach at the mouth of the Gualala River. This hike circles the peninsula along the Gualala River and the Pacific Ocean. Grass and dirt paths branch off the paved path to blufftop overlooks at Whale Watch Point, a rocky, windswept promontory.

Driving directions: From Gualala, just north of the Sonoma County line, drive one mile south on Highway 1, crossing over the Gualala River, to the posted Gualala Point Regional Park turnoff on the right at mile marker 58.20. Turn right and drive 0.6 miles through the park to the visitor center parking lot. A parking fee is required.

The turnoff is located 7.6 miles north of the Sea Ranch Lodge.

Hiking directions: From the visitor center, a paved path crosses the grassy bluffs to the beach. Instead, take the signed grassy path to the right. Descend and pass a short trail on the right that leads through laurel trees to a picnic area on the shore of the Gualala River. Follow the north edge of the bluffs, overlooking the river and the town of Gualala. Merge with the paved path and stay to the right. The paved path ends a short distance ahead and continues as a sand path to the oceanfront and the mouth of the Gualala River. Return to the junction and continue 50 yards south on the paved path. At the restrooms, veer right and take the grassy path along the oceanfront bluffs, with viewing benches of Whale Watch Point. Pass through a cypress tree tunnel to a vista of Gualala Point and a junction. Detour to the right and circle Whale Watch Point, the rocky promontory. Continue south, weaving through a shaded cypress grove to the north boundary of Sea Ranch and a junction. The Coastal Bluff Trail continues into Sea Ranch to Salal Cove (Hike 9) and Walk-On Beach (Hike 10). Bear left and head inland. Stay in the park on the south edge of a meadow along a row of pine trees, returning to the visitor center. ■

9. Coastal Bluff Trail • Salal Cove
GUALALA POINT REGIONAL PARK • SEA RANCH

Hiking distance: 2.8-mile loop
Hiking time: 1.5 hours
Elevation gain: 100 feet
Maps: U.S.G.S. Gualala and Stewarts Point
      The Sea Ranch Trails Map

map
page 38

Summary of hike: The Salal Trail was a seasonal route of the Pomo Indians from their inland camps to a sheltered ocean site near Salal Cove. Gorgeous sculpted rock formations surround the deep U-shaped cove. The Salal Trail follows a heavily vegetated stream-fed ravine to the cove and coastal bluffs. The trail weaves through the lush shaded glen with bishop pines, Monterey cypress, redwoods, red alders, and Pacific wax myrtle. Along the way is a rotunda of redwoods with a waterfall and pool. This hike begins in Gualala Point Regional Park and forms a loop along the coastline with the Sea Ranch public access trail.

Driving directions: From Gualala, just north of the Sonoma County line, drive one mile south on Highway 1, crossing over the Gualala River, to the posted Gualala Point Regional Park turnoff on the right at mile marker 58.20. Turn right and drive 0.6 miles through the park to the visitor center parking lot. A parking fee is required.

The turnoff is located 7.6 miles north of the Sea Ranch Lodge.

Hiking directions: From the visitor center, take the posted Beach Trail along the park's south boundary on the edge of the Sea Ranch Golf Links. Stroll through a hedgerow of towering pines on the south edge of a meadow. At a quarter mile, the grassy path reaches a posted junction at the oceanfront cliffs between Whale Watch Point and Gualala Point. The right fork leads 0.2 miles to Whale Watch Point and 0.6 miles to the beach (Hike 8). Bear left and leave the park into Sea Ranch on the Coastal Bluff Trail, a public access trail. The serpentine path follows the eroding bluffs through pockets of cypress trees. Loop around Gualala Point, with views of the Gualala Point Islands, and pass through a dark tunnel of cypress trees. One mile beyond the park, descend into Salal Cove. Cross a wooden bridge over Salal Creek to a T-junction. The right fork continues on the bluffs 2.2 miles to Walk-On Beach (Hike 10). Bear left on the Salal Trail, and head inland through a lush stream-fed draw with ferns, lichen, and moss-covered rocks. Follow the south edge of the waterway, passing a natural rock-lined pool and a waterfall in a redwood-filled grotto. Cross a bridge to the north side of the stream and follow the watercourse. Cross Leeward Road and continue along the drainage. Climb steps and curve left, parallel Highway 1, and cross the Sea Ranch Golf Links road to the Gualala Point Regional Park entrance. Bear left into the park and skirt the edge of the golf course, returning to the visitor center.■

10. Coastal Bluff Trail:
Salal Trail to Walk-On Beach
GUALALA POINT REGIONAL PARK • SEA RANCH

Hiking distance: 6 miles round trip
Hiking time: 3 hours
Elevation gain: 100 feet
Maps: U.S.G.S. Gualala and Stewarts Point
　　　　The Sea Ranch Trails Map

map
page 38

Summary of hike: The Coastal Bluff Trail follows scalloped sandstone bluffs along the ocean in the Sea Ranch residential community. It is the only portion of coastline on the 10-mile-long stretch of the Sea Ranch that allows public access. The trail is connected to Highway 1 on both ends by the Salal Trail and the Walk-On Beach Trail. The Salal Trail leads through a riparian, stream-fed ravine with redwood groves, a waterfall, and pool. It connects to the Coastal Bluff Trail by Salal Cove, a deep cove with sculpted rock formations. The serpentine Coastal Bluff Trail hugs the coastline past stands of Monterey cypress, a series of coves and points with offshore rocks, Del Mar Point, and a coastal state ecological reserve. This is a great area to observe migrating whales from November through March.

Driving directions: From Gualala, just north of the Sonoma County line, drive one mile south on Highway 1, crossing over the Gualala River, to the posted Gualala Point Regional Park turnoff on the right at mile marker 58.20. Turn right and drive 0.1 mile to the entrance station, and park in the spaces on the left. Additional parking is located directly across from the park entrance. A parking fee is required.

The turnoff is located 7.6 miles north of the Sea Ranch Lodge.

Hiking directions: Walk back to Highway 1 and follow the mowed path, parallel to the highway. Cross the Sea Ranch Golf Links entrance road, and curve right into the stream-fed canyon. Descend steps and follow the watercourse through bishop pine, Douglas fir, alder, and madrone. Cross Leeward Road and follow the north side of the stream. Cross a bridge over the creek to a waterfall in a lush redwood-filled grotto and a natural rock-lined pool. Continue along the south edge of the mossy, fern-lined stream to a junction with the Coastal Bluff Trail at gorgeous Salal Cove. To access the cove, cross the footbridge over the creek to the right, and immediately bear left to the sandy, rock-walled pocket beach fronting the sea stacks. (To the right the trail leads one mile to Gualala Point Regional Park—Hike 9.) For this hike, continue southeast on the Coastal Bluff Trail. Climb steps and emerge on the oceanfront bluffs. Head south along the scalloped coastline with offshore rocks. Weave along the cliffs, curving around coves and passing through dense stands of cypress trees. Cross a bridge over a stream to a stunning rock-walled cove with rounded rocks and driftwood. Pass honeycombed sandstone formations, known as tafoni, and a cove with sea caves. Several more rock formations lie offshore at Del Mar Point at the state ecological reserve. Curve around Del Mar Cove, leaving the reserve, and pass through a mature cypress grove. Cross three more bridges and skirt the west edge of a huge meadow to a posted junction at a cypress grove. Straight ahead, the trail leads 0.2 miles to Walk-On Beach, currently closed due to severe erosion that washed out the trail. The left fork leads 0.3 miles to the Walk-On Beach trailhead at Highway 1. Return by retracing your steps. ∎

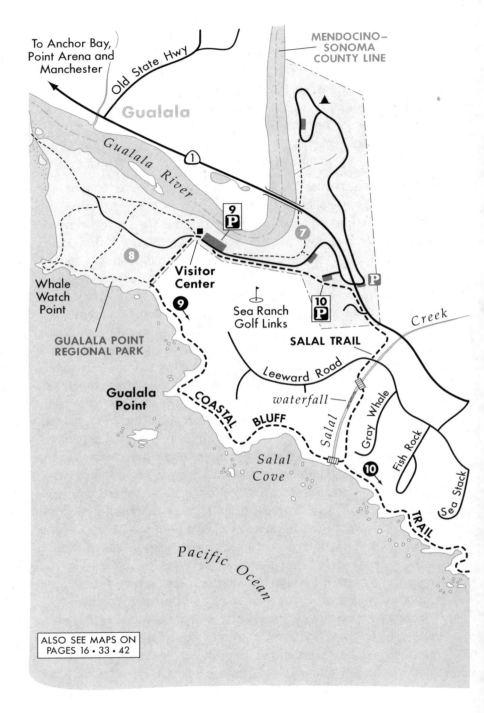

To Anchor Bay,
Point Arena and
Manchester

Old State Hwy

MENDOCINO–
SONOMA
COUNTY LINE

Gualala

Gualala River

1

9 P

7

8

Visitor
Center

9

Whale
Watch
Point

Sea Ranch
Golf Links

10 P

P

Creek

GUALALA POINT
REGIONAL PARK

SALAL TRAIL

Gualala
Point

Leeward Road

COASTAL

BLUFF

waterfall

Salal

Gray Whale

Fish Rock

Salal
Cove

10

Sea Stack

TRAIL

Pacific Ocean

ALSO SEE MAPS ON
PAGES 16 · 33 · 42

Coastal Bluff Trail • Salal Cove
Coastal Bluff Trail:
Salal Trail to Walk-On Beach
GUALALA POINT REGIONAL PARK
SEA RANCH

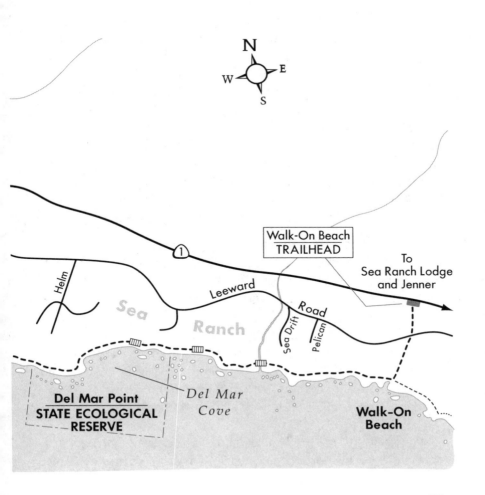

11. Sea Ranch Beaches
ACCESS TRAILS

Hiking distance: 0.4—1.4 miles round trip
Elevation gain: Nearly level
Maps: U.S.G.S. Stewarts Point
 The Sea Ranch Trails Map

map
page 42

Summary of hike: The Sea Ranch has an amazing trail system stretching over ten miles along the dramatic coastline. Within the development's 5,000 acres is a network of more than 45 miles of interconnecting trails that weave through the inland forests and coastal terrace. Unfortunately, the public is only allowed on a court-enforced 3.2 miles of coastal bluffs at the north end of the development (Hike 10) and these beach access trails. A legal battle led to the creation of the California Coastal Commission and the State Coastal Conservancy. To access the extensive trail system, you must rent or own one of the Sea Ranch homes. Otherwise, the public is allowed on a generous five miles of trails. Five short beach-access trails cross the blufftop meadows from Highway 1 to the sandy beach coves with a myriad of offshore rocks. The paths range in length from 0.2 miles to 0.6 miles. Sea Ranch security will issue tickets if you walk beyond these paths. Dogs are allowed on the trails but must be leashed.

Driving directions: The trailheads are listed from north to south. All five trailheads are well-marked and have paved parking lots with restrooms. A parking fee is required.

WALK-ON BEACH TRAIL: 1.7 miles south of Gualala Point Regional Park and 5.9 miles north of Sea Ranch Lodge at mile marker 56.53.

SHELL BEACH TRAIL: 3.0 miles south of Gualala Point Regional Park and 4.6 miles north of Sea Ranch Lodge at mile marker 55.20.

STENGEL BEACH TRAIL: 4.2 miles south of Gualala Point Regional Park and 3.4 miles north of Sea Ranch Lodge at mile marker 53.96. Turn west on Wild Iris and quickly turn right again into the posted parking lot.

PEBBLE BEACH TRAIL: 5.9 miles south of Gualala Point Regional Park and 1.7 miles north of Sea Ranch Lodge at mile marker 52.32.

BLACK POINT TRAIL: 7.35 miles south of Gualala Point Regional Park and 0.25 miles north of Sea Ranch Lodge at mile marker 50.80.

Hiking directions:

WALK-ON BEACH (0.8 miles round trip): From the south end of the lot, descend into a dense pine, fir, and cypress forest. Cross Leeward Road and skirt the south edge of an open bluff meadow. Walk through a towering Monterey cypress grove to a T-junction with the Bluff Trail at 0.3 miles. The right fork leads 2 miles to the Salal Trail (Hike 10) and 3 miles to Gualala Point Regional Park (Hike 9). The left fork, which leads 0.2 miles to Walk-On Beach, has been closed due to severe erosion but may reopen in the future.

SHELL BEACH TRAIL (1.2 miles round trip): Walk into a grove of pines and steadily descend down the trail. Cross Pacific Reach Road and continue downhill through a meadow and thickets of shrub. At 0.6 miles, the path reaches a T-junction with the Bluff Trail, overlooking massive offshore rock formations. Bear right and cross a wooden footbridge over the creek drainage at Shell Beach. Veer left and descend to the sandy beach, backed by a low bluff and endless sea rocks.

STENGEL BEACH TRAIL (0.4 miles round trip): Walk down the path lined with Monterey cypress trees. Parallel a small creek, while views of the ocean stretch out ahead. At the bluffs, curve right to an overlook. A long wooden staircase that is supported by a tilted rock formation descends the cliffs. Descend to the sandy pocket beach, bordered by steep cliffs and offshore rocks. The seasonal stream spills over the bluff, forming a small waterfall.

PEBBLE BEACH TRAIL (0.6 miles round trip): Head west on the grassy, tree-covered path. Slowly descend from the bishop pine forest into an open, grassy meadow, reaching the oceanfront Bluff Trail at 0.3 miles. Bear right and cross a bridge over the lush drainage. Continue 50 yards to steep wooden steps that drop down the cliffs to the black-sand beach cove with tidepools and seastacks.

BLACK POINT TRAIL (0.6 miles round trip): The trailhead is on the northwest corner of the parking lot. Cross the grassland meadow 0.3 miles to the cliffs at the northern edge of Black Point, a huge rock knoll with twisted Monterey cypress. Descend the vertical cliff on a wooden staircase to the long, curving beach. To the south, a private Sea Ranch trail leads out onto the peninsula to an overlook and the west tip of Black Point. ■

Pacific Ocean

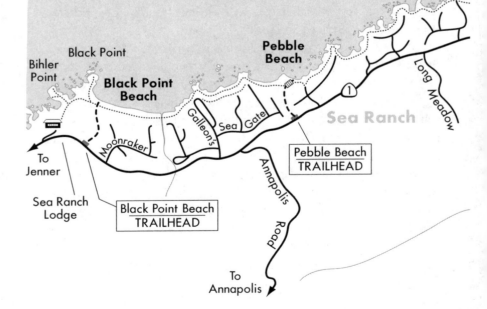

Black Point

Bihler
Point

**Black Point
Beach**

**Pebble
Beach**

Galleon's

Sea Gate

Moonraker

Sea Ranch

Long Meadow

To
Jenner

Sea Ranch
Lodge

Annapolis Road

Pebble Beach
TRAILHEAD

Black Point Beach
TRAILHEAD

To
Annapolis

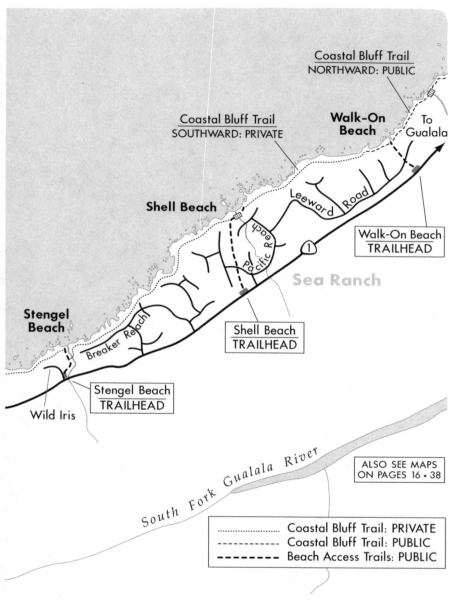

Coastal Bluff Trail
NORTHWARD: PUBLIC

Coastal Bluff Trail
SOUTHWARD: PRIVATE

Walk-On
Beach

To
Gualala

Leeward Road

Shell Beach

Walk-On Beach
TRAILHEAD

(1)

Sea Ranch

Pacific Reach

Stengel
Beach

Shell Beach
TRAILHEAD

Breaker Reach

Stengel Beach
TRAILHEAD

Wild Iris

South Fork Gualala River

ALSO SEE MAPS
ON PAGES 16 • 38

.... Coastal Bluff Trail: PRIVATE
------------ Coastal Bluff Trail: PUBLIC
-------- Beach Access Trails: PUBLIC

HIKE 11
Sea Ranch Beaches
ACCESS TRAILS

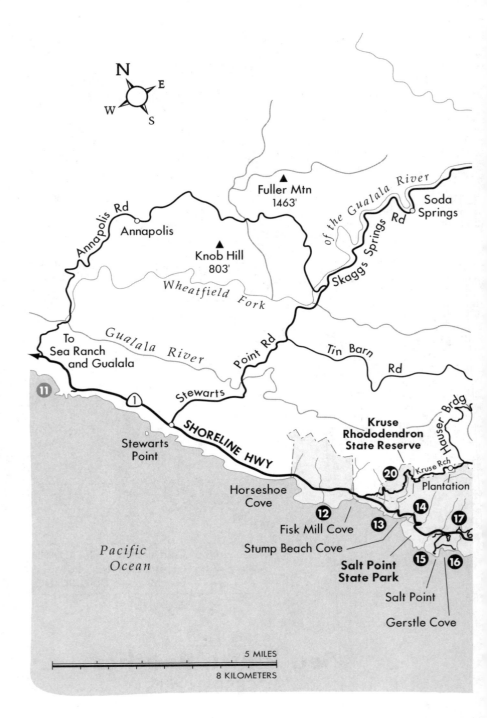

N
W E S

Fuller Mtn
1463'

of the Gualala River

Soda
Springs

Annapolis Rd

Annapolis

Knob Hill
803'

Skaggs Springs Rd

Wheatfield Fork

To
Sea Ranch
and Gualala

Gualala River

Point Rd

Tin Barn

Rd

⑪

Stewarts

Point Rd

SHORELINE HWY

Hauser Brdg

Stewarts
Point

Kruse
Rhododendron
State Reserve

Kruse Rch

Plantation

Horseshoe
Cove

②⓪

Fisk Mill Cove

⑭

⑫

⑬

⑰

Stump Beach Cove

Pacific
Ocean

Salt Point
State Park

⑮

⑯

Salt Point

Gerstle Cove

5 MILES

8 KILOMETERS

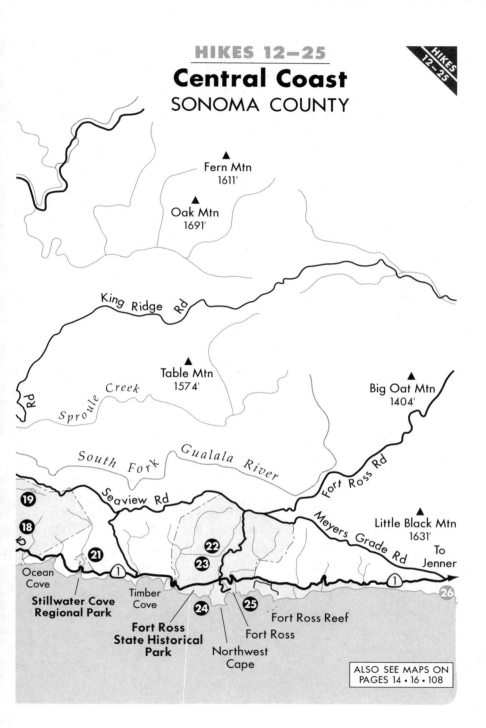

▲
Fern Mtn
1611'

▲
Oak Mtn
1691'

King Ridge Rd

▲
Table Mtn
1574'

▲
Big Oat Mtn
1404'

Creek

Sproule

Rd

South Fork

Gualala River

Fort Ross Rd

Seaview Rd

19

18

21

①

Ocean
Cove

**Stillwater Cove
Regional Park**

Timber
Cove

22

23

**Fort Ross
State Historical
Park**

24

25

Northwest
Cape

Fort Ross

Fort Ross Reef

Meyers Grade Rd

▲
Little Black Mtn
1631'

To
Jenner

①

26

ALSO SEE MAPS ON
PAGES 14 • 16 • 108

Salt Point State Park

HIKES 12 — 19

Salt Point State Park is comprised of 6,000 acres of pristine land 90 miles north of San Francisco. The park has seven miles of incredible coastline. From the ocean, the park stretches two miles inland, rising a thousand feet to the forested coastal ridge. The area is known for its fishing, skin diving, and scuba diving, with rich, undisturbed marine life. Park amenities include two campgrounds and several picnic areas.

The park contains a wide diversity of habitats, including an expansive marine terrace, rolling hills with grassy meadows, sandy beaches, secluded coves, dramatic outcroppings, tide-pools, and sheer rugged cliffs overlooking rocky points. The interior of the park has a dense forest populated with bishop pines, Douglas fir, second-growth redwoods, cypress, tanbark oaks, and madrones. On the upper ridge is a vast 900-foot open prairie. There are sag ponds along the San Andreas Fault and a pygmy forest of stunted cypress, gnarled pines, and redwoods.

The park was once inhabited by the Kashaya Pomo Native Americans. They collected salt from underwater crevices and from catch basins in the sandstone, where the water evaporated and left salt deposits. The salt was used for food preservation and trading. Native American village and midden sites are found throughout the park. The midden sites (ancient refuse piles) contain shell fragments of abalone, mussels, and clams.

A 20-mile network of hiking, biking, and equestrian trails lace through the park. Hikes 12—13 and 15—16 explore the headlands and marine bluffs along this amazing stretch of coastline. Hikes 14 and 17—19 offer remote forested hikes along the ridge backing the coastline.

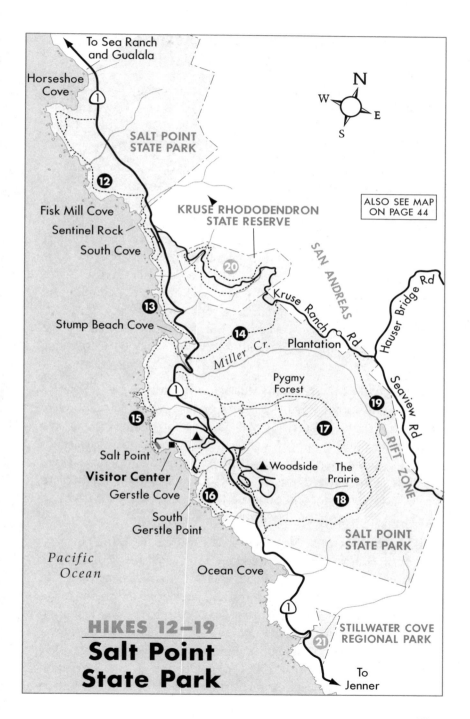

To Sea Ranch and Gualala

Horseshoe Cove

① 1

SALT POINT STATE PARK

⑫

Fisk Mill Cove

Sentinel Rock

South Cove

KRUSE RHODODENDRON STATE RESERVE

ALSO SEE MAP ON PAGE 44

SAN ANDREAS

⑳

⑬

Stump Beach Cove

Kruse Ranch Rd

Hauser Bridge Rd

⑭

Miller Cr.

Plantation

Pygmy Forest

Seaview Rd

⑲

① 1

⑮

⑰

RIFT ZONE

Salt Point

Visitor Center

Gerstle Cove

Woodside

The Prairie

⑯

⑱

South Gerstle Point

SALT POINT STATE PARK

Pacific Ocean

Ocean Cove

① 1

HIKES 12–19

Salt Point State Park

STILLWATER COVE REGIONAL PARK

㉑

To Jenner

12. Fisk Mill Cove to Horseshoe Point

SALT POINT STATE PARK

Hiking distance: 4 miles round trip
Hiking time: 2 hours
Elevation gain: 200 feet
Maps: U.S.G.S. Plantation
Salt Point State Park map

map
next page

Summary of hike: Fisk Mill Cove and Horseshoe Point sit on the northern coastal section of Salt Point State Park. The hike begins from the Fisk Mill Cove picnic area in a forest of bishop pine and Monterey cypress. The trail weaves through the forest to a viewing platform perched atop Sentinel Rock. From the 100-foot high deck is a bird's-eye view into Fisk Mill Cove and far-reaching vistas of the rugged coastline. Between December and April, Sentinel Rock is a great spot for observing gray whales as they migrate to Baja California. The trail continues along the uplifted coastal terrace past Fisk Mill Cove, Cannon Gulch, rocky beaches, and Deadman Gulch en route to Horseshoe Point.

Driving directions: From Gualala, just north of the Sonoma County line, drive 16.3 miles south on Highway 1 (the Shoreline Highway) to the posted Fisk Mill Cove turnoff on the right at mile marker 42.63. The turnoff is located 20.9 miles north of Jenner and 2.7 miles north of the posted Salt Point–Gerstle Cove turnoff. Turn toward the ocean (southwest) to an immediate T-junction. Turn right and continue 0.1 mile to the signed trailhead and parking spaces on the left.

Hiking directions: Walk 50 yards towards the ocean through the thick bishop pine forest and a posted junction. The left fork leads to South Cove and Stump Beach (Hike 13). Bear right and descend through stands of ferns and huckleberries to the edge of the weather-sculpted bluffs. Head north to a signed junction at 0.2 miles. The Bluff Trail continues on the right fork along the coastline. Detour left and climb Sentinel Rock with the aid of log steps. Atop the massive 100-foot formation is an observation platform with amazing coastal vistas above Fisk Mill Cove. Return to the Bluff Trail and weave through the grassy pine forest, with ferns and lace lichen draped from the tree branches, to the south edge of Cannon Gulch. To the left, a path zigzags down to the rocky beach. Bear right through a grove of redwoods, and cross the stream-fed gulch. Climb to the bluffs and curve right, meandering through the grasslands near Highway 1. Bear left towards the sea, and pass through an old wood fence. Descend into a forested gulch with a junction. The left fork leads to another rocky beach. Stay to the right and follow the edge of the cliffs to a headland with rock outcroppings, sea stacks, and views of Sentinel Rock and Fisk Mill Cove. Curve around coves and rock formations. Cross stream-fed Deadman Gulch and continue on the edge of the cliffs. Side paths lead to finely etched sandstone formations on the finger-like extensions of land. Head toward forested Horseshoe Point, overlooking sea palms on the tidal rocks. At the forested 205-foot knoll, veer right and enter the woods. Follow the old road and curve right to the ridge overlooking Horseshoe Cove and Gualala Point. This is a good turnaround spot. The trail reaches Highway 1 at a parking pullout a short distance ahead by mile marker 43.66. Return along the same route. ■

13. Bluff Trail:
Fisk Mill Cove to Stump Beach
SALT POINT STATE PARK

Hiking distance: 2.8 miles round trip
Hiking time: 1.5 hours
Elevation gain: 150 feet
Maps: U.S.G.S. Plantation
Salt Point State Park map

map
next page

Summary of hike: Stump Beach (originally called Big Gulch) is a deep U-shaped sandy cove with calm water backed by sandstone cliffs and forested hills. Miller Creek weaves through the sheltered, white-sand beach, where it empties into the sea. This

CONTINUED PAGE 52

HIKE 12
Fisk Mill Cove to Horseshoe Point
HIKE 13
Fisk Mill Cove to Stump Beach
SALT POINT STATE PARK

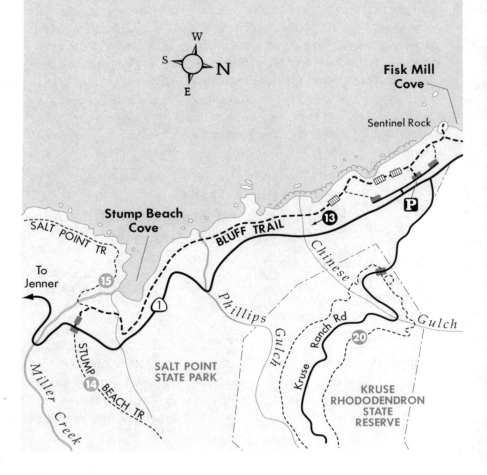

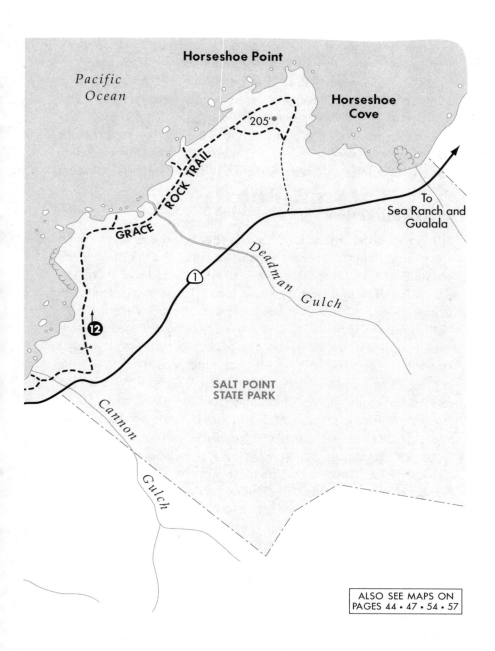

Horseshoe Point

Pacific
Ocean

Horseshoe
Cove

205'

ROCK TRAIL

GRACE

To
Sea Ranch and
Gualala

1

Deadman Gulch

12

SALT POINT
STATE PARK

Cannon

Gulch

ALSO SEE MAPS ON
PAGES 44 • 47 • 54 • 57

hike begins at the Fisk Mill Cove picnic area, on the northern portion of Salt Point State Park, and snakes through a thick forest of bishop pine and Douglas fir. The path follows the jagged 100-foot coastal bluffs through a broad grassy headland to Stump Beach, one of the few sandy beaches on this stretch of coastline. Along the way, the trail overlooks pounding surf, offshore rocks, and picturesque coves at Chinese Gulch and Phillips Gulch. The trail crosses small creeks perched above waterfalls dropping 50 feet from the oceanfront cliffs.

Driving directions: Same as Hike 12.

Hiking directions: Walk 50 yards towards the ocean through the bishop pine forest and a posted junction. The right fork leads to Sentinel Rock, Fisk Mill Cove, and Horseshoe Point (Hike 12). Bear left and head through the pine forest. Cross a wooden footbridge over a gulch and ascend steps to the oceanfront bluffs. Walk through the tall grass, and cross a second stream-fed gulch on a footbridge. Loop around a huge rock outcrop on the edge of the vertical cliffs. Descend steps and merge with the trail from the south end of the trailhead parking lot. Cross a third bridge over a fern-lined gully, and emerge from the wooded bluffs to the open grassy terrace at South Cove. Walk across a small drainage and follow the edge of the bluffs, passing massive rock slabs with tidepools and an abundance of offshore rocks. Cross Chinese Gulch, where a creek waterfall drops 50 feet to the sea. Continue and cross the creek at Phillips Gulch above a 30-foot waterfall. Climb the sloping bluff to an overlook of Stump Beach Cove. Skirt the north edge of the cove, looping around to the east side near Highway 1. Enter a pine forest and drop into a gully to sandy Stump Beach, ringed by sandstone cliffs. Steps on the left lead up to the Stump Beach parking lot and picnic area. This is the turn-around spot.

To extend the hike, the trail continues across the sand at the south end of the beach. The trail climbs up the bluffs and heads south to Salt Point and Gerstle Cove (Hike 15).∎

14. Stump Beach Trail

SALT POINT STATE PARK

Hiking distance: 3 miles round trip
Hiking time: 1.5 hours
Elevation gain: 650 feet
Maps: U.S.G.S. Plantation
      Salt Point State Park map

map
page 54

Summary of hike: Miller Creek begins in the upper slopes of Salt Point State Park along the San Andreas Rift Zone at 800 feet. The perennial creek drains into the sea at Stump Beach. The Stump Beach Trail begins by the beach off Highway 1 and climbs the forested north wall of the Miller Creek canyon to Kruse Ranch Road. The isolated trail is perched on the hillside and weaves through a lush forest of Douglas fir, bishop pine, tanbark oak, and towering redwood groves.

Driving directions: From Gualala, just north of the Sonoma County line, drive 17.7 miles south on Highway 1 (the Shoreline Highway) to the posted Stump Beach turnoff on the right at mile marker 41.20. The turnoff is located 19.5 miles north of Jenner and 1.3 miles north of the posted Salt Point–Gerstle Cove turnoff. Park in either the Stump Beach parking lot on the ocean side (west) or in the pullout on the inland side of the highway by the posted trailhead.

Hiking directions: Walk past the log barrier and head up the forested path. Traverse the steep hillside, perched on a shelf with views into the canyon. At a half mile, cross a footbridge over a side canyon and continue uphill, passing moss-covered tree trunks and coastal redwood groves. The serpentine path steadily climbs up the north wall of the Miller Creek drainage. Near the top, descend and curve right to the end of the trail on Kruse Ranch Road, between Kruse Rhododendron State Reserve and the town of Plantation. ■

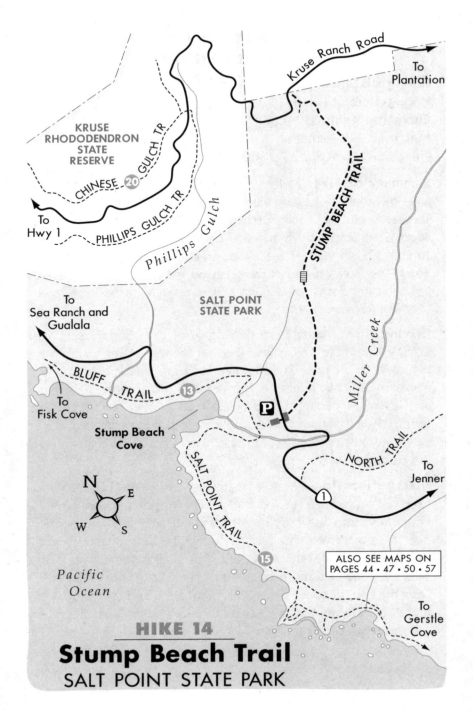

To Plantation

Kruse Ranch Road

KRUSE
RHODODENDRON
STATE
RESERVE

CHINESE GULCH TR.

20

PHILLIPS GULCH TR.

Phillips Gulch

To
Hwy 1

STUMP BEACH TRAIL

SALT POINT
STATE PARK

To
Sea Ranch and
Gualala

Miller Creek

BLUFF TRAIL

13

To
Fisk Cove

P

Stump Beach
Cove

NORTH TRAIL

1

To
Jenner

SALT POINT TRAIL

N
E
W
S

15

Pacific
Ocean

ALSO SEE MAPS ON
PAGES 44 • 47 • 50 • 57

To
Gerstle
Cove

HIKE 14

Stump Beach Trail
SALT POINT STATE PARK

15. Salt Point Trail:
Gerstle Cove to Stump Beach
SALT POINT STATE PARK

Hiking distance: 3.2 miles round trip
Hiking time: 1.5 hours
Elevation gain: 100 feet
Maps: U.S.G.S. Plantation
Salt Point State Park map

map
page 57

Summary of hike: The Salt Point Trail is an amazing, world-class hike with a geologically unique stretch of coastal bluffs. The hike explores ancient conglomerate sandstone rock lifted from the ocean bottom. Delicate formations are carved into the cliff faces, forming natural earth sculptures with pits, knobs, ribs, and ridges. Concretions—hard rounded rocks—sit on isolated pedestals. Natural depressions in the bedrock collect seawater, forming pools. Most dramatic are the intricate wind and wave-sculpted honeycomb formations in the sandstone called tafoni. The waffle-shaped formations have a complex lacy pattern etched into the weathering sandstone. This hike begins on Salt Point at the north end of Gerstle Cove and follows the rolling coastal bluffs north to horseshoe-shaped Stump Beach, protected by 80-foot bluffs. The trail passes sandstone outcroppings with Native American midden sites, wave-pounded rocky points, sea stacks, sea caves, and tidepools.

Driving directions: From Gualala, just north of the Sonoma County line, drive 19 miles south on Highway 1 (the Shoreline Highway) to the posted Salt Point–Gerstle Cove turnoff on the right at mile marker 39.90. The turnoff is located 18.2 miles north of Jenner and 6.7 miles north of Fort Ross. Turn towards the ocean (west), and drive 0.7 miles to the oceanfront parking lot at Salt Point. A parking fee is required.

Hiking directions: From the northwest corner of Gerstle Cove, take the posted trail along the edge of Salt Point. The paved path leads to the point, overlooking tidepools, sea stacks, sea caves, sculpted sandstone formations, sea lions, and a frequently turbulent sea. The pavement ends at the southwest tip and continues as a dirt path. Leave the promontory and head north on the 40-foot bluffs to a Y-fork. The left fork follows the edge of the bluffs. The parallel right path meanders through a meadow with rock outcroppings and boulders. Cross over ephemeral Warren Creek, and meander through rattlesnake grass and California poppies. The two paths merge ahead at a dramatic cove with offshore sea stacks, tilted rock formations, and vertical eroding cliffs. The bluff path passes a series of rock-strewn coves and a Kashaya Pomo midden. The site is scattered with shell fragments of abalone, clams, crabs, and mussels on the leeward base of a knoll. To the left, a side path leads 50 yards on a finger of land between two coves. A short distance ahead is a fantastic, moonscape-looking rock garden with pools in the water-carved formations. Using extreme caution, explore the pock-marked tafoni formations and pools, following your own path. Return to the main trail, and continue to sandy Stump Beach in a deep cove at the mouth of Miller Creek. Descend to the beach, then cross the creek to a trail split at the canyon drainage. This is the turn-around spot.

To extend the hike, steps on the right lead up to the Stump Beach parking lot and picnic area. Across the highway is the Stump Beach Trail (Hike 14). The Bluff Trail climbs up the gulch to the left (northwest) and crosses the stream, returning to the bluffs (Hike 13). The trail continues to South Cove, Sentinel Rock, Fisk Mill Cove, and Horseshoe Point (Hike 12). ■

HIKE 15 →
Salt Point Trail:
Gerstle Cove to Stump Beach
SALT POINT STATE PARK

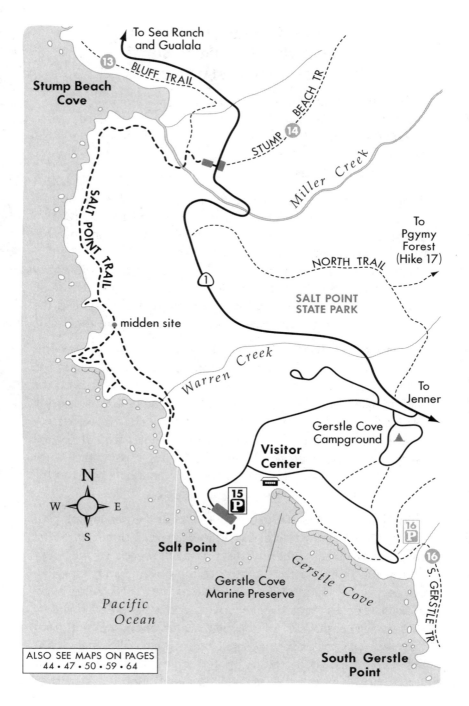

To Sea Ranch
and Gualala

⑬ BLUFF TRAIL

STUMP BEACH TR.

**Stump Beach
Cove**

Miller Creek

⑭

SALT POINT TRAIL

To
Pgymy
Forest
(Hike 17)

NORTH TRAIL

①

**SALT POINT
STATE PARK**

• midden site

Warren Creek

To
Jenner

Gerstle Cove
Campground

**Visitor
Center**

N

W ✦ E

**15
P**

S

Salt Point

Gerstle Cove
Marine Preserve

**16
P**

⑯

S. GERSTLE TR.

*Pacific
Ocean*

Gerstle Cove

ALSO SEE MAPS ON PAGES
44 · 47 · 50 · 59 · 64

**South Gerstle
Point**

16. South Gerstle Trail and the Southern Bluffs

SALT POINT STATE PARK

Hiking distance: 1 mile round trip
Hiking time: 40 minutes
Elevation gain: 50 feet
Maps: U.S.G.S. Plantation
Salt Point State Park map

Summary of hike: Gerstle Cove is an underwater ecological reserve at the southern end of Salt Point State Park. The reserve supports and protects a diverse community of fish, invertebrates, and aquatic plants. The South Gerstle Trail explores eroding sandstone cliffs and the jagged, chiseled headland with rocky promontories that jut out into the ocean at South Gerstle Point. The views include wave-carved caves, natural bridges, and the crashing surf constantly slamming against the offshore rocks.

Driving directions: From Gualala, just north of the Sonoma County line, drive 19 miles south on Highway 1 (the Shoreline Highway) to the posted Salt Point–Gerstle Cove turnoff on the right at mile marker 39.90. The turnoff is located 18.2 miles north of Jenner and 6.7 miles north of Fort Ross. Turn towards the ocean (west), and drive 0.5 miles to the signed turnoff for the visitor center. Turn left and continue 0.5 miles, passing the visitor center, to South Gerstle Cove and a picnic area parking lot at the end of the road. A parking fee is required.

Hiking directions: From the south end of the parking lot, pass the posted trailhead gate and follow the old dirt road. Cross over Squaw Creek, where a steep path descends to the rocky beach. This trail is an access route to the cove, used by snorkelers and scuba divers. Skirt the edge of the bluffs while overlooking rock terraces, beach coves, and offshore formations. Pass through a grove of bishop pines to an open, grassy terrace covered with rock outcroppings. A faint path follows the cliffs and a two-track road crosses the terrace by South Gerstle Point. This exposed marine terrace invites exploration. Cross a small stream and follow a footpath south through a pine grove to finely etched sandstone formations. Loop around a deep, vertical-walled cove. The path ends above ephemeral Wildcat Creek and a rock-filled beach cove near the southern park boundary. Return by retracing your steps. ∎

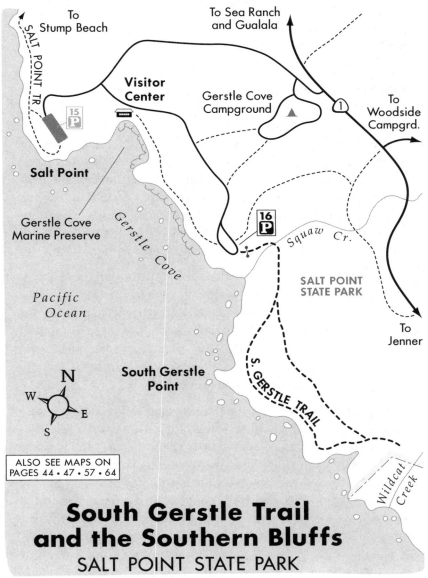

South Gerstle Trail and the Southern Bluffs
SALT POINT STATE PARK

17. Pygmy Forest:
North Trail—Central Trail Loop
SALT POINT STATE PARK

Hiking distance: 3-mile loop
Hiking time: 1.5 hours
Elevation gain: 600 feet
Maps: U.S.G.S. Plantation
Salt Point State Park map

map
page 64

Summary of hike: Three trails form two loops from the Woodside Campground in the dense interior of Salt Point State Park. This hike on old logging roads combines the North Trail and Central Trail through a mixed forest of redwoods, Douglas fir, tanbark oak, bishop pine, madrone, manzanita, trillium, ferns, and rhododendrons. The North Trail parallels Warren Creek to the pygmy forest, a rare grove with stunted versions of bishop pines, Mendocino cypress, and coastal redwoods. The trees grow in highly acidic, nutrient-deficient soil with a shallow hard-pan surface, preventing tree roots and water to penetrate.

Driving directions: From Gualala, just north of the Sonoma County line, drive 19 miles south on Highway 1 (the Shoreline Highway) to the posted Woodside Campground turnoff on the left at mile marker 39.78. The turnoff is located 0.1 mile south of the posted Salt Point—Gerstle Cove turnoff and 18.1 miles north of Jenner. Turn inland (northeast) and drive 0.1 mile to the day use parking lot. A parking fee is required.

Hiking directions: Take the posted Central Trail past the gate and head uphill into the dense forest. At 0.1 mile is a posted junction. Leave the Central Trail and bear left, beginning the loop on the Huckleberry Trail. Traverse the hillside and cross over Warren Creek to a signed junction with the North Trail at 0.4 miles. The left fork leads to Highway 1, just south of Stump Beach. Go to the right and weave up the hill. Parallel the seasonal creek through a forest of coastal redwoods, bishop pines, tanbark oak, madrone, and bay laurel trees to a trail split. The right fork—the Water Tank Trail—leads 0.2 miles to the Central Trail. Stay to the left as the trail levels out. Pass the headwaters of Warren Creek, and enter the pygmy forest at just over one mile. Meander through the quiet grove for a quarter mile, and descend to a T-junction with the Central Trail. The left fork leads to the Prairie Trail and the South Trail (Hike 18). Bear right and descend under the towering Douglas fir and redwoods. Pass a row of four wooden water tanks by the connector trail to the North Trail. Continue downhill, completing the loop.■

18. The Prairie:
Central Trail—South Trail Loop
SALT POINT STATE PARK

Hiking distance: 4-mile loop
Hiking time: 2 hours
Elevation gain: 600 feet
Maps: U.S.G.S. Plantation
　　　 Salt Point State Park map

map
page 64

Summary of hike: The Central Trail and South Trail are located in the heart of Salt Point State Park, forming a large loop around Woodside Campground. The trails are fire roads that climb through a dense conifer forest to the crest of the coastal ridge. At the ridge is The Prairie, a vast grassland meadow frequented by deer and hawks. The wooded, atmospheric route meanders under towering second-growth redwoods, Douglas fir, and bishop pines, with an understory of ferns, salal, huckleberry, rhododendrons, and manzanita.

Driving directions: Same as Hike 17.

Hiking directions: Take the posted Central Trail past the gate, and head up the fire road through the lush forest with towering Douglas fir. At 0.1 mile is a junction with the Huckleberry Trail. Stay on the Central Trail and steadily climb towards the ridge. Pass a row of four wooden water tanks on the left by the Water Tank Trail, leading to the pygmy forest (Hike 17). Stay on the Central Trail, and curve right, climbing to a junction with the upper end of the North Trail. Stay straight and slowly descend to

The Prairie, a long, open meadow at 900 feet. Skirt the south-west edge of the meadow to a trail split. The Prairie Trail bears left through the meadow to the sag ponds on Miller Creek along the San Andreas Fault (Hike 19). For this hike, go straight on the South Trail and curve right, reentering the forest. Descend through the redwoods and moss-filled forest. Near the bottom of the hill, as the trees submit to the open sky, watch for a trail sign on the right, located 70 yards shy of the highway. Bear right on the Powerline Trail, a footpath in a forested utility corridor. Cross Wildcat Creek and ascend the slope, parallel to Highway 1. Pass the campground access trail that leads to Gerstle Cove. Join the paved campground road, and follow either the road back to the trailhead or take the footpath through the campground.■

19. Plantation and Prairie Trails along the San Andreas Rift Zone
SALT POINT STATE PARK

Hiking distance: 4 miles round trip
Hiking time: 2 hours
Elevation gain: 250 feet
Maps: U.S.G.S. Plantation
       Salt Point State Park map

map
page 64

Summary of hike: The Plantation and Prairie Trails follow the crest of a coastal ridge along the San Andreas Rift Zone in Salt Point State Park. The two trails meander through a dense forest of towering redwoods, pine, fir, and madrones. The Prairie Trail leads to a vast, 900-foot hilltop meadow where deer and hawks are frequently spotted. En route to The Prairie, the trail passes sag ponds—water-filled depressions formed by the sinking ground along the San Andreas Fault. The quiet trails offer an away-from-the-crowds hike. They are accessed from Kruse Ranch Road, Seaview Road, and the Woodside Campground via the Central–South Trail loop (Hike 18).

Driving directions: From Gualala, just north of the Sonoma County line, drive 16.2 miles south on Highway 1 (the Shoreline

Highway) to the posted Kruse Ranch Road turnoff on the left at mile marker 42.75. The turnoff is located 21 miles north of Jenner and 2.8 miles north of the posted Salt Point–Gerstle Cove turnoff. Turn inland (northeast) and drive 3.7 miles up the narrow, winding road to the posted trailhead on the right. The trailhead is 0.3 miles past the community of Plantation. A parking pullout is by the trailhead.

Hiking directions: Descend past the trailhead sign on the Plantation Trail. Traverse the hillside through the isolated forest, passing massive redwoods and moss-covered downfall. Continue descending into the forest. The path levels out and meanders through the quiet of the forest. Ascend the hillside and curve to the left to a T-junction with the Prairie Trail (also called the Seaview Trail), an old ranch road. The left fork leads 0.2 miles to Seaview Road. Bear right and descend on the forested dirt road along the south wall of the canyon. Cross over Miller Creek and the sag ponds on the left along the San Andreas Fault. Head uphill, weaving through the lush forest to the ridge at a massive open meadow called The Prairie. Walk through the meadow to a posted T-junction with the South Trail. Both routes lead downhill ·to the Woodside Campground and Highway 1 (Hike 18). The right fork also merges with the North Trail to the pygmy forest (Hike 17). Return by retracing your route. ∎

20. Chinese Gulch—Phillips Gulch Loop
KRUSE RHODODENDRON STATE RESERVE

Hiking distance: 2.5-mile loop
Hiking time: 1.5 hours
Elevation gain: 400 feet
Maps: U.S.G.S. Plantation
      Salt Point State Park map

map
page 67

Summary of hike: Kruse Rhododendron State Reserve encompasses 317 acres adjacent to Salt Point State Park. California rhododendrons, the namesake of the park, grow in

CONTINUED PAGE 66

HIKE 17
Pygmy Forest:
North Trail—Central Trail

HIKE 18
The Prairie:
Central Trail—South Trail

HIKE 19
Plantation Trail and
Prairie Trail

SALT POINT STATE PARK

Kruse Ranch

STUMP BCH TR

14

SALT POINT TRAIL

15

NORTH TRAIL

1

HUCKLEBERRY
TRAIL

17
18
P

Warren Cr.

Visitor
Center

Gerstle Cove
Campground

15

Salt
Point

Gerstle Cove

SOUTH

16

GERSTLE TR

South
Gerstle Point

Plantation

19 P

Hauser Bridge Road

Plantation Road

Miller Creek

Seaview Road

N
W E
S

PLANTATION TRAIL

SAN ANDREAS

19

P

Pygmy Forest

sag ponds

RIFT ZONE

PRAIRIE TRAIL

water tanks

NORTH TRAIL

17

WATER TANK TRAIL

CENTRAL TRAIL

The Prairie

18

SALT POINT STATE PARK

Squaw Cr.

Woodside Campground

▲

Wildcat Creek

SOUTH TRAIL

ALSO SEE MAPS ON PAGES 44 · 47 · 57 · 59

POWERLINE TR

①

To Jenner

profusion. Their brilliant pink blossoms bloom in clusters from April through June. The fast-growing rhododendrons flourished after a forest fire around 1900 removed most of the existing vegetation. The reserve also contains a mixed forest of second-growth redwoods, Douglas fir, grand fir, tanbark oaks, madrones, manzanita, and eucalyptus. Fern-lined Chinese Gulch and Phillips Gulch flow through the reserve. The undeveloped land was donated to the state in 1933. It was part of the Kruse Ranch, a sheep and logging ranch dating back to the 1880s. Five miles of hiking trails weave through the reserve's forested coastal hills.

Driving directions: From Gualala, just north of the Sonoma County line, drive 16.2 miles south on Highway 1 (the Shoreline Highway) to the posted Kruse Ranch Road turnoff on the left at mile marker 42.75. The turnoff is located 21 miles north of Jenner and 2.8 miles north of the posted Salt Point—Gerstle Cove turnoff. Turn inland (northeast) and drive 0.45 miles up the narrow road to the posted trailhead on the left. Parking pullouts are on both sides of the road.

Hiking directions: Begin the loop on the upper north side of the road. Ascend steps to the map kiosk. At the map, two post-lined paths form the short Rhododendron Loop. Begin on either path and weave through the lush forest, passing groves of redwoods and moss-covered tree trunks to the far end of the loop. Continue straight on the north slope of Chinese Gulch through Douglas fir, tanbark oaks, coastal redwoods, and ferns. Zigzag down to a junction in Chinese Gulch. The right fork leads 20 yards to Kruse Ranch Road at a U-shaped bend. (For a shorter loop, return 0.4 miles down the dirt road.) Bear left and cross the wooden footbridge over the fern-lined creek. Ascend the south canyon wall and cross a small bridge. Climb two switchbacks and traverse the canyon wall, steadily gaining elevation to a junction. Bear right on the Phillips Gulch Trail, and sharply descend to Kruse Ranch Road at Phillips Gulch. Walk 20 yards up the road to the signed trail. Descend steps and stroll through the tanbark oak forest. Veer right at a trail sign and pass a gorgeous hollow of redwoods. Switchbacks lead down the draw, returning to Chinese

Gulch. Cross a wood bridge over the stream and wind up the hillside. Near the top, pass restrooms and continue 50 yards to Kruse Ranch Road at the trailhead. ■

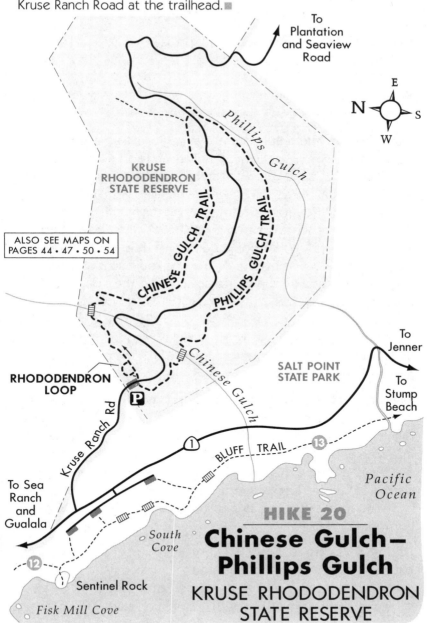

To Plantation and Seaview Road

E
N · S
W

KRUSE RHODODENDRON STATE RESERVE

ALSO SEE MAPS ON PAGES 44 · 47 · 50 · 54

CHINESE GULCH TRAIL

PHILLIPS GULCH TRAIL

Phillips Gulch

RHODODENDRON LOOP

P

Kruse Ranch Rd

Chinese Gulch

SALT POINT STATE PARK

To Jenner

To Stump Beach

To Sea Ranch and Gualala

1

BLUFF TRAIL

13

Pacific Ocean

South Cove

12

Sentinel Rock

Fisk Mill Cove

HIKE 20
Chinese Gulch— Phillips Gulch
KRUSE RHODODENDRON STATE RESERVE

21. Stockhoff Creek Loop:
Fort Ross Schoolhouse • Stillwater Cove
STILLWATER COVE REGIONAL PARK

Hiking distance: 1.6 miles round trip
Hiking time: 1 hour
Elevation gain: 200 feet
Maps: U.S.G.S. Plantation
　　　　Stillwater Cove Regional Park map

Summary of hike: Stillwater Cove Regional Park encompasses 363 acres between Salt Point State Park and Fort Ross State Park. The park sits amid pine-covered hillsides, while perennial Stockhoff Creek flows through a canyon filled with redwood, fir, and red alder. Stillwater Cove, situated at the mouth of the creek, is a gorgeous beach protected by 100-foot cliffs (cover photo). The historic Fort Ross Schoolhouse sits in a tree-lined meadow in the hills above Stockhoff Creek. The one room schoolhouse was originally erected on the bluffs adjacent to the village of Fort Ross in 1885 and was active through 1920. It has since been moved to the present site and restored. This hike explores the forested canyon, climbs to North Meadow and the schoolhouse, and returns to the scenic beach cove. Within the park is a picnic area and campground.

Driving directions: From Gualala, just north of the Sonoma county line, drive 22 miles south on Highway 1 (the Shoreline Highway) to the posted Stillwater Cove turnoff on the left at mile marker 37.02. It is located 2.9 miles south of the Salt Point State Park entrance. Turn inland and drive 0.2 miles to the day use parking lot on the left. A parking fee is required.

　　The turnoff is located 15 miles north of Jenner and 3.8 miles north of Fort Ross.

Hiking directions: From the northwest corner of the parking lot, descend on the signed trail into the dense, dark forest on the south canyon wall. At 0.1 mile is a posted 3-way junction by a bridge over Stockhoff Creek. The left fork leads 0.2 miles to

Stillwater Cove across Highway 1. Straight ahead the trail crosses the bridge over the creek—the return route. For now, bear right and begin the loop. Follow the path along the fern-covered canyon wall through redwoods and firs. Cross a bridge over a tributary stream, following the course of the main creek. Cross two more bridges over small gullies to the signed park boundary.

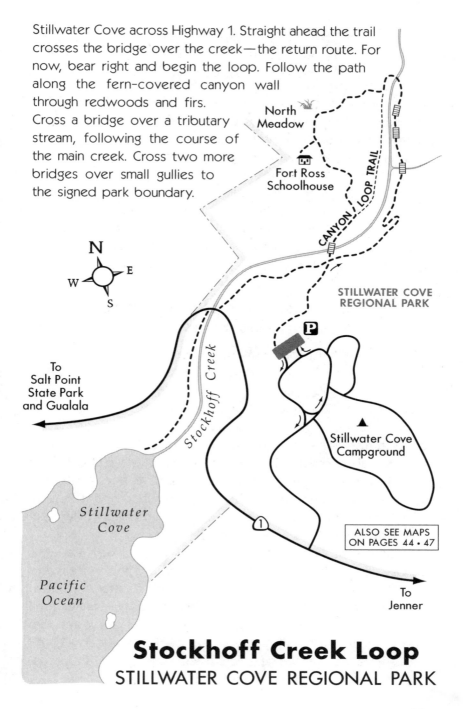

North Meadow

Fort Ross Schoolhouse

CANYON LOOP TRAIL

STILLWATER COVE REGIONAL PARK

P

N
W   E
S

To
Salt Point
State Park
and Gualala

Stockhoff Creek

Stillwater Cove
Campground

Stillwater
Cove

Pacific
Ocean

①

ALSO SEE MAPS
ON PAGES 44 • 47

To
Jenner

Stockhoff Creek Loop
STILLWATER COVE REGIONAL PARK

Cross the creek and return on the north side of Stockhoff Creek. A short distance ahead is an unsigned trail on the right. Veer right and climb the south-facing slope. Traverse the hillside to a posted junction. The left fork is the return route. Detour 50 yards straight ahead to the historic schoolhouse on the left and North Meadow on the right. After exploring the schoolhouse and the interpretive displays, return to the junction. Descend the hill to the Canyon Loop Trail. Bear right and cross the long wooden bridge, completing the loop.

To reach Stillwater Cove, follow the south side of the creek through the darkness of the dense redwood forest. The forest soon gives way to the sky and Highway 1. Cross the highway and pick up the paved path to the sandy beach pocket beneath towering rock walls and numerous offshore rocks. ■

Fort Ross State Historic Park
HIKES 22 — 25

Fort Ross State Historic Park encompasses 3,200 acres, 11 miles north of Jenner. Kashaya Pomo Native Americans inhabited this land for over 7,000 years.

In the early 19th century, it became an outpost for Russian fur traders. Trappers followed seal and sea otter colonies down the coast from Alaska and settled the area in 1812. The Russian stronghold was abandoned in 1841. A few original settlement buildings remain, and many of the fort structures have been restored, including hand-hewn log barracks, blockhouses, and a Russian Orthodox chapel. The fort sits atop the wind-washed terrace overlooking Fort Ross Cove and the Pacific Ocean.

Bisecting the state park is Highway 1. To the west are high, windswept bluffs with dramatic headlands and rocky sheltered coves. To the east are the heavily forested coastal mountains with second-growth redwood groves and a mixed conifer forest of Bishop pine, Douglas fir, wax myrtle, and bay laurel. The eastern end of the park borders Seaview Road, winding 1,500 feet above the sea. The next four hikes explore both the broad marine terrace and the upland hills.

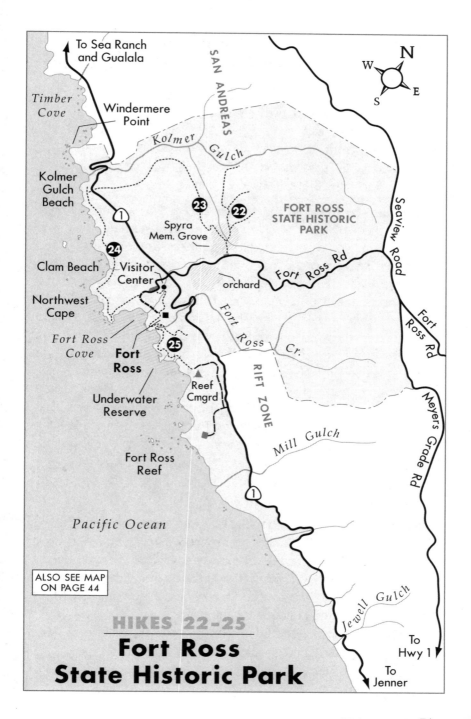

To Sea Ranch and Gualala

SAN ANDREAS

N
W E
S

Timber Cove

Windermere Point

Kolmer Gulch

Kolmer Gulch Beach

23

22

FORT ROSS STATE HISTORIC PARK

Seaview Road

1

24

Spyra Mem. Grove

Fort Ross Rd

Clam Beach

Visitor Center

orchard

Fort Ross Rd

Northwest Cape

Fort Ross Cove

Fort Ross

25

Fort Ross Cr.

RIFT ZONE

Meyers Grade Rd

Underwater Reserve

Reef Cmgrd

Mill Gulch

Fort Ross Reef

Pacific Ocean

ALSO SEE MAP ON PAGE 44

Jewell Gulch

HIKES 22-25

Fort Ross
State Historic Park

To Hwy 1

To Jenner

22. Kolmer Gulch Camp
Fort Ross Orchard • Spyra Memorial Grove
FORT ROSS STATE HISTORIC PARK

Hiking distance: 1.8 miles round trip

Hiking time: 1 hour

map
page 74

Elevation gain: 200 feet

Maps: U.S.G.S. Fort Ross and Plantation
Fort Ross State Historic Park map

Summary of hike: In the center of Fort Ross State Historic Park is the Fort Ross Orchard, a three-acre garden filled with apple, plum, and pear trees dating back to 1814. Across the road from the historic orchard is the Stanley Spyra Memorial Grove. The grove has the world's oldest known second-growth coastal redwoods. The San Andreas Fault runs through the orchard and the memorial grove. During the infamous 1906 San Francisco earthquake, the ground suddenly shifted more than 12 feet. The grove has visible remnants of the earthquake, including offset creeks, sag ponds (water-filled depressions along the fault), escarpments, and damaged trees. The ancient redwoods had their trunks split and their tops snapped off. The branches have since grown in a deformed manner. This hike takes an old logging road from the Stanley Spyra Memorial Grove and follows the fractured land to Kolmer Gulch Camp, an old mining camp on the edge of the creek, where there are benches, a fire pit, spring water, a wood shelter, and an old wooden fence.

Driving directions: From Gualala, just north of the Sonoma County line, drive 25.7 miles south on Highway 1 (the Shoreline Highway) to the posted Fort Ross State Park turnoff on the right at mile marker 33.00. Turn left (inland) on Fort Ross Road, and drive 0.55 miles to the posted Stanley Spyra Memorial Grove on the left. Park in the pullout near the grove.

Fort Ross Road is located 11.5 miles north of Jenner.

Hiking directions: Walk through the metal vehicle gate, and follow the old logging road into the dense redwood forest. Pass a circle of massive redwoods on the left to a signed trail split. The Lower Kolmer Gulch Trail veers left (Hike 23). Go right towards Upper Kolmer Gulch. Reenter the deep forest along a canyon on the left, passing posted Steer Field Road on the right. Cross a bridge over a seasonal tributary of Kolmer Gulch, pass Tan Oak Trail on the right, and continue down the gradual descent. Walk past a sag pond and enter Kolmer Gulch Camp, an old logging camp on the banks of Kolmer Creek. After exploring the creekside area, return along the same route. ■

23. Lower Kolmer Gulch to Coastal Overlook
FORT ROSS STATE HISTORIC PARK

Hiking distance: 3.4 miles round trip
Hiking time: 1.75 hours
Elevation gain: 200 feet
Maps: U.S.G.S. Fort Ross and Plantation
    Fort Ross State Historic Park map

map
page 74

Summary of hike: The majority of the Fort Ross State Historic Park lies east of Highway 1. The undeveloped uplands rise over 1,500 feet to the coastal ridge. Old logging roads wind through the dense conifer forest with second-growth coastal redwoods and timbered meadows. This hike weaves through the deep forest, meadows, and open grassland along the San Andreas Rift Zone to an overlook of the ocean above Windermere Point. Along the way are close-up views of fault trenches and sag ponds, formed from sinking ground along the fault zone.

Driving directions: Same as Hike 22.

Hiking directions: Walk past the trailhead gate, and head down the old logging road through the Stanley Spyra Memorial Grove. Notice the redwoods that lost their tops from the 1906 earthquake. Pass a magnificent circle of redwoods on the left to a posted trail split. The right fork leads to Kolmer Gulch Camp (Hike 22). Veer left and pass a sag pond on the left covered in

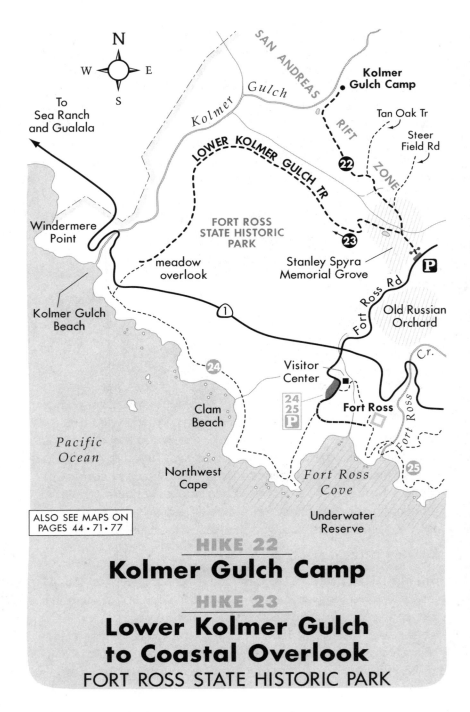

HIKE 22
Kolmer Gulch Camp

HIKE 23
Lower Kolmer Gulch
to Coastal Overlook
FORT ROSS STATE HISTORIC PARK

reeds and cattails, another visible feature of the San Andreas Fault. Curve left on a sweeping S-curve through the meadow with a view of the ocean. Enter a Douglas fir and redwood forest on the west edge of a gulch, and meander at a near-level grade. Gradually descend and curve left along the south side of Kolmer Gulch. Head uphill and weave through the forested grasslands. Descend through Bishop pines to a huge meadow with a view of Windermere Point, the ocean, beautiful offshore rocks, and the sound of barking sea lions. This is a good turn-around spot.

To extend the hike, drop down to Highway 1, just under a mile from the park entrance. Carefully cross the highway and walk along the oceanfront bluffs toward Northwest Cape (Hike 24). Hikes 23 and 24 can be combined for a 4-mile loop hike, con-

24. Fort Ross North Headlands
FORT ROSS STATE HISTORIC PARK

Hiking distance: 2.6 miles round trip
Hiking time: 1.5 hours
Elevation gain: 75 feet
Maps: U.S.G.S. Fort Ross and Plantation
Fort Ross State Historic Park map

map
page 77

Summary of hike: The Fort Ross North Headlands are 100-foot windswept bluffs with serrated, wave-pounded cliffs; deep, stream-cut canyons; and sheltered coves. The route does not follow a designated trail, but rather traverses the expansive coastal plateau along the edge of the grassy bluffs. The hike explores the high marine terrace from Northwest Cape to an overlook of Kolmer Gulch Beach, just shy of Windermere Point. Throughout the hike are far-reaching vistas, including Sonoma's Lost Coast and Point Reyes.

Driving directions: From Gualala, just north of the Sonoma County line, drive 25.7 miles south on Highway 1 (the Shoreline Highway) to the posted Fort Ross State Park turnoff on the right at mile marker 33.00. Turn right (towards the ocean), and drive 0.2 miles to the parking lot at the visitor center. An entrance fee is required.

The turnoff is located 11.5 miles north of Jenner.

Hiking directions: From the far end of the parking lot, follow the dirt road southwest. As the road curves left toward the fort, veer right on a grassy path by the distinct rock outcropping. Climb the ladder over the fence, and head to the oceanfront edge of Northwest Cape at the western tip of Fort Ross Cove. Follow the edge of the grassy coastal bluff to the right, passing a series of rocky beaches along Northwest Cape. The bluffs overlook jagged offshore formations with barking sea lions. At the western tip of Northwest Cape, veer north and cross a series of small seasonal drainages. A steep side path descends to the rocky shoreline and tidepools at Clam Beach. The hike ends just shy of Windermere Point at an overlook of Kolmer Gulch Beach, where the protected sandy cove meets Highway 1. Return along the same route. ■

25. Fort Ross Cove— Russian Cemetery—Southern Bluffs
FORT ROSS STATE HISTORIC PARK

Hiking distance: 2.8 miles round trip

Hiking time: 1.5 hours

Elevation gain: 200 feet

Maps: U.S.G.S. Fort Ross
Fort Ross State Historic Park map

map
page 79

Summary of hike: Fort Ross, dating back to 1812, sits atop the wind-sculpted terrace overlooking Fort Ross Cove and the ocean. A few original settlement buildings remain, and many of the fort structures have been restored, including hand-hewn log barracks, blockhouses, and a Russian Orthodox chapel. Fort Ross Cove is a protected beach below the fort. The cove was the site of the first shipyard in California. The Russian Orthodox Cemetery

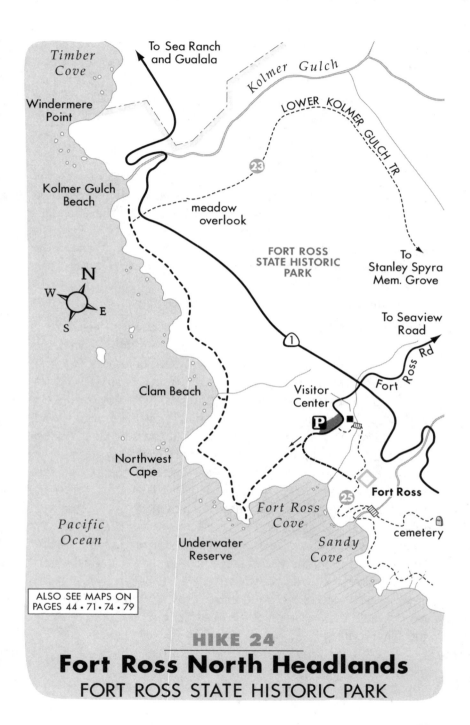

To Sea Ranch
and Gualala

*Timber
Cove*

Kolmer *Gulch*

LOWER KOLMER GULCH TR.

Windermere
Point

23

Kolmer Gulch
Beach

meadow
overlook

FORT ROSS
STATE HISTORIC
PARK

To
Stanley Spyra
Mem. Grove

N
W   E
S

To Seaview
Road

1

Fort Ross Rd

Clam Beach

Visitor
Center

P ■

Fort Ross

Northwest
Cape

25

*Pacific
Ocean*

*Fort Ross
Cove*

cemetery

Underwater
Reserve

*Sandy
Cove*

ALSO SEE MAPS ON
PAGES 44 • 71 • 74 • 79

HIKE 24

Fort Ross North Headlands
FORT ROSS STATE HISTORIC PARK

sits atop a grassy knoll above the cove and across the creek-fed gulch from the fortress. The cemetery has Russian Orthodox crosses marking the burial sites. The grassy southern bluffs rise nearly 200 feet and lead to Reef Campground, with 20 primitive campsites. This hike begins at the visitor center and explores the historic fort, the isolated cove, and the cemetery. The trail then crosses the undulating coastal terrace, passing gullies and transient streams to the campground.

Driving directions: From Gualala, just north of the Sonoma County line, drive 25.7 miles south on Highway 1 (the Shoreline Highway) to the posted Fort Ross State Park turnoff on the right at mile marker 33.00. Turn right (towards the ocean), and drive 0.2 miles to the parking lot at the visitor center. An entrance fee is required.

The turnoff is located 11.5 miles north of Jenner.

Hiking directions: Take the paved path along the right (south) side of the visitor center. Descend through a Monterey cypress forest, and cross a wood bridge over a transient creek. Pass the historic Call Ranch buildings on the right to the west wall of Fort Ross at 0.3 miles. From the fort's west (main) gate, follow the dirt lane across the bluff to the edge of the cliffs. Curve left and descend into U-shaped Fort Ross Cove. At the base of the deep cove, walk toward a footbridge over Fort Ross Creek. Cross the bridge and climb the vegetated east slope of the stream-fed gulch through bay laurel, willow, and alder. Leave the forest to the open, grassy slopes and enter the historic Russian cemetery, with old wood crosses and views of the fort and cove. Return to Fort Ross Cove, and follow the gated dirt road to the beach. Bear left and climb the wood steps up the cliffs to the headland bluffs. Follow the open coastal terrace past rocky coves and sea stacks. Loop around the deep cove, crossing three footbridges over gullies. The trail ends at the Reef Campground. Return along the same route. ■

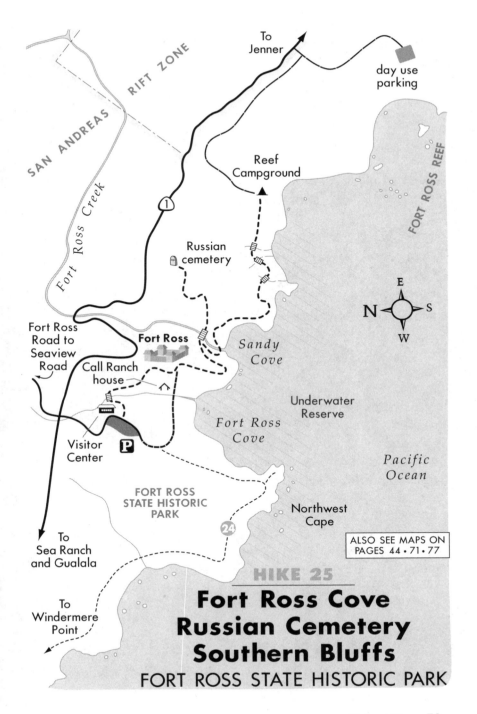

To
Jenner

day use
parking

SAN ANDREAS RIFT ZONE

Fort Ross Creek

FORT ROSS REEF

Reef
Campground

Russian cemetery

1

N E
S W

Fort Ross
Road to
Seaview
Road

Fort Ross

*Sandy
Cove*

Call Ranch
house

Visitor
Center

P

*Fort Ross
Cove*

Underwater
Reserve

*Pacific
Ocean*

**FORT ROSS
STATE HISTORIC
PARK**

24

Northwest
Cape

To
Sea Ranch
and Gualala

ALSO SEE MAPS ON
PAGES 44·71·77

To
Windermere
Point

HIKE 25

Fort Ross Cove
Russian Cemetery
Southern Bluffs
FORT ROSS STATE HISTORIC PARK

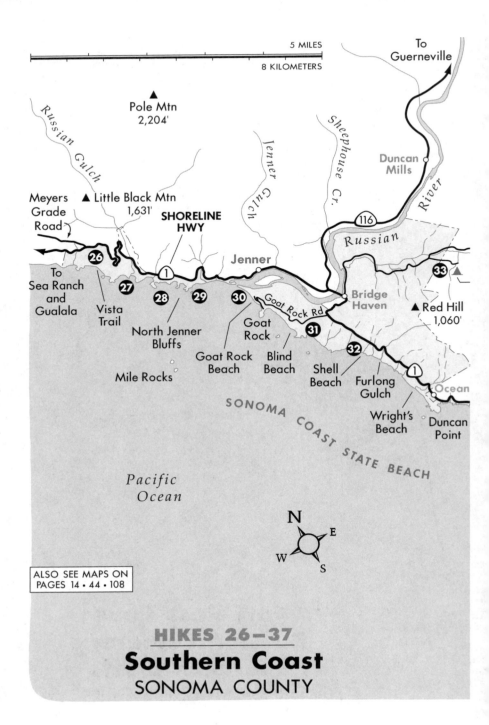

5 MILES

8 KILOMETERS

To
Guerneville

▲ Pole Mtn
2,204'

Russian Gulch

Jenner Gulch

Sheephouse Cr.

Duncan
Mills

Meyers
Grade
Road

▲ Little Black Mtn
1,631'

**SHORELINE
HWY**

116

Russian River

Jenner

1

To
Sea Ranch
and
Gualala

26

27

Vista
Trail

28

29

30

Goat Rock Rd

Bridge
Haven

33 ▲

▲ Red Hill
1,060'

North Jenner
Bluffs

Goat
Rock

31

Goat Rock
Beach

Blind
Beach

Shell
Beach

32

1

Ocean

Mile Rocks

Furlong
Gulch

Wright's
Beach

Duncan
Point

SONOMA COAST STATE BEACH

*Pacific
Ocean*

N
E
W
S

ALSO SEE MAPS ON
PAGES 14 • 44 • 108

HIKES 26–37

Southern Coast
SONOMA COUNTY

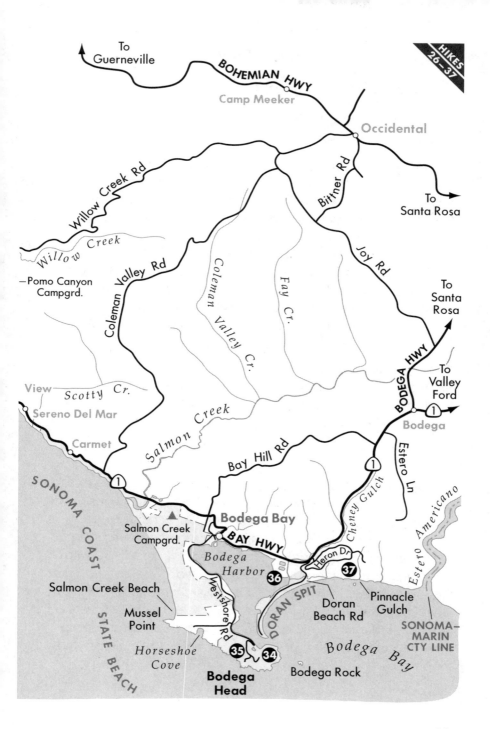

To Guerneville

BOHEMIAN HWY

Camp Meeker

Occidental

Bittner Rd

To Santa Rosa

Willow Creek Rd

Joy Rd

Willow Creek

Coleman Valley Rd

Coleman Valley Cr.

Fay Cr.

—Pomo Canyon Campgrd.

To Santa Rosa

BODEGA HWY

To Valley Ford

View

Scotty Cr.

Sereno Del Mar

Salmon Creek

Bay Hill Rd

Bodega

Carmet

1

1

Estero Ln

Cheney Gulch

Estero Americano

SONOMA COAST

Salmon Creek Campgrd.

Bodega Bay

BAY HWY

Bodega Harbor

36

Heron Dr.

37

Salmon Creek Beach

Westshore Rd

Doran Beach Rd

Pinnacle Gulch

SONOMA–MARIN CTY LINE

STATE BEACH

Mussel Point

DORAN SPIT

Bodega Bay

Horseshoe Cove

35

34

Bodega Rock

Bodega Head

26. Vista Trail

Hiking distance: 1-mile loop
Hiking time: 30 minutes
Elevation gain: 50 feet
Maps: U.S.G.S. Arched Rock

Summary of hike: The Vista Trail provides some of the most spectacular coastal vistas in California. The one-mile loop sits atop the Jenner Grade on a high plateau 600 feet above the sea. From the trail are unobstructed panoramic vistas of the chiseled coastline and jagged cliffs. The 272-acre open grassland rests at the southern base of Little Black Mountain, high above the ocean and Russian Gulch. Access to the trail is via the twisting, corkscrew route of Highway 1, cut into the edge of the rugged coastal cliffs. This blufftop trail (a wheelchair-accessible path) circles the natural area, with picnic areas and an observation deck.

Driving directions: From Jenner, drive 5 miles north on Highway 1 to the posted Vista Trail on the left at mile marker 26.30. It is at the summit, directly across from Meyers Grade Road. The turnoff is 32 miles south of Gualala and 6.5 miles south of Fort Ross State Park. Turn towards the ocean and park in the paved lot.

Hiking directions: Walk past the trailhead kiosk on the paved path to a Y-fork. Begin the loop on the left fork, heading south. At the southern end are magnificent views into the deep, creek-fed Russian Gulch (Hike 27). Loop around the south end of the expansive plateau to another Y-fork. The left fork leads 50 yards to a platform overlook with a bench and sweeping coastal views, including Point Reyes National Seashore, Bodega Head, Goat Rock, the Russian River, Russian Gulch, and Northwest Cape at Fort Ross. Return to the junction and continue across the grassland beneath forested Little Black Mountain, completing the loop. ■

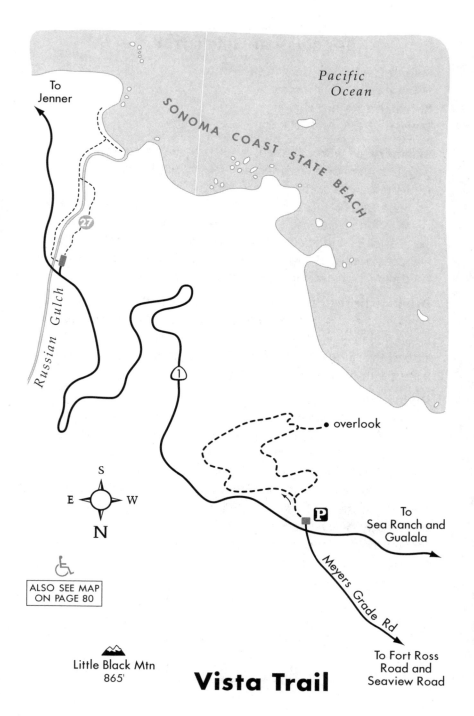

Pacific
Ocean

To
Jenner

SONOMA COAST STATE BEACH

27

Russian Gulch

1

overlook

S
E W
N

To
Sea Ranch and
Gualala

P

Meyers Grade Rd

ALSO SEE MAP
ON PAGE 80

Little Black Mtn
865'

To Fort Ross
Road and
Seaview Road

Vista Trail

27. Russian Gulch Trail

Hiking distance: 0.7 miles round trip
Hiking time: 30 minutes
Elevation gain: Level
Maps: U.S.G.S. Arched Rock

Summary of hike: Russian Gulch is a stream-fed canyon that begins in the upper reaches of Little Black Mountain. The creek flows through a sheltered valley to the sea and forms a lagoon on the crescent-shaped beach. The expansive sandy beach, part of the Sonoma Coast State Beach, is bordered by 120-foot vertical cliffs and scattered offshore rocks. This trail begins on the coastal side of Highway 1 and weaves through a thick riparian forest to the scenic beach cove.

Driving directions: From Jenner, drive 3.2 miles north on Highway 1 to the posted Russian Gulch turnoff at mile marker 24.55, located on the ocean side of the highway on the north side of the bridge. The turnoff is 34 miles south of Gualala and 8.3 miles south of Fort Ross State Park.

Hiking directions: Two trails leave from the parking lot. From the northeast corner, a gated dirt road leads to the rocky creekbed. This is the least desirable route. The main trail begins from the far south end of the parking lot. Descend through thick brush with above-ground tree roots, willows, red alders, mossy tree trunks, and ferns. Meander on the serpentine path and emerge on the rocky Russian Gulch creekbed. Continue to the huge sandy beach nestled beneath 120-foot unstable bluffs. To the north is a lagoon at the mouth of the creek, with two 25-foot-high rock formations. ■

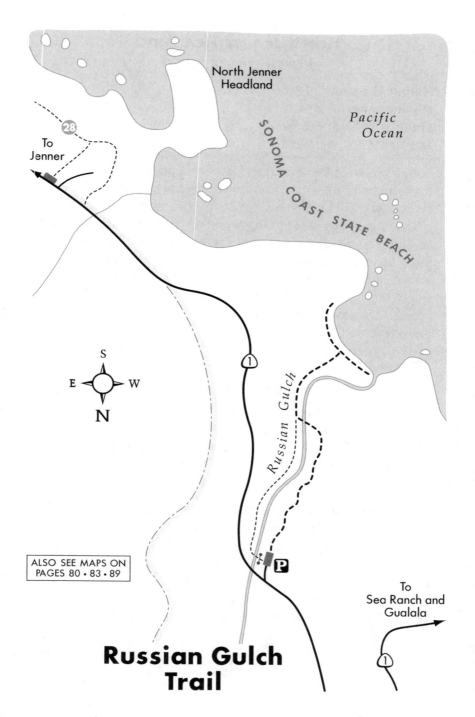

North Jenner
Headland

Pacific
Ocean

SONOMA COAST STATE BEACH

To
Jenner

28

S
E ⟡ W
N

1

Russian Gulch

ALSO SEE MAPS ON
PAGES 80 • 83 • 89

P

To
Sea Ranch and
Gualala

1

Russian Gulch
Trail

28. North Jenner Headland
NORTH JENNER BLUFFS

Hiking distance: 1.2 miles round trip
Hiking time: 30 minutes
Elevation gain: 50 feet
Maps: U.S.G.S. Arched Rock

map
page 88

Summary of hike: North of Jenner, Highway 1 clings to the rugged, breath-taking cliffs with winding bends and steep hairpin switchbacks. This dramatic and pristine stretch of coastline offers sweeping vistas of craggy cliffs plunging into the turbulent sea and jagged offshore rocks. The North Jenner Headland sits atop the steep oceanfront bluffs between Russian Gulch and Jenner. The massive 100-foot-high monolith rises out of the ocean, connected to the mainland by a narrow ridge. This hike crosses the marine terrace from Highway 1 to the headland. A cliff-edge trail follows the serrated bluffs across the 200-foot plateau, passing a series of secluded pocket beaches and elevated overlooks. The panoramic vistas include beach coves, sea stacks, oceanfront mountains, and sweeping coastal views.

Driving directions: From Jenner, drive 2.5 miles north on Highway 1 to North Jenner Headland at mile marker 23.83. The turnoff is 34.7 miles south of Gualala and 9 miles south of Fort Ross State Park. Park in the large pullout on the ocean side of the highway by a gated road.

Hiking directions: The posted trail is just south of the metal gate. Cross the grassy oceanfront terrace to the 200-foot cliffs that front the massive North Jenner Headland. Bear right to an elevated bluff with amazing vistas of the rugged, scalloped coastline. Rocks with wave-cut arches lie offshore. The path ends at Highway 1 on the south edge of a deep stream-fed gulch. Return and head southeast through the low, coastal scrub. A steep side path descends to a pocket beach. The blufftop trail follows the edge of the North Jenner Bluffs to a promontory. The trail continues south and connects with Hike 29. Choose your own turn-around spot. ■

29. North Jenner Bluffs

Hiking distance: 1 mile round trip
Hiking time: 30 minutes
Elevation gain: 50 feet
Maps: U.S.G.S. Arched Rock

map
page 88

Summary of hike: The North Jenner Bluffs sit along a three-mile stretch of coastline between the Russian River at Jenner and Russian Gulch to the north. The road, which is now Highway 1, was originally built in the 1870s. It is perched on the rolling contours of the angular cliffs high above the sea. This area is among the finest coastal displays in California. The 200-foot oceanfront bluffs stretch across a rolling marine terrace to rocky headlands and a series of beach coves. The trail includes an overlook of the crenulated coast and the Russian River as it joins the sea. The offshore rock islands are isolated remnants of the former coastline.

Driving directions: From Jenner, drive 1.9 miles north on Highway 1 to the North Jenner Bluffs at mile marker 23.21. The turnoff is 35 miles south of Gualala and 9.6 miles south of Fort Ross State Park. Park in the narrow pullout on the oceanside edge of the highway by the trail sign. Fifty yards north is a deeper parking pullout with more off-highway breathing room.

Hiking directions: Head west across the grassy plateau to the edge of the 200-foot cliffs. On the right is a gorgeous U-shaped bay with offshore rocks covered in bird guano. A narrow footpath descends the cliffs to the beach cove. Walk out onto the peninsula to the narrow, razor-sharp spine. The path extends out on the vertigo-inducing ridge. If this route is attempted, use caution and good judgement. Continue south on the main footpath, skirting the edge of the bluffs to a trail fork. The left fork returns to Highway 1 at mile marker 23.17. Stay to the right, following the bluffs to a knoll, and continue to a trail split. The right fork descends to the beach on an easy grade. From the beach, it is possible to walk south to the Russian River at low tide. The other route on the blufftop leads to an overlook on the edge of a deep, spring-fed drainage, where there are views of offshore rocks with natural arches and the Russian River mouth. Return by retracing your route.■

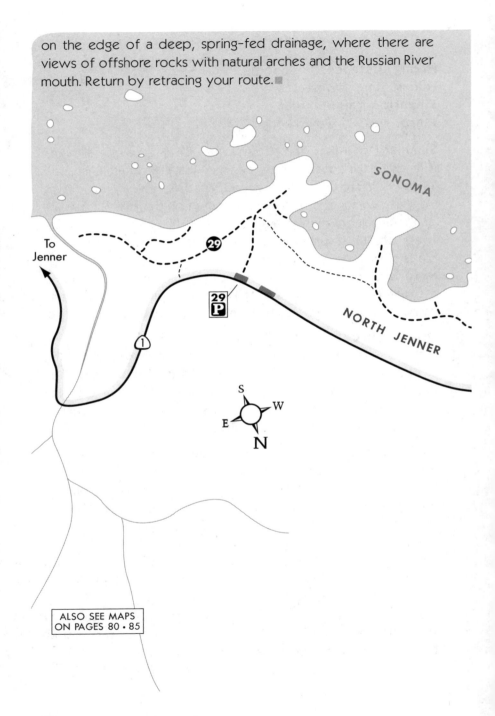

North Jenner Headland

North Jenner Bluffs

Pacific Ocean

COAST STATE BEACH

North Jenner Headland

28

BLUFFS

28 P

1

Russian Gulch

27

To
Sea Ranch
and
Gualala

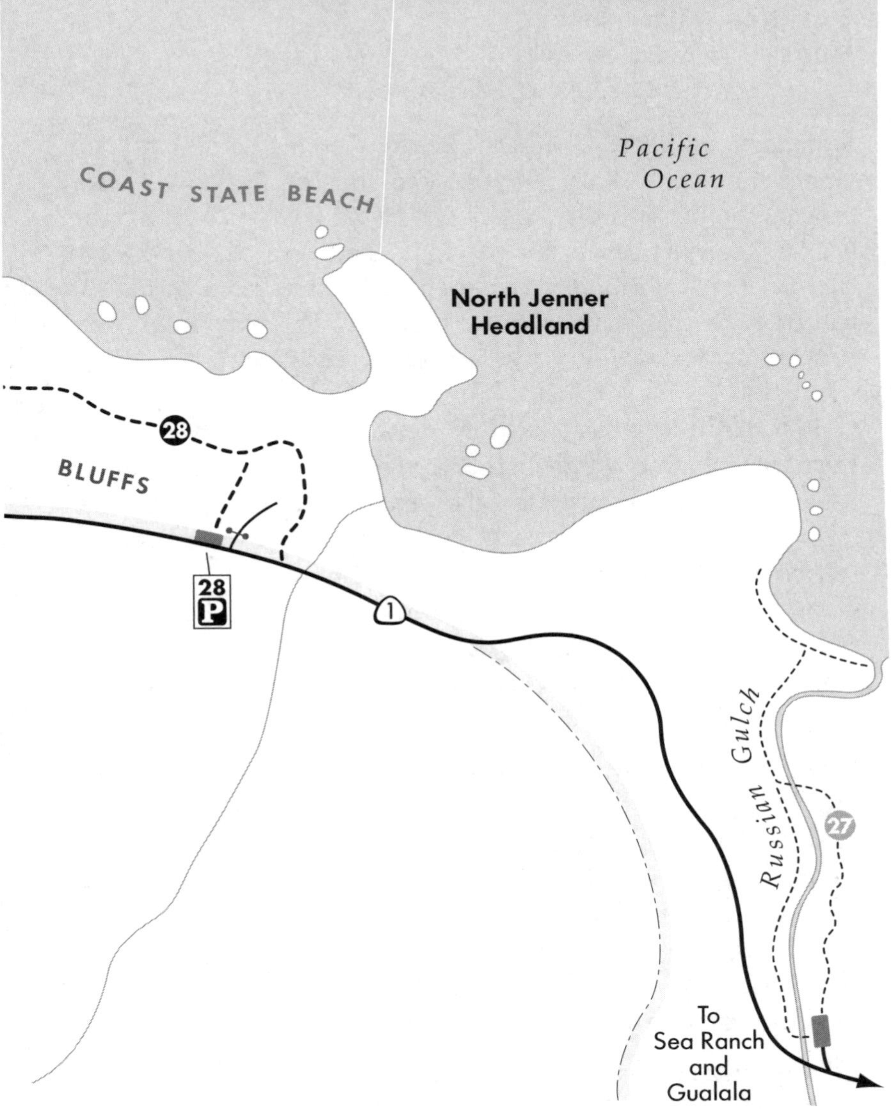

30. Goat Rock Beach
to Harbor Seal Nursery
SONOMA COAST STATE BEACH • RUSSIAN RIVER

Hiking distance: 0.75 miles round trip
Hiking time: 40 minutes
Elevation gain: 50 feet
Maps: U.S.G.S. Duncan Mills
       Sonoma Coast State Beach map

Summary of hike: Goat Rock Beach is on a sand spit formed where the Russian River empties into the sea. The low, north-pointing peninsula is wedged between the Russian River and the Pacific Ocean, ending at the mouth of the river below the town of Jenner. The north end of the strand is home to a colony of harbor seals that number in the hundreds. It is the largest seal rookery in Sonoma County. Seal pups are born from March through June.

This hike begins just north of Goat Rock, a towering, flat-topped promontory connected to the mainland by a manmade causeway. The path crosses the sandspit to the harbor seal nursery, where the seals bask on the sand. During the pupping season, adult seals can be protective. Safely stay at least 50 yards from the pups to avoid disturbing the seals and their habitat. From March through August, docents are at the site with binoculars and spotting scopes to offer information about the harbor seals.

Driving directions: From Highway 1 and Highway 116 (just south of Jenner) cross the Russian River bridge on Highway 1, and drive 0.65 miles south to Goat Rock Road at mile marker 19.15. Turn right and continue 1.9 miles to the lower parking lot at the north end of the road.

From Bodega Bay, drive 8 miles north on Highway 1 to Goat Rock Road at mile marker 19.15. Turn left and continue 1.9 miles to the lower parking lot at the north end of the road.

Hiking directions: Head north past Whale Point on the sandy peninsula between the Russian River and the Pacific Ocean. The panoramic views include Penny Island in the river, Goat Rock jutting out to sea, and gorgeous off-shore rocks. The quaint town of Jenner sits on the cliffs above the river. Cross the sand spit along Goat Rock Beach on the low scrub dunes, passing driftwood and old wood pilings. Continue toward the northern end of the peninsula near the mouth of the river, overlooking the harbor seal rookery. ■

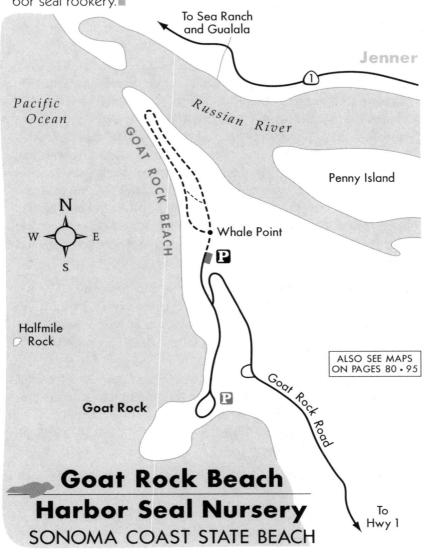

Goat Rock Beach
Harbor Seal Nursery
SONOMA COAST STATE BEACH

31. Kortum Trail:
Blind Beach to Shell Beach
SONOMA COAST STATE BEACH

Hiking distance: 4.6 miles round trip or 2.3-mile one-way shuttle

map
page 94

Hiking time: 2.5 hours
Elevation gain: 300 feet
Maps: U.S.G.S. Duncan Mills
Sonoma Coast State Beach map

Summary of hike: Sonoma Coast State Beach stretches 16 miles from Bodega Head (Hike 34) to the Vista Trail (Hike 26), located four miles north of Jenner. The state beach is actually a series of sandy beaches separated by rocky 100-foot bluffs and headlands. The craggy coastline includes secluded coves, reefs, fertile tidepools, rugged headlands, natural rock arches, sand dunes, and wildflower-covered meadows. This hike follows the north section of the Kortum Trail on the coastal plateau. The trail starts from an overlook above Blind Beach and Goat Rock and leads to Shell Beach, a sandy pocket beach surrounded by jagged offshore rocks.

Driving directions: From Highway 1 and Highway 116 (just south of Jenner) cross the Russian River bridge on Highway 1, and drive 0.65 miles south to Goat Rock Road at mile marker 19.15. Turn right and continue 0.75 miles to the Blind Beach parking lot on the left side of the high bluffs.

From Bodega Bay, drive 8 miles north on Highway 1 to Goat Rock Road at mile marker 19.15. Turn left and continue 0.75 miles to the Blind Beach parking lot on the left.

For a one-way shuttle hike, leave a second car at the Shell Beach parking lot—follow the driving directions for Hike 32.

Hiking directions: From the parking lot is a great bird's-eye view of Goat Rock and Blind Beach. A steep path descends the cliffs to Blind Beach, 200 feet below. For this hike, walk 30 yards back down the road to the posted Kortum Trail on the right.

Ascend the grassy slope toward prominent Peaked Hill. Climb to the saddle between the 377-foot peak on the right and the rocky outcrop on the left. From the ridge, the southern views stretch past Bodega Head to Point Reyes. Descend the southeast slope, and pass through a fence to a giant rock formation on the marine terrace. Curve right to the oceanfront cliffs and continue south. Pass dramatic formations on the grassy bluffs and offshore rocks, including Gull Rock, a nesting site for gulls and cormorants. Cross a small gully and continue atop the plateau. Cross a larger gully with the aid of stairs and a footbridge. Follow a 300-foot boardwalk over a wetland. Curve inland, walk across another 150-foot boardwalk, and return to the oceanfront cliffs. Pass through a fence and continue on a graveled path to the Shell Beach parking lot. A path on the right descends the bluffs to the beach. Return by retracing your steps.

To extend the hike, continue with Hike 32 to Wright's Beach.■

32. Kortum Trail: Shell Beach to Wright's Beach
SONOMA COAST STATE BEACH

Hiking distance: 3.2 miles round trip or 1.6-mile one-way shuttle

Hiking time: 1.5 hours

Elevation gain: 200 feet

Maps: U.S.G.S. Duncan Mills
Sonoma Coast State Beach map

map
page 94

Summary of hike: Shell Beach is a sandy sheltered inlet with jagged shoreline rocks that support tidepools. The beach sits at the crossroad of four trails. To the west, a trail descends the bluffs to Shell Beach, strewn with driftwood. To the east, the Pomo Canyon Trail crosses over Red Hill to Pomo Canyon Campground (Hike 33). To the north, the Kortum Trail leads to Blind Beach and Goat Rock (Hike 31). This hike heads 1.6 miles south to Wright's Beach, a wide sandy beach with a picnic area

KORTUM TRAIL:

HIKE 31
Blind Beach to Shell Beach
HIKE 32
Shell Beach to Wright's Beach
SONOMA COAST STATE BEACH

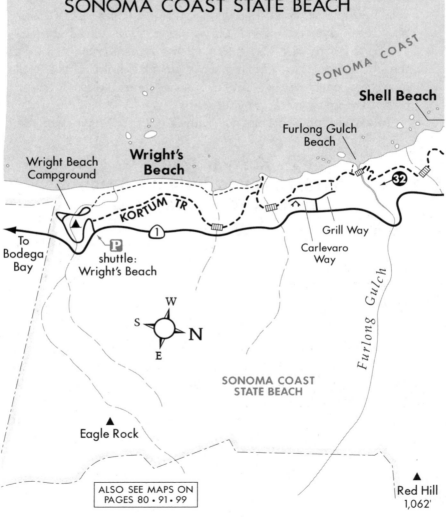

SONOMA COAST

Shell Beach

Furlong Gulch
Beach

Wright Beach
Campground

Wright's
Beach

KORTUM TR

32

To
Bodega
Bay

P
shuttle:
Wright's Beach

1

Grill Way

Carlevaro
Way

Furlong Gulch

W

S

E

N

SONOMA COAST
STATE BEACH

Eagle Rock

ALSO SEE MAPS ON
PAGES 80 • 91 • 99

Red Hill
1,062'

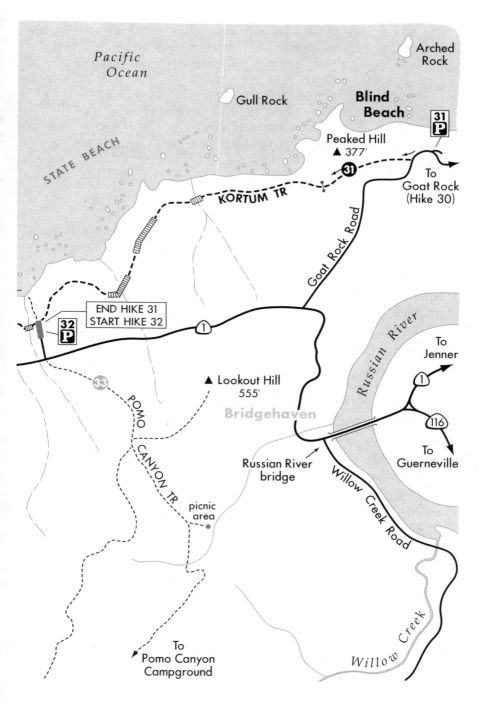

Pacific
Ocean

Arched
Rock

Gull Rock

Blind
Beach

31 P

STATE BEACH

Peaked Hill
▲ 377'

31

KORTUM TR

Goat Rock Road

To
Goat Rock
(Hike 30)

END HIKE 31
START HIKE 32

32 P

1

Russian River

To
Jenner

1

33

▲ Lookout Hill
555'

POMO CANYON TR

Bridgehaven

116

To
Guerneville

Russian River
bridge

picnic
area

Willow Creek Road

To
Pomo Canyon
Campground

Willow Creek

and tree-sheltered campground. The trail follows the coastal bluffs past abundant wildflowers and large sea stacks. En route, the path crosses Furlong Gulch, an isolated beach beneath the 80-foot bluffs.

Driving directions: From Highway 1 and Highway 116 (just south of Jenner) cross the Russian River bridge on Highway 1, and drive 1.6 miles south to the posted Shell Beach turnoff at mile marker 18.22. Turn right into the parking lot.

From Bodega Bay, drive 7 miles north on Highway 1 to the posted Shell Beach turnoff at mile marker 18.22. Turn left into the parking lot.

For a one-way shuttle hike, leave a second car at the Wright's Beach parking lot. The lot is located 1.4 miles south of the Shell Beach turnoff at mile marker 16.8.

Hiking directions: From the west end of the parking lot, a trail descends 150 yards to scenic Shell Beach, surrounded by jagged sea stacks. Take the posted Kortum Trail south, and weave down into a stream-fed drainage. Cross a wooden footbridge over the first of five seasonal creeks. Climb out of the gully to the coastal terrace and the oceanfront cliffs at an overlook of Shell Beach and the dramatic off-shore rocks. Follow the edge of the bluffs and curve east, away from the ocean. Drop into a second drainage and cross the bridge over the ephemeral stream. Return to the bluffs, with views of Red Hill and the sandy beach at the mouth of Furlong Gulch. Zigzag down three switchbacks into Furlong Gulch. Cross another bridge over the creek and a shorter bridge over a feeder stream. After the second bridge is a junction. The right fork descends steps to Furlong Gulch Beach on the south edge of the creek. Continue straight ahead, climbing the 100-foot bluffs. Atop the terrace, pass a connecting trail from Grill Way. Curve left toward the house near the end of Carlevaro Way. Before reaching the house, veer to the right, staying on the trail. Drop down and cross a bridge over the fourth stream to a posted junction. Straight ahead, the right path leads to a sandy beach at the mouth of the stream. At low tide, this route can be taken to Wright's Beach, forming a loop with the blufftop trail. The main trail curves left and weaves across the bluffs, crossing a bridge over a winter stream near Highway 1. Follow the south wall of the drainage, and return to the ocean-front, where the path joins a gravel utility road. The gravel ends at the paved access road leading down to Wright's Beach and campground. Wind a quarter mile downhill to the sandy beach and campground. ∎

33. Pomo Canyon Trail:
Pomo Canyon Campground to Shell Beach
SONOMA COAST STATE BEACH

Hiking distance: 6.6 miles round trip or
3.3-mile one-way shuttle

Hiking time: 3.5 hours

Elevation gain: 650 feet

Maps: U.S.G.S. Duncan Mills
Sonoma Coast State Beach map

map
page 99

Summary of hike: Pomo Canyon Campground sits on the alluvial flats above broad Willow Creek canyon in a beautiful redwood grove. The Pomo Canyon Trail begins at the campground and winds up and over the rolling coastal hills, skirting the north slope of Red Hill. The trail weaves through lush redwood forests, oak and fir woodlands, open grasslands, and crosses seasonal streams en route to the ocean at Shell Beach. The path was an ancient trading route of the Pomo and Miwok people. The hike offers panoramic vistas of the lower Russian River, Willow Creek, the town of Jenner, and the serrated coastline.

Driving directions: From Highway 1 and Highway 116 (just south of Jenner) cross the south side of the Russian River ridge on Highway 1. Immediately turn left on Willow Creek Road at mile marker 19.79. Drive 2.6 miles on the narrow, paved road to the posted Pomo Canyon Campground turnoff. Park near the gated road but not in front of the gate. The campground is open from

April through November. During that time, drive a half mile up the campground road and park by the kiosk.

From Bodega Bay, drive 9 miles north on Highway 1 to Willow Creek Road at mile marker 19.79. The road is just before the Russian River bridge. Turn right and follow the directions above.

For a one-way shuttle hike, leave a second car at the Shell Beach parking lot—follow the driving directions for Hike 32.

Hiking directions: Walk past the gate and follow the unpaved campground access road. Stroll a half mile through a grassy valley between forested hills to the campground entrance. Head into the campground on the right as the road veers off to the left. Go 15 yards and bear right on the posted Dr. David Joseph Memorial Pomo Canyon Trail. Enter the gorgeous redwood forest and stay to the right past two paths on the left and the campsites on each side of the main trail. Climb up the ridge through tanbark oak, bay laurel, Douglas fir, circular stands of redwoods, sword ferns, and trillium. Emerge from the forest to a Y-fork at 0.8 miles, located in a clearing with views of Jenner and the mouth of the Russian River. The left fork leads to the 1,062-foot summit of Red Hill and forms a loop with this trail. Stay to the right toward Shell Beach, and traverse the hill. Cross a bridge over a seasonal creek and curve right, skirting a rock outcrop. Descend through brush to the open, rolling slopes with ocean views. Cross a small stream and reenter a fir and redwood forest. Cross a third stream and gradually descend through the thick brush. Curve left into the gulch, cross the creek, and head down the draw. Ascend the hill to a knoll with a picnic area and vista point on the right. The main trail continues straight, with a view of the serpentine Russian River. Head up another hill on the wide, grassy path to a knoll atop the 500-foot oceanfront ridge and a junction with the west end of the Red Hill Trail. Pass a trail on the right leading to Lookout Hill, and descend the slope, with views of Point Reyes, Bodega Head, Gull Rock, and Goat Rock. Drop down a partially paved utility road to the trailhead gate, across the road from the Shell Beach parking lot. ■

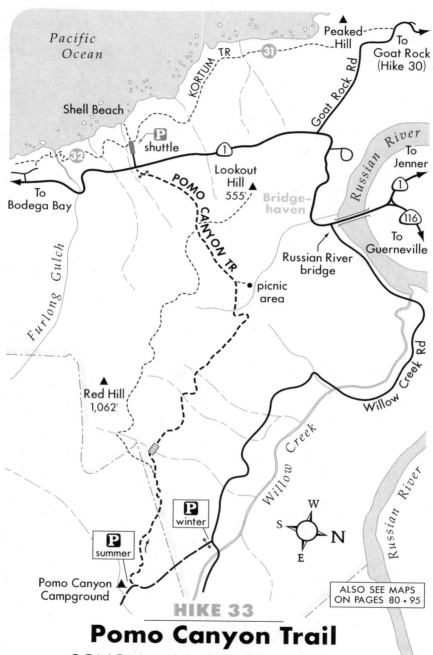

Pacific
Ocean

Shell Beach

KORTUM TR

Peaked Hill

To Goat Rock (Hike 30)

Goat Rock Rd

31

32

shuttle

1

To Bodega Bay

POMO CANYON TR

Lookout Hill 555'

Bridge-haven

Russian River

To Jenner

1

116

To Guerneville

Russian River bridge

picnic area

Furlong Gulch

Red Hill 1,062'

Willow Creek Rd

Willow Creek

Russian River

W
N
S
E

P winter

P summer

ALSO SEE MAPS ON PAGES 80 · 95

Pomo Canyon Campground

HIKE 33

Pomo Canyon Trail
SONOMA COAST STATE BEACH

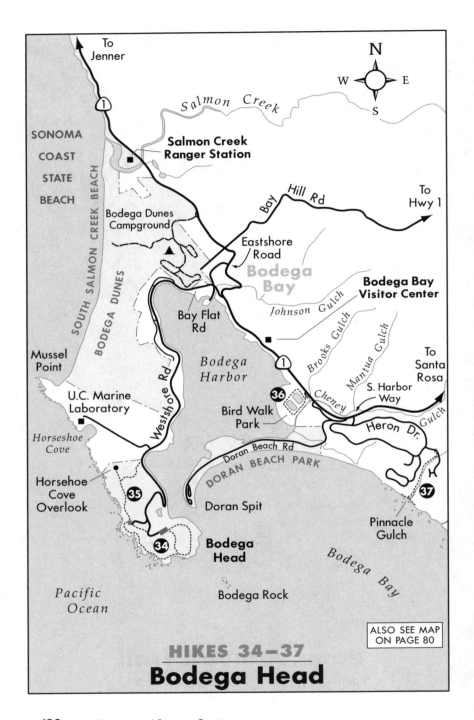

To
Jenner

N

SONOMA
COAST
STATE
BEACH

Salmon Creek

Salmon Creek
Ranger Station

Bay Hill Rd

To
Hwy 1

SOUTH SALMON CREEK BEACH

Bodega Dunes
Campground

Eastshore
Road

Bodega
Bay

Bodega Bay
Visitor Center

BODEGA DUNES

Bay Flat
Rd

Johnson Gulch

Brooks Gulch

Mussel
Point

Bodega
Harbor

To
Santa
Rosa

Westshore Rd

Mantua Gulch

U.C. Marine
Laboratory

Cheney

S. Harbor
Way

Heron Dr.

Gulch

Horseshoe
Cove

Bird Walk
Park

36

Horsehoe
Cove
Overlook

35

Doran Beach Rd

DORAN BEACH PARK

37

Doran Spit

Pinnacle
Gulch

34

Bodega
Head

Bodega Bay

Pacific
Ocean

Bodega Rock

ALSO SEE MAP
ON PAGE 80

HIKES 34–37
Bodega Head

34. Bodega Head Trail

Hiking distance: 1.7-mile loop
Hiking time: 1 hour
Elevation gain: 200 feet
Maps: U.S.G.S. Bodega Head
      Sonoma Coast State Beach map

map
page 103

Summary of hike: Bodega Head, a massive granite promontory jutting out into the sea, marks the entrance into Bodega Harbor. The 800-acre harbor is protected and enclosed from Bodega Bay by a narrow two-mile-long sand spit known as Doran Spit. This hike circles the exposed, southern tip of the grassy headland 200 feet above Bodega Harbor and Doran Spit. The trail loops around to the open sea, overlooking the rocky shores, hidden caves and coves, untouched beaches, sea stacks, natural arches, bird-nesting cliffs, coastal bluffs, a series of eroded spires, and the open ocean. The nearly treeless landscape is covered with scrub vegetation and coastal grass. Gray whale pods migrate with new calves from December through April, following a northerly route from Baja California to Alaska. The high cliffs offer an excellent vantage spot for observation. Docents offer information about the whale migration and share their binoculars every weekend from January through April.

Driving directions: From downtown Bodega Bay, drive north on Highway 1 to East Shore Road and turn left. (The turnoff is one mile north of the Bodega Bay Visitor Center.) Continue 0.3 miles to Bay Flat Road and turn right. Drive 3.3 miles to a road fork. (En route, Bay Flat Road becomes Westshore Road.) Veer left and go 0.4 miles to the east trailhead parking area. A parking fee is required.

Hiking directions: From the far east end of the parking lot by the restrooms, head east. The trail overlooks the sandy beach of the Doran Spit, enclosed Bodega Harbor, Bodega Bay, Point Reyes, and the ocean. Curve around to the south end of the headland. Off the steep cliffs are offshore outcroppings, the sound of barking sea lions, and Bodega Rock, less than a half mile from shore. Follow the south edge of the cliffs through scrub vegetation and coastal grassland, passing offshore rocks and a small inaccessible pocket beach. Climb the open, grassy slope to the highest point of the hike, passing vertical rock cliffs, stunning sea stacks, and far-reaching vistas. Pass a memorial to fishermen lost at sea and a popular overlook for observing migrating whales by the west parking lot. Pick up the footpath on the left (north) side of the restroom. Traverse the sloping grassland and pass through a small grove of windswept cypress to the east parking lot access road. Walk around the vehicle gate and follow the road

35. Horseshoe Cove Overlook

Hiking distance: 1.2 miles round trip
Hiking time: 40 minutes
Elevation gain: 200 feet
Maps: U.S.G.S. Bodega Head
      Sonoma Coast State Beach map

Summary of hike: Horseshoe Cove sits on the west (ocean) side of Bodega Head, adjacent to the Bodega Marine Laboratory and Marine Reserve. The laboratory and reserve are part of the University of California Natural Reserve System. The research and teaching facility protects 362 acres of undisturbed intertidal habitat, a salt marsh, mudflats, sandy beaches, coastal prairie, dunes, and a mile of coastline. Horseshoe Cove is exactly as the name implies, a deep, U-shaped sandy beach cove. The cove is part of the marine reserve. Unfortunately, public access is restricted. It is a place you can see but not touch. The Horseshoe Cove Overlook sits atop the peninsula's highest point at 265 feet, where there are sweeping 360-degree vistas. Scattered around the windswept summit are weathered rock outcroppings covered with lichen. The trail begins from the western trailhead of Bodega Head and gently climbs 200 feet to the summit while overlooking the Pacific.

Driving directions: From downtown Bodega Bay, drive north on Highway 1 to East Shore Road and turn left (one mile north of

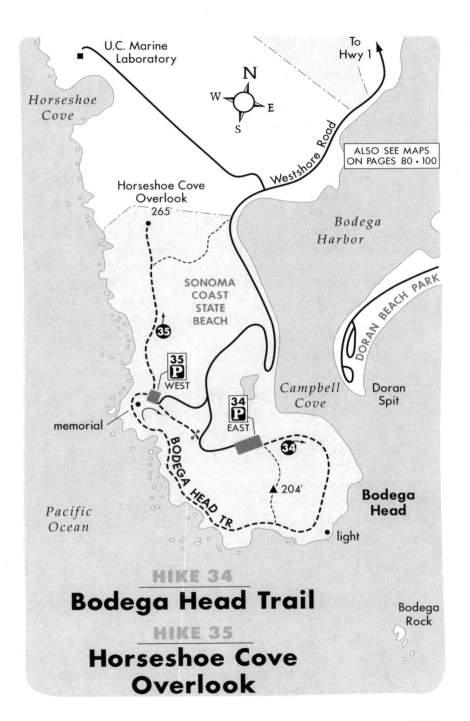

U.C. Marine
Laboratory

To
Hwy 1

N
W   E
S

*Horseshoe
Cove*

Westshore Road

ALSO SEE MAPS
ON PAGES 80 · 100

Horseshoe Cove
Overlook
265'

*Bodega
Harbor*

SONOMA
COAST
STATE
BEACH

DORAN BEACH PARK

35

35
P
WEST

34
P
EAST

*Campbell
Cove*

Doran
Spit

34

memorial

BODEGA HEAD TR

▲ 204'

**Bodega
Head**

*Pacific
Ocean*

light

Bodega
Rock

HIKE 34

Bodega Head Trail

HIKE 35

Horseshoe Cove
Overlook

the Bodega Bay Visitor Center). Continue 0.3 miles to Bay Flat Road and turn right. Drive 3.3 miles to a road fork. (En route, Bay Flat Road becomes Westshore Road.) Veer right and go 0.2 miles to the west trailhead parking area. A parking fee is required.

Hiking directions: From the north end of the parking lot, take the posted trail north. Climb the hill overlooking the ocean to a posted Y-fork at 0.4 miles. The right fork claims Salmon Creek Beach is 2.2 miles. This is true, but it entails quite a bit of walking on Westshore Road. The old trail used to cut through the Bodega Marine Reserve en route to the massive dune fields, but is currently not accessible. Take the left fork toward the Horseshoe Cove Overlook. Gently climb to the 265-foot summit amid granite rock formations and 360-degree vistas. Views of the Sonoma and Marin County coast include Mussel Point, the massive 900-acre Bodega Dunes, Horseshoe Cove, Bodega Marine Labs, Bodega Harbor, the town of Bodega Bay, Doran Sand Spit, Tomales Bay, Point Reyes Peninsula, and the open sea. Return by retracing your steps.■

36. Bird Walk Coastal Access Park
DORAN PARK MARSH
355 Highway 1 · Bodega Bay

Hiking distance: 0.75-mile loop
Hiking time: 30 minutes
Elevation gain: Level
Maps: U.S.G.S. Bodega Head

Summary of hike: The Bird Walk Coastal Access Park lies at the mouth of Cheney Gulch where it empties into Bodega Harbor, just north of the Doran Spit. The coastal access trail follows old levees built to hold silt dredged from Bodega Harbor. The elevated walkway circles the freshwater ponds held within the levees. The trail overlooks Doran Park Marsh (a revitalized saltwater marsh) and the 800-acre harbor. With thousands of birds throughout the year, it is a superb bird observation area for waterfowl, shore-

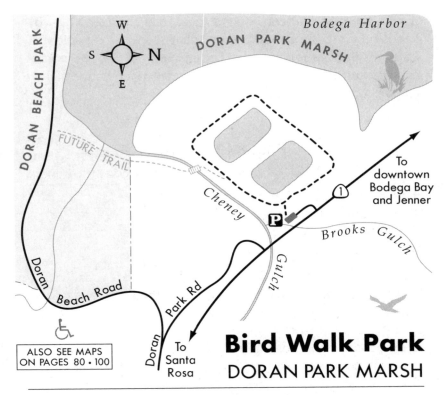

ALSO SEE MAPS
ON PAGES 80 • 100

Bird Walk Park
DORAN PARK MARSH

birds, and songbirds. Future trail plans include a bridge connecting the Bird Walk Coastal Access Park with Doran Beach Park along the sand spit. Leashed dogs are allowed on the trail.

Driving directions: From the south end of Bodega Bay, just before Highway 1 leaves the coast, turn right at the posted Bird Walk Coastal Access turnoff. (The turnoff is 0.7 miles south of the Bodega Bay Visitor Center.) Drive 0.1 mile to the trailhead parking lot. A parking fee is required.

Hiking directions: Walk up the slope on the paved, handicapped-accessible path to the east pond. The loop path can be hiked in either direction. These directions go to the left, hiking clockwise. Cross the south end of the first pond, parallel to the Cheney Gulch channel on the left. Continue to the far end of the second (west) pond, overlooking the expansive Doran Park Marsh, a protected mudflat. The vistas include Point Reyes in

Marin County; prominent Bodega Head; and the narrow, two-mile-long arm of Doran Spit, a crescent-shaped sand spit that separates Bodega Harbor from Bodega Bay. Walk to the northwest corner of Doran Beach Park and curve right. Return alongside the pond, skirting the edge of Bodega Harbor. ■

37. Pinnacle Gulch
20600 Mockingbird Road · Bodega Harbor

Hiking distance: 1.2 miles round trip
Hiking time: 40 minutes
Elevation gain: 350 feet
Maps: U.S.G.S. Bodega Head
Pinnacle Gulch–Shorttail Gulch Coastal Access map

Summary of hike: Pinnacle Gulch sits at the south end of the town of Bodega Bay between Doran Spit and the Sonoma–Marin county line. The half-mile gulch leads to Pinnacle Beach, a quiet sandy beach cove with a distinctive off-shore rock. This stream-fed gulch and beach is used mainly by locals . The trailhead is tucked away in a newer housing development by a golf course. The Coastal Access Trail, part of the Sonoma County Regional Parks, leads down the narrow gulch alongside a winter stream to the beach. Pinnacle Rock lies just off shore. Dogs are allowed on the trail.

Driving directions: From the south end of Bodega Bay, just after Highway 1 leaves the coast, turn south on South Harbor Way. (The turnoff is 1.2 miles south of the Bodega Bay Visitor Center.) Drive one block to the end of the street. Turn left on Heron Drive, and continue 0.9 miles to Mockingbird Road. Turn left and go 0.1 mile to the posted trailhead on the right. Park in the lot on the left. A parking fee is required.

Hiking directions: Cross Mockingbird Road to the posted trailhead. Descend through a canopy of cypress and wax myrtle. Follow the dirt path, paralleling Mockingbird Road, and curve right to the head of Pinnacle Gulch. Zigzag down five short switchbacks into the lush drainage overgrown with coastal scrub, coyote brush, and berry vines. The creekbed is lined with willows and salmonberry. Cross a wood footbridge on the north wall of the narrow stream-fed canyon. Coastal scenery and homes perched on the bluffs above the gulch soon come into view. The trail hugs the canyon wall while crossing two more bridges over small water channels. Descend to the isolated quarter-mile-long sandy beach on Bodega Bay, with a close-up view of Pinnacle Rock. The gorgeous coastal views include Tomales Bay; Point Reyes; Bodega Head; and the narrow, two-mile-long Doran Beach Park, the crescent-shaped sand spit that separates Bodega Harbor from Bodega Bay. ■

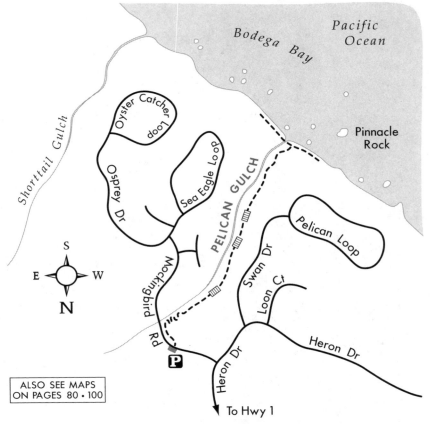

Pinnacle Gulch

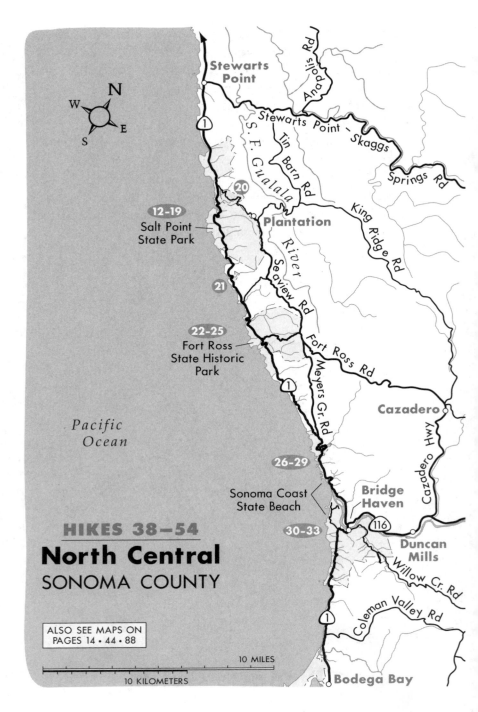

N
W · E
S

Stewarts Point

Annapolis Rd

Stewarts Point – Skaggs Springs Rd

S. F. Gualala

Tin Barn Rd

King Ridge Rd

12-19
Salt Point
State Park

Plantation

River

Seaview Rd

21

20

22-25
Fort Ross
State Historic
Park

Fort Ross Rd

Meyers Gr. Rd

Cazadero

Cazadero Hwy

Pacific
Ocean

26-29

Sonoma Coast
State Beach

**Bridge
Haven**

HIKES 38–54
North Central
SONOMA COUNTY

30-33

116

**Duncan
Mills**

Willow Cr. Rd

ALSO SEE MAPS ON
PAGES 14 · 44 · 88

Coleman Valley Rd

10 MILES

10 KILOMETERS

Bodega Bay

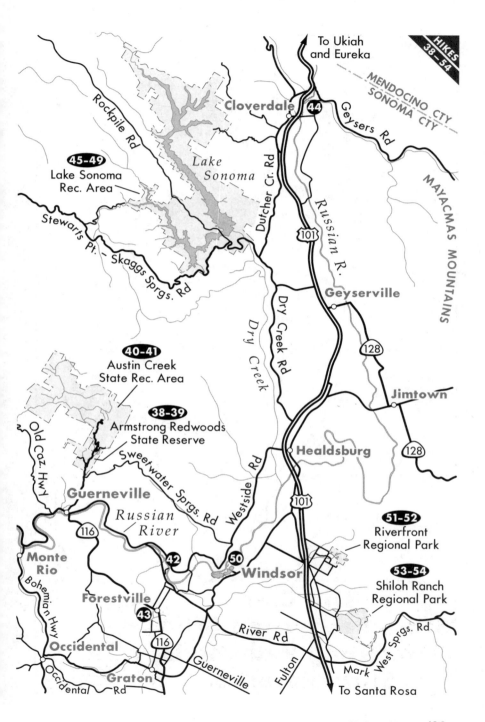

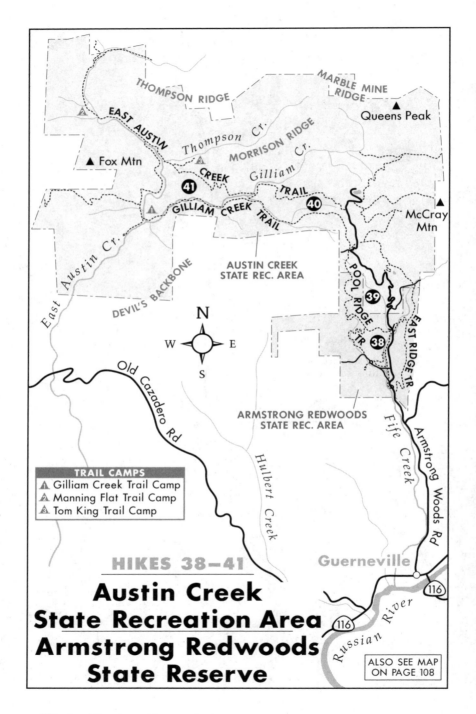

THOMPSON RIDGE

MARBLE MINE RIDGE

▲ Queens Peak

EAST AUSTIN

MORRISON RIDGE

Thompson Cr.

Gilliam Cr.

▲ Fox Mtn

CREEK

Gilliam

41

TRAIL

GILLIAM CREEK TRAIL

40

▲ McCray Mtn

East Austin Cr.

AUSTIN CREEK
STATE REC. AREA

DEVIL'S BACKBONE

POOL RIDGE TR

39

East Austin Cr.

N

W ✦ E

S

EAST RIDGE TR

38

Old Cazadero Rd

ARMSTRONG REDWOODS
STATE REC. AREA

Hulbert Creek

Fife Creek

Armstrong Woods Rd

TRAIL CAMPS
⛺ Gilliam Creek Trail Camp
⛺ Manning Flat Trail Camp
⛺ Tom King Trail Camp

Guerneville

HIKES 38—41

Austin Creek
State Recreation Area
Armstrong Redwoods
State Reserve

116

116

Russian River

ALSO SEE MAP
ON PAGE 108

38. Armstrong Nature Trail:
Pioneer Trail, Icicle Tree Trail and Discovery Trail
ARMSTRONG REDWOODS STATE RESERVE
17020 Armstrong Woods Road · Guerneville

Hiking distance: 1.7 miles
Hiking time: 1 hour
Elevation gain: Level
Maps: U.S.G.S. Guerneville and Cazadero
Armstrong Redwoods State Reserve map

map
page 113

Summary of hike: In the 1870s, lumberman Colonel James Armstrong, a Union officer in the Civil War, realized that if not preserved, this gorgeous area of primeval redwoods would be destroyed by logging. He set aside the land as a natural park and botanical garden. Due to this early preservation, the 805-acre reserve contains the largest remaining first-growth coast redwoods in Sonoma County. It is also the only grove of first generation redwoods open to the public in the county. This ancient grove flourishes along Fife Creek in a cool and dark valley floor at 3,316 feet. Scattered among the stately redwoods are tanbark oak, California bay laurel, and big-leaf maple. The shady forest floor, highlighted by filtered sunlight, is carpeted with redwood sorrel, trillium, fairy bells, redwood orchid, mushrooms, lichens, and mosses. This hike strolls through the heart of the redwood cathedral under the forest canopy. The Armstrong Nature Trail and Icicle Tree Trail are self-guided nature trails with interpretive displays and a printed guide. The Discovery Trail is a Braille Trail for the visually impaired. Both trails are connected to the Pioneer Trail, leading from the visitor center to the large group picnic area. Dogs are allowed on the paved roads and in picnic areas.

Driving directions: From downtown Guerneville on Main Street (Highway 116), drive 2.3 miles north on Armstrong Woods Road to the visitor center on the right, just before the state park entrance station. Park in the large lot on the right by the visitor center.

Hiking directions: From the visitor center parking lot, walk up the park road past the park entrance kiosk to the posted nature trail. Bear left and parallel Fife Creek through a forest of massive redwoods. Cross the park road to the 1,300-year-old Parson Jones Tree. It is the tallest tree in the grove at 310 feet and a diameter of 13.8 feet. Stroll through the redwoods and cross another road to Burbank Circle, an enormous ring of redwood trees. Continue to a junction with the Discovery Trail. For now, stay to the right on the Pioneer Trail. Follow Fife Creek upstream to a second junction with the Icicle Tree Trail, our return route. Continue straight, crossing a bridge over Fife Creek and a second bridge over a tributary stream. At 0.75 miles, the trail reaches a road fork by the picnic area. Return to the Icicle Tree Trail, and curve right to Icicle Tree, with clusters of icicle-shaped burl formations (nodules) growing on the side of the tree's trunk. Cross a wooden footbridge over Fife Creek. Climb steps and weave through the forest to the Colonel James Armstrong Tree near the park road. The tree is at least 1,400 years old and is the largest tree (in mass) within the reserve. The towering tree reaches 308 feet high with a diameter of 14.6 feet. Veer left on the Discovery Trail. This portion of the hike is a Braille Trail. It is equipped with a guide wire and interpretive stations in Braille and English that describe trailside features through touch and smell. Complete the loop by the Burbank Circle. Go to the right, retracing your steps, or return on the park road. ■

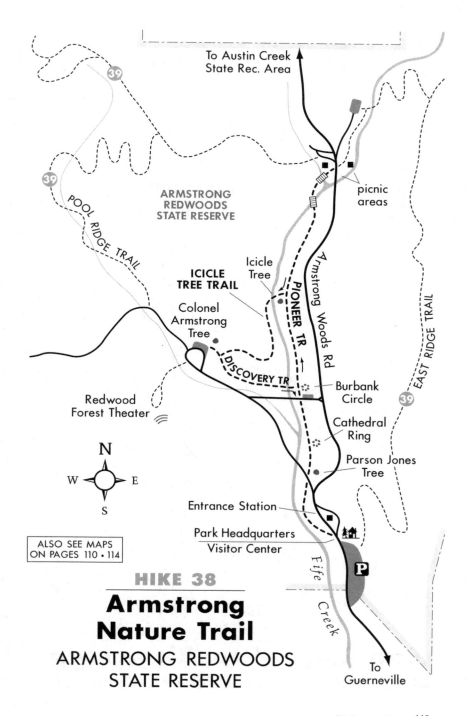

To Austin Creek
State Rec. Area

picnic
areas

ARMSTRONG
REDWOODS
STATE RESERVE

POOL RIDGE TRAIL

Icicle
Tree

ICICLE
TREE TRAIL

Armstrong Woods Rd

PIONEER TR

EAST RIDGE TRAIL

Colonel
Armstrong
Tree

DISCOVERY TR

Burbank
Circle

Redwood
Forest Theater

Cathedral
Ring

Parson Jones
Tree

N
W   E
S

Entrance Station

Park Headquarters
Visitor Center

ALSO SEE MAPS
ON PAGES 110 • 114

Fife

P

HIKE 38

Armstrong
Nature Trail
ARMSTRONG REDWOODS
STATE RESERVE

Creek

To
Guerneville

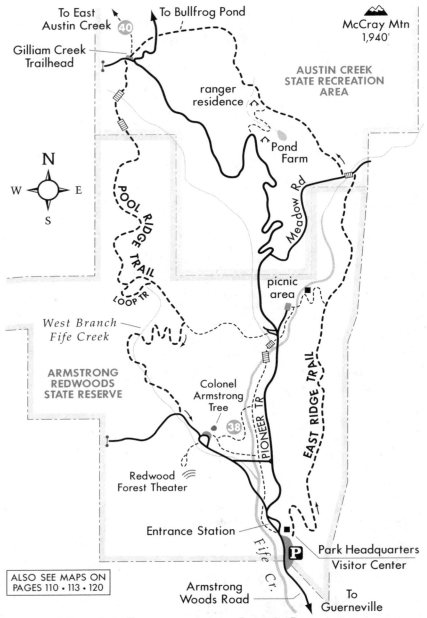

To East Austin Creek 40

To Bullfrog Pond

McCray Mtn 1,940'

Gilliam Creek Trailhead

AUSTIN CREEK STATE RECREATION AREA

ranger residence

Pond Farm

N
W   E
S

Meadow Rd

POOL RIDGE TRAIL

LOOP TR

picnic area

West Branch Fife Creek

ARMSTRONG REDWOODS STATE RESERVE

EAST RIDGE TRAIL

Colonel Armstrong Tree 38

PIONEER TR

Redwood Forest Theater

Entrance Station

Park Headquarters Visitor Center

P

ALSO SEE MAPS ON PAGES 110 • 113 • 120

Fife Cr.

Armstrong Woods Road

To Guerneville

East Ridge—Pool Ridge Loop
ARMSTRONG REDWOODS—AUSTIN CREEK

39. East Ridge—Pool Ridge Loop

ARMSTRONG REDWOODS STATE RESERVE
AUSTIN CREEK STATE RECREATION AREA

17020 Armstrong Woods Road · Guerneville

Hiking distance: 5.6-mile loop
Hiking time: 4 hours
Elevation gain: 1,100 feet
Maps: U.S.G.S. Guerneville and Cazadero
     Armstrong Redwoods State Reserve map

Summary of hike: The East Ridge—Pool Ridge Loop circles the heart of Armstrong Redwoods State Reserve on two ridges that overlook the first-growth redwood forest deep in the Fife Creek Canyon. The hike begins and ends on the canyon floor among the magnificent giant sentinels. The East Ridge Trail climbs 1,100 feet through Douglas fir, tanbark oak, California bay laurel, and madrones, emerging to far-reaching views across the tops of the ancient forest. En route, the trail crosses the headwaters of Fife Creek and passes Pond Farm, which was home, workshop, and school of well-known ceramic artist Marguerite Wildenhain from 1949 to 1980. The Pool Ridge Trail parallels the opposite side of the canyon from the Gilliam Creek Trailhead in the Austin Creek State Recreation Area. The trail leads to the canyon floor and the Colonel Armstrong Tree, passing open grassy slopes and skirting the West Branch of Fife Creek. The trail descends through gnarled oaks, bay laurels, and Douglas fir. The two trails are also equestrian routes

Driving directions: Same as Hike 38.

Hiking directions: Begin at the posted East Ridge Trailhead on the south (right) side of the visitor center. Head up the hillside on the west-facing slope, steadily gaining elevation through the shaded forest. Thick tree roots form a mosaic pattern on the trail. Climb up two switchbacks to the ridge. Follow the rises and dips on the rolling ridge to a junction at 1.2 miles. The left fork descends 0.3 miles to the picnic area at Fife Creek and the

Pioneer Trail on the canyon floor (Hike 38) for a shorter 2.2-mile loop. Continue straight, climbing and descending the hilly route toward McCray Mountain. Emerge from the forest to a sloping meadow with vistas of the densely forested canyon. Drop down to Fife Creek and a T-junction with Meadow Road on the park boundary at 1.8 miles. Bear left on the unpaved service road, and cross a bridge over the creek in Austin Creek State Recreation Area. Pick up the East Ridge Trail on the right, 20 yards ahead. Climb to an overlook of a pond in a scenic, grassy depression. Follow the east side of the pond to a Y-fork. The left branch leads to Pond Farm and the park road. Stay to the right and continue uphill through Douglas fir, passing a ranger's residence on the left. Cross over a small stream on an S-curve, and emerge to an open slope, with vistas across the Russian River to Mount Tamalpais. Follow the slope to the ridge with a viewing bench and a junction. To the right, the East Ridge Trail continues 1.3 miles to Bullfrog Pond. Take the left fork 150 yards to the park road, with views into the East Austin Creek drainage. Cross the road, descend steps, and curve left. Enter a redwood forest and return to the road at the Gilliam Creek Trailhead. (Hike 40 heads to the north.) Follow the narrow road 85 yards to the right to the posted Pool Ridge Trail. Bear left on the footpath and head downhill into the forest, leaving the panoramic views. Weave along the contours of the cliffs and skirt around deep ravines. Descend on three switchbacks and cross two bridges, hugging the hillside over two steep drainages through oak groves. Reenter Armstrong Redwoods State Reserve, and pass two junctions with the posted Loop Trail on the right at 4 miles. The side path leads to an abandoned apple orchard and an overlook. A short distance ahead is a trail split. The left fork, straight ahead, leads 0.6 miles to the Pioneer Trail on the valley floor. Go to the right and descend on six switchbacks along the West Branch of Fife Creek. Cross the creek four times, following it downstream to a park road. Bear left 0.1 mile to the main road. Veer right and continue 0.4 miles through the stately redwoods, returning to the visitor center. ■

40. Gilliam Creek Trail—
East Austin Creek: East Loop
AUSTIN CREEK STATE RECREATION AREA

Hiking distance: 4.2-mile loop
Hiking time: 3 hours

*map
page 120*

Elevation gain: 1,000 feet
Maps: U.S.G.S. Cazadero
       Austin Creek State Recreation Area map

Summary of hike: Austin Creek State Recreation Area encompasses 5,683 acres in a largely undeveloped area. The isolated wilderness is adjacent to, and accessed through, Armstrong Redwoods State Reserve. The rugged topography includes rolling grassland meadows, oak-covered knolls, deep valleys, forested ridges, chaparral hillsides, oak woodlands, conifer forests, and year-round streams. There are three backcountry camps and more than 20 miles of hiking and equestrian trails. This hike begins with vistas across the Russian River Valley from 1,100 feet. The path contours across grassy slopes and tree-lined creek ravines on the Gilliam Creek Trail. En route, the trail fords Schoolhouse Creek three times. The hike returns on the East Austin Creek Trail, an unpaved service road, and steeply winds up the canyon through meadows with spectacular vistas.

Driving directions: From downtown Guerneville on Main Street (Highway 116), drive 2.3 miles north on Armstrong Woods Road to the visitor center on the right, just before the state park entrance station. Continue 2.5 miles past the entrance station, staying to the right, to the Gilliam Creek Trailhead parking area. The last 1.7 miles winds up a narrow, paved mountain road on a 12% grade. An entrance fee is required.

Hiking directions: From the trailhead map, head downhill on the Gilliam Creek Trail. Wind down the mountain slope, crossing two forks of Schoolhouse Creek by its headwaters. Cross Gilliam Ridge, a rolling, grassy ridge dotted with oaks, then traverse the north slope of the canyon. Walk over a few seasonal tributaries to the canyon floor and Schoolhouse Creek at just under a mile. Rock-hop over the creek, and follow the southwest wall of the canyon. Stroll through the lush, wet forest with fern-covered hills. Thick green moss covers the rocks and tree trunks. Rock-hop over Schoolhouse Creek two consecutive times to a posted junction at 2 miles. The trail straight ahead leads to Gilliam Creek Camp. To extend the hike for a 9-mile double loop, continue with Hike 41. For this hike, wade across Schoolhouse Creek and curve right, looping around a hill to the south bank of Gilliam Creek. Head upstream to a junction with the East Austin Creek Trail by a bridge. Veer right, staying on the south side of the creek. Head up the hill along Gilliam Creek. Curve away from the creek, and steadily climb the well-named Panorama Grade, gaining 1,000 feet over 1.5 miles. Steadily climb, with barely a break, to the trail gate by the park road, where the climb mercifully ends. The left fork leads to Bullfrog Pond Campground. Bear right and follow the paved road 0.6 miles back to the trailhead. ■

41. Gilliam Creek Trail—
East Austin Creek: Double Loop
AUSTIN CREEK STATE RECREATION AREA

Hiking distance: 9-mile double loop
Hiking time: 5.5 hours
Elevation gain: 1,700 feet
Maps: U.S.G.S. Cazadero
       Austin Creek State Recreation Area map

**map
page 120**

Summary of hike: The 3.7-mile Gilliam Creek Trail, in the Austin Creek State Recreation Area, contours across grassy slopes and drops down tree-lined ravines to three creeks—Schoolhouse Creek, Gilliam Creek, and East Austin Creek. The trail continues parallel to Gilliam Creek in an oak-shaded woodland, crossing the creek nine times. The East Austin Creek Trail is a 4.7-mile unpaved service road, dropping from 1,200 feet to 300 feet. The road winds down the remote canyon through a mix of forested groves, grassy meadows, and spectacular vistas of the rugged coastal mountains and the Russian River Valley. This secluded hike continues from the west end of Hike 40, forming a second loop. En route, the hiking and equestrian trail passes Gilliam Creek Trail Camp (at the confluence of Gilliam Creek and East Austin Creek) and the Tom King Trail Camp (on the banks of Thompson Creek). Biking is allowed on the East Austin Creek Trail.

NOTE: During the winter, the lower Gilliam Creek Trail can be impassable due to high water. Check with the rangers at the visitor center before heading out.

Driving directions: Same as Hike 40.

Hiking directions: Follow the hiking directions for Hike 40 to the posted junction at 2 miles by Schoolhouse Creek. From the junction, continue straight along the south edge of Schoolhouse Creek, which soon converges with Gilliam Creek. Continue along Gilliam Creek in a lush forest with thick, mossy tree trunks and lichen-covered boulders. The East Austin Creek Trail—our return route—can be seen on the north side of the creek. Cross Gilliam Creek at a major tributary stream. This is the first of nine consecutive creek crossings which all require wading. After the ninth soaking, head up the north slope and traverse the canyon wall across minor dips and rises. At 3.8 miles, return to the creek at Gilliam Creek Trail Camp, a rustic camp at the confluence with East Austin Creek. Wade across larger East Austin Creek wherever the best spot can be found. Walk up the slope 100 yards to an old dirt road being reclaimed by nature. Veer right above East Austin Creek and head upstream. Cross a side stream and climb through a meadow to a posted junction at 4 miles. The Fox Mountain Trail bears left. Continue straight, weaving through the forest on the dirt road overlooking East Austin Creek. At 5.3 miles, wade across the creek for the last time to a posted junction with the East Austin Creek Trail. To detour, the left fork leads 0.7 miles to Manning Flat Trail Camp, perched on the west bank of the creek. For this hike, bear right and head downstream along the north side of East Austin Creek. Pass redwoods and cross the Thompson Creek bridge. Climb to a junction with the trail to Tom King Trail Camp on the left. Stay straight, with a view of Devil's

Backbone to the south, Thompson Ridge to the north, and Morrison Ridge to the east. Steadily climb, skirting the north edge of Knoll 702. Weave back down on four sweeping bends to Gilliam Creek. Cross a bridge over Gilliam Creek to a junction with the Gilliam Creek Trail at 7 miles. Stay to the left and continue with the return hiking directions for Hike 40. ■

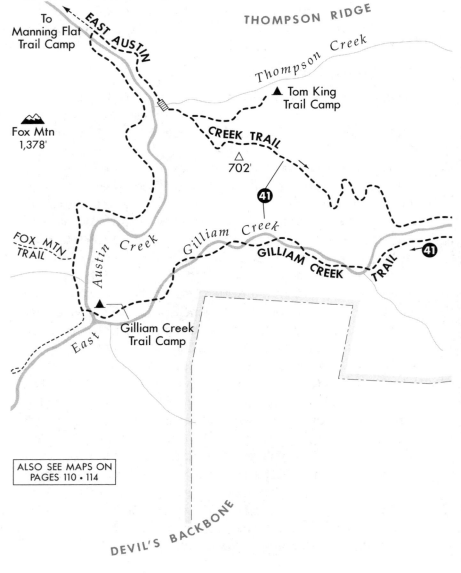

N
W · E
S

Queens Peak
1,948'

AUSTIN CREEK
STATE RECREATION
AREA

MORRISON RIDGE

McCray Mtn
1,940'

Gilliam Creek

Bullfrog
Pond

EAST AUSTIN CREEK TRAIL

PANORAMA GRADE

Bullfrog
Pond
Campgrd. ▲

40

CONTINUE
HIKE 41

Schoolhouse

40

GILLIAM CREEK TRAIL

GILLIAM

RIDGE

Creek

EAST
RIDGE
TR

39

POOL

P

RIDGE TR

HIKES 40 · 41

Gilliam Creek Trail–
East Austin Creek

Hike 40: East Loop
Hike 41: Double Loop

AUSTIN CREEK
STATE RECREATION AREA

42. Willow—Osprey Loop
STEELHEAD BEACH REGIONAL PARK
9000 River Road · Forestville

Hiking distance: 1.5-mile loop
Hiking time: 45 minutes
Elevation gain: Level
Maps: U.S.G.S. Camp Meeker and Guerneville
　　　　Steelhead Beach Regional Park map

Summary of hike: The Russian River originates in the Mayacmas Mountains above Lake Mendocino. The twisting river winds through vineyards, plains, redwood forests and canyons, draining a million acres over 120 miles before emptying into the sea at Jenner (Hike 30). Steelhead Beach Regional Park is a 26-acre oasis on the banks of the Russian River at the north end of Forestville and east of Guerneville. The park is a popular river access site for fishing, kayaking, rafting, and canoeing. This natural stretch of the Russian River has endangered coho salmon and threatened steelhead (rainbow) trout. A loop trail follows the south side of the river and connects Steelhead Beach with Children's Beach. The hike weaves through three plant communities: an alluvial stand of large redwoods; riparian scrub with thickets of willows; and a riparian forest with cottonwoods, walnuts, Oregon ash, big-leaf maple, California bay, bamboo, and box elder.

Driving directions: From Highway 116 in Forestville, drive 1.4 miles north on Mirabel Road to River Road. Turn left and continue a quarter mile to the posted park entrance on the right. Turn right and park in the lot 0.1 mile ahead.

From Guerneville, drive 7 miles east on River Road to the park entrance on the left. A parking fee is required.

Hiking directions: Take the paved path west to the group picnic area, where the paving ends. Continue on the dirt path, crossing the boat ramp road near the boat launch, to the posted Willow Trail. Weave through the mixed riparian forest on the low bluffs above the Russian River. Pass a junction with the Seasonal Trail on the right, and follow the river downstream to a junction with the Osprey Trail. The right fork leads to sandy Children's Beach. Return on the Osprey Trail, meandering through the forest between River Road and the Willow Trail. Cross the boat ramp road, returning to the parking lot. ■

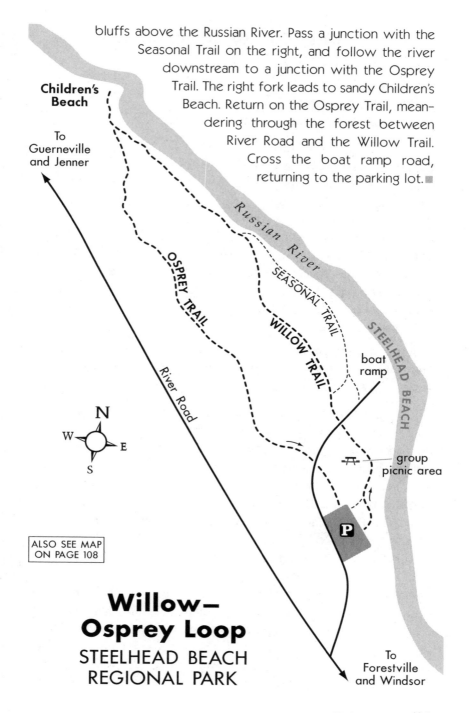

Children's Beach

To Guerneville and Jenner

Russian River

OSPREY TRAIL

SEASONAL TRAIL

WILLOW TRAIL

River Road

STEELHEAD BEACH

boat ramp

group picnic area

P

N
W   E
S

ALSO SEE MAP ON PAGE 108

Willow– Osprey Loop
STEELHEAD BEACH REGIONAL PARK

To Forestville and Windsor

43. West County Regional Trail

Hiking distance: 4 miles round trip
Hiking time: 2 hours
Elevation gain: Level
Maps: U.S.G.S. Camp Meeker and Sebastopol
West County and Rodota Trails map

Summary of hike: The West County Regional Trail is on the old Petaluma and Santa Rosa Railroad line, connecting Petaluma and Santa Rosa with Sebastopol and Forestville. When completed, the entire Rails-to-Trails system will extend 13 miles, connecting the towns. This hike follows a portion of the trail in a tree-lined corridor from Forestville to the small town of Graton. The trail parallels a water channel, meanders alongside pastures and vineyards, and passes through the Fish and Game's Atascadero Marsh Ecological Reserve. The mostly paved path is a hiking, biking, and dog-walking route.

Driving directions: From downtown Forestville on Highway 116, park along the south side of the street between Second Street and Mirable Road, or pull into the open area off the road.

Hiking directions: Walk down the gravel road alongside houses and buildings on the left. As the road curves left, leave the road to the right. Walk toward the tree grove to the posted trailhead. Take the paved path through a tunnel of trees alongside a stream and a vineyard on the right. Follow the tree-lined corridor, cross a bridge over the creek, and cross Kay Lane, a private road. Cross a second bridge over a stream. Continue south to Ross Branch Road at 0.8 miles. Bear left 30 yards to Ross Station Road. Walk 40 yards to the right, and pick up the posted trail on the left. Stroll between vineyards and a few farm houses, gradually descending past horse stables and corrals. Pass the Graton Sanitation Pond on the right, then cross a bridge over the creek and another over a wetland pond. Curve right, where the pavement ends, and follow the dirt path between a pond and a vineyard. Curve left through the Atascadero Marsh Ecological Reserve. Cross the wetland on a 160-yard boardwalk to Green

Valley Road. This is our turn-around spot.

To extend the hike, walk a quarter mile to the left on Green Valley Road, picking up the trail again on the right. The path continues south 1.5 miles through the town of Graton to Occidental

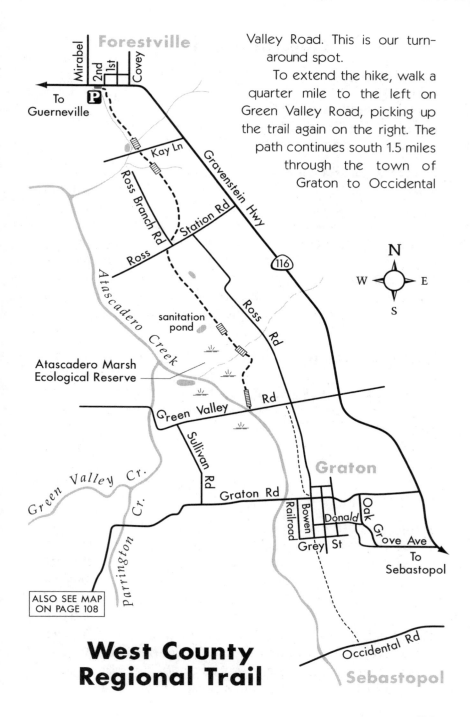

West County Regional Trail

44. Cloverdale River Park

Hiking distance: 2.2 miles round trip
Hiking time: 1 hour
Elevation gain: Level
Maps: U.S.G.S. Cloverdale
Cloverdale River Park map

Summary of hike: The town of Cloverdale is tucked into the rolling hills of northern Sonoma County on the banks of the Russian River. Cloverdale River Park stretches 1.3 miles along the west bank of the river from First Street, near downtown, to McCray Road at the north end. A mile-long paved trail follows the river through the 72-acre park, passing freshwater marshes, grassland meadows, oak woodlands, riparian scrub, and riparian forest. This hike begins from the southern entrance, but the trail can be started from either trailhead. Dogs are allowed on the trail.

Driving directions: South Trailhead: From downtown Cloverdale on Cloverdale Boulevard, take East First Street 0.5 miles east towards the Russian River. Turn left on Crocker Road, 40 yards before the Russian River bridge, and park in the trailhead spaces on the right.

North Trailhead: From the north end of Cloverdale on Cloverdale Boulevard, cross under Highway 101. Continue 0.1 mile to McCray Road and turn right. Drive 0.5 miles to the posted trailhead parking lot on the left.

Hiking directions: Walk 40 yards down East First Street to the posted trailhead by the Russian River bridge. Bear left and follow the west bank of the Russian River upstream. At the city water treatment plant, curve right on the paved path, skirting the facility to the Makahmo Trail. Continue along the river through the riparian forest with walnut, maple, willow, buckeye, bay, and box elder trees. Weave through the woodland and cross a metal bridge over Oak Valley Creek and an interpretive panel. Meander through open grassland meadows to the northern trailhead parking lot off of McCray Road. Return along the same route. ■

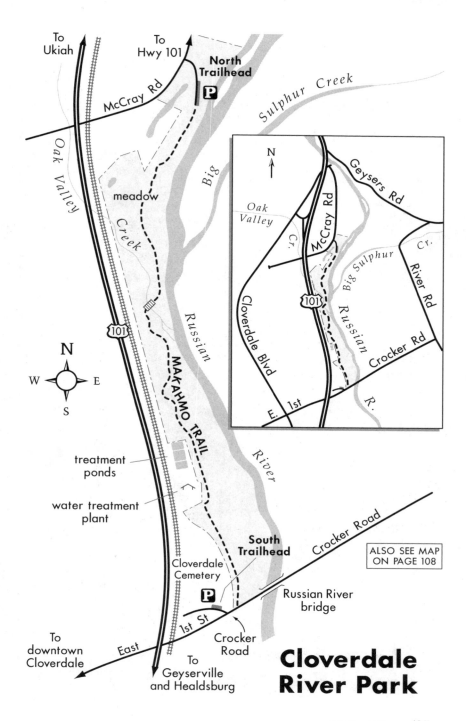

To
Ukiah

To
Hwy 101

**North
Trailhead**

🅿

McCray Rd

Sulphur Creek

Oak Valley

Big

meadow

Creek

Russian

🅽

Oak
Valley

Cr.

McCray Rd

Geysers Rd

Cr.

River Rd

101

Big Sulphur

Russian

Crocker Rd

Cloverdale Blvd

E. 1st

R.

101

MAKAHMO TRAIL

N

W ⊹ E

S

River

treatment
ponds

water treatment
plant

**South
Trailhead**

Crocker Road

Cloverdale
Cemetery

🅿

Russian River
bridge

ALSO SEE MAP
ON PAGE 108

1st St

Crocker
Road

To
downtown
Cloverdale

East

To
Geyserville
and Healdsburg

Cloverdale
River Park

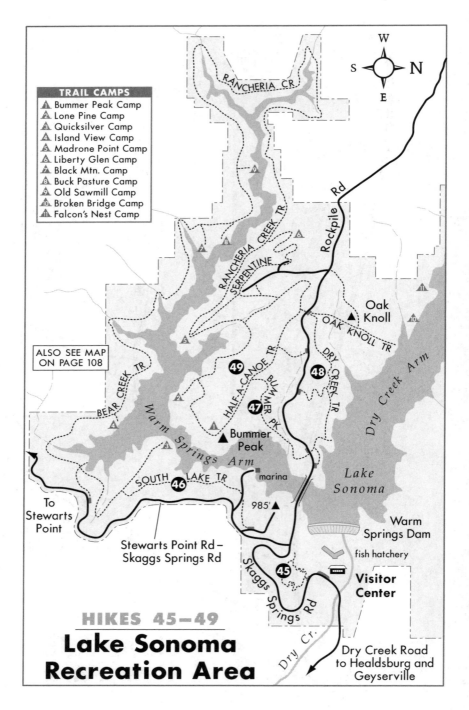

TRAIL CAMPS
- Bummer Peak Camp
- Lone Pine Camp
- Quicksilver Camp
- Island View Camp
- Madrone Point Camp
- Liberty Glen Camp
- Black Mtn. Camp
- Buck Pasture Camp
- Old Sawmill Camp
- Broken Bridge Camp
- Falcon's Nest Camp

RANCHERIA CR.

Rockpile Rd

RANCHERIA CREEK TR

SERPENTINE

Oak Knoll

OAK KNOLL TR

ALSO SEE MAP ON PAGE 108

BEAR CREEK TR

DRY CREEK TR

HALF-A-CANOE TR

BUMMER PK.

49

48

47

Bummer Peak

Warm Springs Arm

Dry Creek Arm

SOUTH LAKE TR

46

marina

Lake Sonoma

To Stewarts Point

985'

Stewarts Point Rd – Skaggs Springs Rd

Warm Springs Dam

fish hatchery

Skaggs Springs Rd

45

Visitor Center

Dry Cr.

HIKES 45–49
Lake Sonoma
Recreation Area

Dry Creek Road to Healdsburg and Geyserville

Lake Sonoma Recreation Area

3333 Skaggs Springs Road · Geyserville

HIKES 45—49

Lake Sonoma Recreation Area is an expansive parkland with a sprawling manmade lake at the north end of Sonoma County. Within its boundaries are 17,600 acres of rolling, coastal foothills. The lake takes in 2,700 of these acres, with 53 miles of undulating shoreline stretching into the steep canyons of the Mendocino Highlands. The recreation area includes a visitor center; marina; and primitive campgrounds that can be accessed via car, boat, bike, horse, or on foot. Dogs are allowed on all the trails.

The long and narrow lake was formed by Warm Springs Dam, an earthen embankment dam built in 1983. The 3,000-foot-long dam stands 319 feet high. The lake has two main arms with many finger-shaped inlets and scores of coves. The Dry Creek Arm extends nine miles to the northwest, while the southern Warm Springs Arm reaches four miles. The lake is rich with steelhead trout, perch, catfish, salmon, and is among the best bass fishing lakes in California.

This popular outdoor recreation area is also known for swimming, picnicking, boating, camping, and hiking. More than 40 miles of hiking, equestrian, and mountain biking trails loop around the lake on the steep hills, weaving through grassy slopes, redwood groves, Douglas fir forests, and oak woodlands. A variety of trails lead to overlooks of the lake and to many backcountry camps.

The following five hikes explore the varied terrain along the shoreline and high above both arms of Lake Sonoma.

Driving directions: FROM HEALDSBURG: From Highway 101, head 10.3 miles northwest on Dry Creek Road to the base of Warm Springs Dam and Lake Sonoma Visitor Center on the right. (Dry Creek Road becomes Skaggs Springs Road in the park.)

FROM GEYSERVILLE (located 8 miles south of Cloverdale and 8 miles north of Healdsburg): Exit Highway 101 on Canyon Road. Drive 2.1 miles west to a T-junction with Dry Creek Road. Turn right and continue 3.2 miles to the base of Warm Springs Dam and the Lake Sonoma Visitor Center on the right.

45. Woodland Ridge Trail
LAKE SONOMA RECREATION AREA

Hiking distance: 1.5-mile loop
Hiking time: 1 hour
Elevation gain: 150 feet
Maps: U.S.G.S. Warm Springs Dam
Lake Sonoma map

Summary of hike: The Woodland Ridge Trail is an easily accessible loop trail that offers an introduction to the various habitats around Lake Sonoma. The trail moderately climbs through four different plant communities: chaparral, coast redwood, Douglas fir, and oak woodland. At the ridge are sweeping vistas of Alexander Valley, the Mayacmas Mountains, Warm Springs Dam,

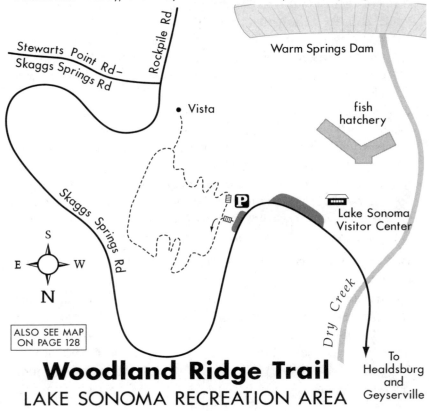

Woodland Ridge Trail
LAKE SONOMA RECREATION AREA

and the lower portion of Lake Sonoma. The interpretive trail has 19 learning stations and an accompanying nature guide available at the Lake Sonoma Visitor Center. The learning stations describe how plants adapt, how the climate effects plants, the effects of fire, edible and medicinal plants, bark, and wildlife.

Driving directions: Follow the driving directions on page 129 to the Lake Sonoma Visitor Center. From the visitor center, drive 0.2 miles to the parking area on the right by the trailhead.

Hiking directions: Cross the wood footbridge and begin the loop to the left. Enter a grove of towering redwoods, and climb a long series of wood steps. Traverse the hillside through bay laurel trees, high above Skaggs Springs Road. Climb another set of steps, and zigzag up to the ridge through a mixed forest of Douglas fir, madrone, and a variety of oaks. From the bald ridge are views of Dry Creek Valley, Alexander Valley, and the Mayacmas Mountains, high above Sonoma Valley and Napa Valley. Follow the ridge through live oaks and black oaks, cresting the ridge. A short path on the left leads through a brushy canyon to a vista point with a view of Warm Springs Dam and the lower portion of Lake Sonoma. Return to the main loop and descend on wood steps, winding down a stream-fed draw shaded by madrones. Continue down to the base of the hill, cross a wood bridge, and complete the loop at the trailhead bridge. ■

46. South Lake Trail to Skaggs Springs Vista
LAKE SONOMA RECREATION AREA

Hiking distance: 3.8 shuttle or 7.6 miles round trip
Hiking time: 2 hours or 4 hours
Elevation gain: 500 feet
Maps: U.S.G.S. Warm Springs Dam
      Lake Sonoma map

map
page 133

Summary of hike: The South Lake Trail traverses the steep, upper hillside along the wooded south side of Lake Sonoma. Throughout the hike are spectacular vistas of the Warm Springs

Arm of the lake, including the marina, private coves, fingers of land extending into the lake, Bummer Peak, and the rolling hills surrounding the lake (back cover photo). This hike begins below the observation deck and picnic area at the 985-foot overlook high above the south end of the dam. The trail passes forested stream-fed drainages and an access path to Quicksilver Camp en route to Skaggs Springs Vista. Quicksilver Camp has eleven campsites along the oak-filled hillside and near the water.

Driving directions: Follow the driving directions on page 129 to the Lake Sonoma Visitor Center. From the visitor center, drive 1.7 miles to a posted junction. Turn left on Stewarts Point/Skaggs Springs Road, and continue 0.5 miles to the Lake Sonoma Overlook turnoff. Turn right 100 yards and turn left into the posted trailhead parking lot.

For a one-way shuttle hike, the signed Skaggs Springs Vista Trailhead is located 2.3 miles farther on Stewarts Point/Skaggs Springs Road. Turn right into the parking lot.

Hiking directions: Pass the trailhead fence at the southwest end of the lot. Traverse the hillside overlooking Lake Sonoma, and cross the marina access road. Steadily descend through oaks, pines, and madrones high above the marina. Weave along the hillside contours. The views extend across the Warm Springs Arm of Lake Sonoma to Bummer Peak, with its rounded, oak-covered summit. Bummer Peak Camp can be spotted on the lower (west) knoll. Curve in and out of a series of lush drainages and grottos, and walk through a grove of moss-covered oak trees. Continue along the trail with several small dips and rises. After topping a minor ridge, drop down 50 yards to a posted junction at 2 miles. The right fork descends 0.7 miles to Quicksilver Camp at the lakeshore. Bear left and continue traversing the hill. Descend to a stream-fed drainage at 2.7 miles, and cross the rolling grasslands. Descend to within 50 yards of the lake and a 4-way junction at 3.2 miles. The right fork leads 0.1 mile to the lake. One mile straight ahead is Island View Camp at the shoreline. Bear left and climb through the forest to an open ridge. Veer left to the Skaggs Springs Vista Trailhead. Return by retracing your steps.▪

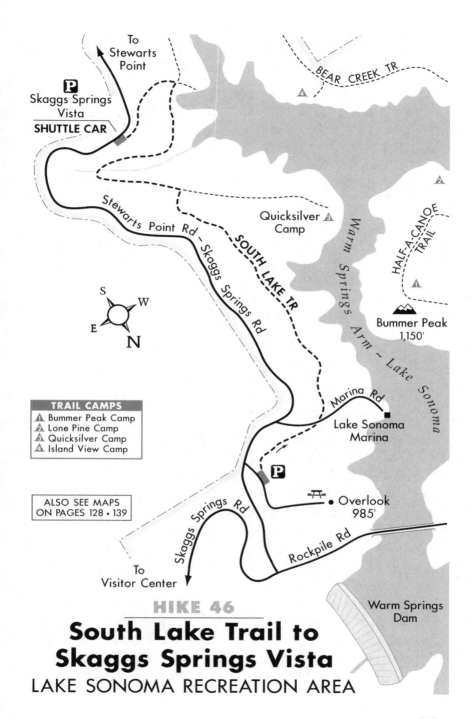

To
Stewarts
Point

P
Skaggs Springs
Vista
SHUTTLE CAR

BEAR CREEK TR

Stewarts Point Rd ~ Skaggs Springs Rd

SOUTH LAKE TR

Quicksilver Camp

Warm Springs Arm ~ Lake Sonoma

HALF-A-CANOE TRAIL

S W
E N

Bummer Peak
1,150'

Marina Rd

TRAIL CAMPS
Bummer Peak Camp
Lone Pine Camp
Quicksilver Camp
Island View Camp

Lake Sonoma
Marina

P

ALSO SEE MAPS
ON PAGES 128 • 139

Skaggs Springs Rd

Overlook
985'

Rockpile Rd

To
Visitor Center

Warm Springs
Dam

HIKE 46

South Lake Trail to
Skaggs Springs Vista
LAKE SONOMA RECREATION AREA

47. Little Flat to Bummer Peak
LAKE SONOMA RECREATION AREA

Hiking distance: 3.4 miles round trip
Hiking time: 2 hours
Elevation gain: 600 feet
Maps: U.S.G.S. Warm Springs Dam
Lake Sonoma map

Summary of hike: Bummer Peak lies at the end of the ridge high above the Warm Springs Arm of Lake Sonoma. The peak is a 1,150-foot knoll overlooking Lake Sonoma and the surrounding rugged foothills. Adjacent to the peak is Bummer Peak Camp, a primitive two-site camp open to hikers, bikers, and equestrians. Several trails access the ridge—this hike begins at Little Flat on the Bummer Peak Trail. The mile-long trail climbs through oak, madrone, and redwood groves to great views along the ridge.

Driving directions: Follow the driving directions on page 129 to the Lake Sonoma Visitor Center. From the visitor center, continue 2.7 miles, crossing the bridge over Lake Sonoma, to the posted Little Flat parking lot on the right. (En route, the road becomes Rockpile Road.)

Hiking directions: From the trailhead kiosk, enter the oak and madrone forest. Traverse the contours of the hills, crossing small stream-fed drainages with mossy boulders and tree trunks. Zigzag up to the ridge while overlooking the Lake Sonoma Marina on the Warm Springs Arm of the lake. Descend and cross Rockpile Road, heading toward the lake. Curve right, continue downhill, and cross a stream. Head up the hillside, following the ridge into a grove of redwoods. Climb to an overlook of the redwood grove and Lake Sonoma, reaching the upper ridge and a T-junction with the Half-A-Canoe Loop. The right fork leads to No Name Flat and Lone Rock Flat (Hike 49). Bear left and weave along the roller coaster ridge to Bummer Peak Camp. The camp sits on an terraced, oak-covered knoll with picnic benches, fire pits, and great views of the lake. This is the turn-around spot.

To extend the hike, loop around the camp and descend a stream-fed canyon to Lone Pine Camp at the lakeshore. Return by retracing your route, or continue on the Half-A-Canoe Loop— Hike 49.■

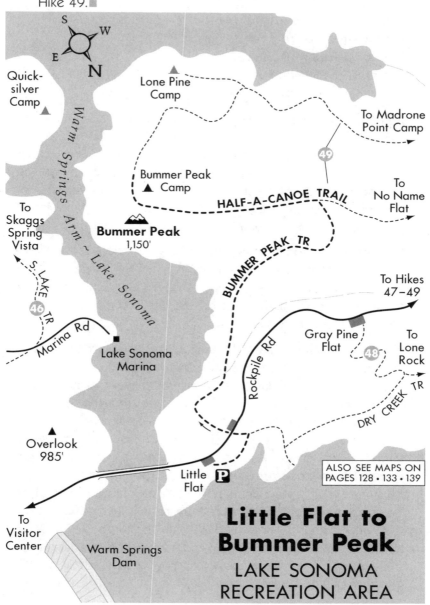

ALSO SEE MAPS ON
PAGES 128 • 133 • 139

Little Flat to Bummer Peak
LAKE SONOMA
RECREATION AREA

48. Dry Creek Trail:
Lone Rock to Gray Pine Flat
LAKE SONOMA RECREATION AREA

Hiking distance: 2.3-mile shuttle or 4.6 miles round trip
Hiking time: 1.5 hours or 3 hours
Elevation gain: 400 feet
Maps: U.S.G.S. Warm Springs Dam
Lake Sonoma map

Summary of hike: The Dry Creek Arm of Lake Sonoma is nine miles long with multiple finger-like channels. The Dry Creek Trail follows the lower end of the Dry Creek Arm near Warm Springs Dam. The trail weaves through oak woodlands, redwood groves, grasslands, and wildflower-covered meadows to overlooks of the lake. This hike begins from Lone Rock, the western access of the Dry Creek Trail, and heads east to Gray Pine Flat.

Driving directions: Follow the driving directions on page 129 to the Lake Sonoma Visitor Center. From the visitor center, continue 4.3 miles, crossing the bridge over Lake Sonoma, to the posted Lone Rock parking lot on the right. (En route, the road becomes Rockpile Road.)

Hiking directions: From the trailhead mapboard, bear left and descend, looping clockwise around the knoll in an oak forest. Zigzag down into the lush, shady redwood grove, crossing small feeder streams. Slowly gain elevation while returning to the oak and madrone forest. Cross the rolling terrain, with views through the trees of the Dry Creek Arm of Lake Sonoma. At 1.5 miles, the Warm Springs Dam comes into view. At an unsigned Y-fork, veer right and drop into a fern-filled grotto. Cross a footbridge over the stream to a posted junction. The left fork leads to Little Flat, the lakeshore, and a boat ramp. Stay to the right toward Gray Pine Flat. Ascend the slope and wind up the hillside to the large parking lot overlooking the dam and surrounding hills. Return by retracing your steps, or follow Rockpile Road one mile to the right, completing a loop. ∎

Dry Creek Trail:
Lone Rock to Gray Pine Flat
LAKE SONOMA RECREATION AREA

49. Half-A-Canoe Loop
LAKE SONOMA RECREATION AREA

Hiking distance: 5.5-mile loop
Hiking time: 3 hours
Elevation gain: 1,100 feet
Maps: U.S.G.S. Warm Springs Dam
          Lake Sonoma map

map
page 139

Summary of hike: The Half-a-Canoe Loop Trail is a circular hiking and biking path that follows a rolling ridge between the two arms of Lake Sonoma. It is the only biking trail in the park. The trail leads to Bummer Peak Camp atop the ridge overlooking the Warm Springs Arm of Sonoma Lake, then drops down to the lakeshore at Lone Pine Camp. The Half-a-Canoe Trail has connector trails from Liberty Glen Camp, Lone Rock Flat, No Name Flat, and Little Flat (Hike 47). This hike follows the No Name Flat Trail to the ridge through oak woodlands and grasslands.

Driving directions: Follow the driving directions on page 129 to the Lake Sonoma Visitor Center. From the visitor center, continue 3.6 miles, crossing the bridge over Lake Sonoma, to the posted No Name Flat parking lot on the left. (En route, the road becomes Rockpile Road.)

Hiking directions: From the trailhead kiosk, take the No Name Flat Trail downhill. Cross a footbridge over a small stream, and head up the oak-dotted hillside to sweeping vistas of the rolling hills. Cross a second wooden bridge to a T-junction on the ridge with the Half-A-Canoe Trail at 0.6 miles, overlooking the Warm Springs Arm of Lake Sonoma. Begin the loop to the left, and follow the rolling ridge. Pass the Bummer Peak Trail (Hike 47) at just over a mile. Weave along the contours of the hills past rock outcroppings, overlooking the Rockpile Road bridge and the Lake Sonoma Marina en route to Bummer Peak Camp. The camp sits on a terraced, oak-covered knoll below the 1,150-foot peak. Loop around the camp and descend to the floor of a stream-fed canyon, passing moss-covered tree trunks and rocks. Continue down to the edge of the lake and a junction. The left fork leads a short distance to Lone Pine Camp in a grove of oaks. Go to the right along the edge of the lake to the north end of the inlet. Leave the shore and wind up the hill. Head northeast, steadily gaining elevation. Pass a junction to Madrone Point Camp, the bike route on the left. Continue climbing up the creek-fed canyon to a junction. The left fork leads to Liberty Glen Camp and another access to Madrone Point Camp. Bear right, heading uphill on the north wall of the valley. Parallel Rockpile Road, passing a trail to Lone Rock on the left. Curve right to the No Name Flat Trail, completing the loop. Bear left and return 0.6 miles to the trailhead. ■

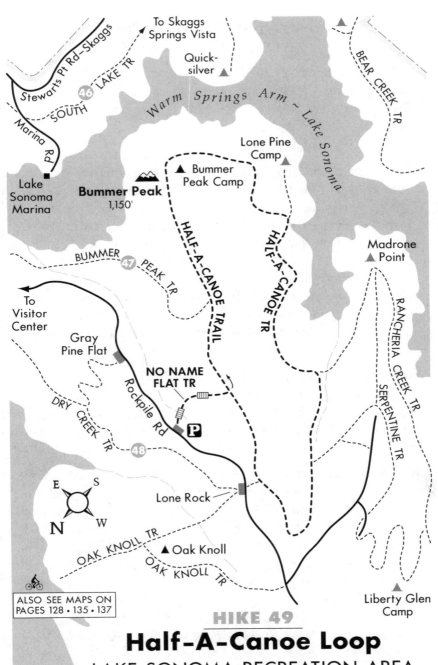

To Skaggs
Springs Vista

Quick-
silver

Stewarts Pt Rd–Skaggs

46 SOUTH LAKE TR

Marina Rd

Warm Springs Arm ~ Lake Sonoma

BEAR CREEK TR

Lake
Sonoma
Marina

Bummer Peak
1,150'

▲ Bummer
Peak Camp

Lone Pine
Camp ▲

Madrone
▲ Point

BUMMER 47 PEAK TR

HALF-A-CANOE TRAIL

HALF-A-CANOE TR

RANCHERIA CREEK TR

To
Visitor
Center

Gray
Pine Flat

DRY CREEK TR

Rockpile Rd

NO NAME
FLAT TR

P

SERPENTINE TR

48

E S

N W

Lone Rock

OAK KNOLL TR

▲ Oak Knoll

OAK KNOLL TR

Liberty Glen
Camp

ALSO SEE MAPS ON
PAGES 128 • 135 • 137

HIKE 49

Half-A-Canoe Loop
LAKE SONOMA RECREATION AREA

50. Riverfront Regional Park

7821 Eastside Road · Windsor

Hiking distance: 2-mile loop
Hiking time: 1 hour
Elevation gain: Level
Maps: U.S.G.S. Healdsburg
       Riverfront Regional Park map

Summary of hike: Riverfront Regional Park is adjacent to the Russian River in the town of Windsor. The 300-acre park, once a gravel quarry, was opened to the public in 2005. It includes a picnic area in a large redwood grove and two recreational lakes used for fishing and non-motorized boating. The park has more than two miles of lakeshore trails that circle the lakes. From January through July, the area is a nesting site for the great blue heron, North America's largest wading water bird. Their nests can be spotted high in the trees. This hike follows the perimeter of Lake Benoist and skirts the banks of the Russian River and the east shore of Lake Wilson. Dogs are allowed on the trails.

Driving directions: From Highway 101 in Windsor, exit on Central Windsor. Drive 2.1 miles west on Windsor River Road to Eastside Road. Turn left and continue 1.8 miles to the signed park entrance on the right. Turn right and drive 0.5 miles to the trailhead parking lot. A parking fee is required.

Hiking directions: Walk past the trailhead kiosk, and follow the Lake Trail southwest (a dirt road). Skirt a dense redwood forest and picnic area on the left and Lake Wilson on the right. Continue to a junction at the north end of Lake Benoist at 0.3 miles. The right fork, our return route, crosses a berm separating the two lakes. Begin the loop on the left fork, and follow the southwest side of the lake on the forested path through redwoods, willow, bamboo, and bay laurel. Cross over an inlet stream at a concrete spillway and a few other rocked inlet streams. At the far west end of the lake is a great view across the length of the lake. Cross a stream and begin the return. A lower footpath skirts the edge of the lake. If the water level is high, cross the rocky dam and follow the top of the berm along the Russian River. The two paths merge atop the ridge and continue east, overlooking the lake. Descend and cross a stream, completing the loop. ∎

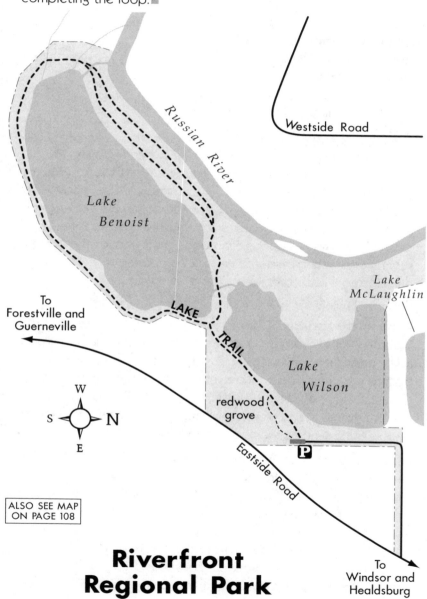

Westside Road

Russian River

Lake Benoist

Lake McLaughlin

To Forestville and Guerneville

LAKE TRAIL

Lake Wilson

redwood grove

W
S — N
E

Eastside Road

P

ALSO SEE MAP
ON PAGE 108

Riverfront Regional Park

To Windsor and Healdsburg

51. Perimeter Loop:

Three Lakes—Alta Vista—Oakwood—Westside Trails
FOOTHILL REGIONAL PARK
1351 Arata Lane · Windsor

Hiking distance: 2.6-mile loop

Hiking time: 1.5 hours

Elevation gain: 460 feet

Maps: U.S.G.S. Healdsburg
Foothill Regional Park map

map
page 144

Summary of hike: Foothill Regional Park sits in the rolling hills at the northeast corner of Windsor between Highway 101 and Chalk Hill Valley. The 211-acre parkland was a cattle ranch until the mid-1980s. The land is covered in oak savanna that is scattered with several species of oaks, bay, madrone, and buckeye trees. Many of the trails that weave through the rolling hills are old ranch roads. This hike loops around the perimeter of the park on several connecting trails. The hike passes three ponds and climbs oak-dotted hills to scenic overlooks of the Santa Rosa Plain and the Russian River Valley. Dogs are allowed on the trails.

Driving directions: From Highway 101 in Windsor, exit on Central Windsor. Drive 0.7 miles southeast on Old Redwood Highway to Hembree Lane and turn left. Continue 1.3 miles to the posted park entrance on the right. A fee for parking in the lot is required. Free parking is available along both sides of the road.

From the north end of Windsor, drive 1.4 miles east of Highway 101 on Arata Lane to the park entrance on the left.

Hiking directions: Walk up the gravel road past the restrooms and vehicle gate to a trail junction. Stay to the right on the Three Lakes Trail for about 100 yards to a junction with the Pond A Trail on the left. Stay straight along the south side of the pond through an open oak grove. Climb to the crest of the hill to a junction on the left with the Westside Trail. Stay on the Three Lakes Trail, and descend to the edge of Pond B. Cross the earthen dam. Pass the second Pond B trail junction and the Oakwood Trail, reaching

Pond C. Cross a bridge over the outlet stream. Skirt the southern edge of Pond C to a trail split at the end of the Three Lakes Trail at 0.8 miles. Take the right fork on the posted Alta Vista Trail, and climb the oak-dotted hillside. Steadily climb the spine to the upper reaches of Foothill Park. At 1.1 miles, the trail reaches an overlook at 660 feet, the highest point in the park. Curve to the left and descend across the rolling grasslands to a junction with the Oakwood Trail at a post-and-rail fence. Take the Oakwood Trail to the right, continuing along the east perimeter of the park. Pass the Ravine Trail on the left, and cross a wooden bridge over a seasonal stream. Weave through the forest, overlooking the ponds, the town of Windsor, and the Russian River Valley. Continue to a Y-fork with the Westside Trail at 2.4 miles. Veer to the right, passing the Bobcat Trail on the left, and steadily descend through oak-dotted grasslands. Pass the Pond A Trail and walk 150 yards, completing the loop at the trailhead. ■

52. The Three Ponds
FOOTHILL REGIONAL PARK
1351 Arata Lane · Windsor

Hiking distance: 1.4-mile multi-loop
Hiking time: 1 hour
Elevation gain: 100 feet
Maps: U.S.G.S. Healdsburg
      Foothill Regional Park map

map
page 144

Summary of hike: Foothill Regional Park has three manmade ponds that were built in the 1960s when it was a ranch. The ponds are now a drinking source for wild animals and may be used for fishing but not swimming. This hike begins on the Three Lakes Trail and circles the perimeter of all three ponds, forming three loops. Dogs are allowed on the trails.

Driving directions: Same as Hike 51.

Hiking directions: Walk up the gravel road past the restrooms and trailhead gate to a trail junction. Stay to the right on the Three

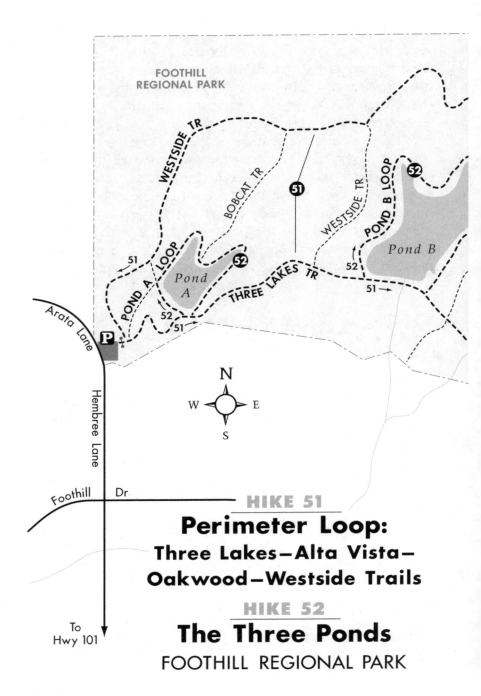

FOOTHILL
REGIONAL PARK

WESTSIDE TR.

BOBCAT TR.

51

WESTSIDE TR.

POND B LOOP

52

Pond B

POND A LOOP

51

Pond
A

THREE LAKES TR.

52

51→

52

52

51

Arata Lane

P

Hembree Lane

N
W E
S

Foothill Dr.

HIKE 51

Perimeter Loop:
Three Lakes–Alta Vista–
Oakwood–Westside Trails

HIKE 52

The Three Ponds
FOOTHILL REGIONAL PARK

To
Hwy 101

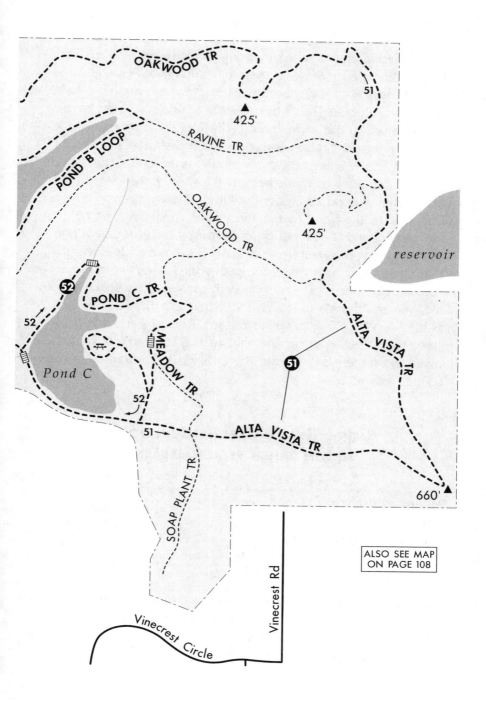

OAKWOOD TR

51

▲ 425'

RAVINE TR

POND B LOOP

OAKWOOD TR

▲ 425'

reservoir

52

52

POND C TR

ALTA VISTA TR

51

Pond C

MEADOW TR

52

51→

ALTA VISTA TR

▲ 660'

SOAP PLANT TR

ALSO SEE MAP
ON PAGE 108

Vinecrest Rd

Vinecrest Circle

Lakes Trail for about 100 yards to a junction with the Pond A Loop on the left. Bear left on the west side of the pond. Head up the hillside on the footpath, rising above the dam to an overlook of the pond. Stay to the right, skirting the pond's edge through manzanita and oak. Follow the curvature of the lake, passing the Bobcat Trail. After looping around two arms of the pond, return to the wide Three Lakes Trail and continue to the left. Crest the hill and descend to the southeast corner of Pond B. Bear left and follow the west side of the second pond. Loop around both arms of the largest of the three ponds. At the far end of the second arm, pass the Ravine Trail and return on the east side of the pond to the Three Lakes Trail. Continue to the left to the Pond C Trail, just before crossing the wooden bridge. Bear left along the west shore of Pond C. Cross a bridge over the inlet stream and curve right. The path soon leaves the lake at its northeast corner to a T-junction with the Meadow Trail. Go to the right and cross a footbridge to a trail split. Stay to the right, as the Soap Plant Trail curves to the left. Twenty yards shy of the Three Lakes Trail, a path on the right leads 0.1 mile to a picnic area overlooking the pond. At the Three Lakes Trail, return 0.6 miles to the trailhead. ∎

53. Ridge Trail—Creekside Loop
SHILOH RANCH REGIONAL PARK
5750 Faught Road · Santa Rosa

Hiking distance: 2.8-mile loop
Hiking time: 2 hours

map
page 149

Elevation gain: 550 feet
Maps: U.S.G.S. Healdsburg and Mark West Springs
Shiloh Ranch Regional Park map

Summary of hike: Shiloh Ranch Regional Park is located at the east edge of Windsor. It was a cattle ranch until 1988. The 860-acre park stretches from the base of the valley floor into the wild foothills. The hilly terrain has rugged stream-fed canyons

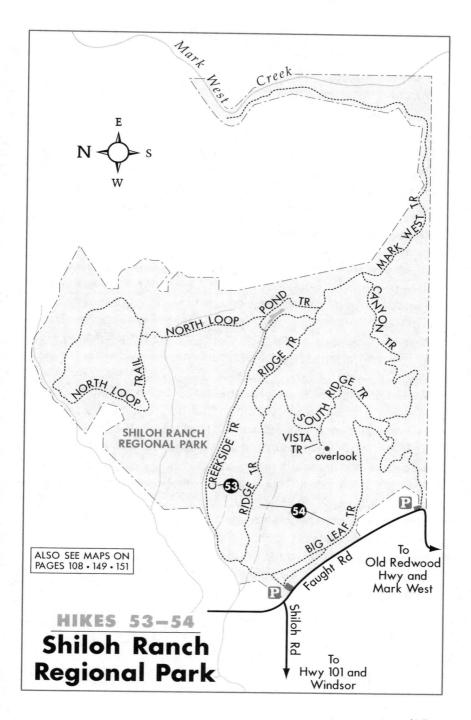

N E S W

Mark West Creek

MARK WEST TR

POND TR

NORTH LOOP

CANYON TR

RIDGE TR

NORTH LOOP TRAIL

SOUTH RIDGE TR

SHILOH RANCH
REGIONAL PARK

CREEKSIDE TR

VISTA TR
overlook

RIDGE TR

53

54

BIG LEAF TR

ALSO SEE MAPS ON
PAGES 108 • 149 • 151

To
Old Redwood
Hwy and
Mark West

Faught Rd

Shiloh Rd

To
Hwy 101 and
Windsor

HIKES 53–54
Shiloh Ranch
Regional Park

and a variety of habitats, including valley oak woodlands, coast redwood groves, stands of Douglas fir, big leaf maple, grasslands, and mixed chaparral. This loop hike follows a ridge with sweeping vistas, returning through a canyon in a riparian corridor along a creek. Dogs are not allowed in the park.

Driving directions: From Highway 101 in Windsor, exit on Shiloh Road. Drive 1.4 miles east to Faught Road at the base of the hills. Turn right (south) and continue 0.1 mile to the posted park entrance on the left. A fee for parking in the lot is required. Free parking is available along the shoulder of Faught Road.

Hiking directions: Walk past the trailhead map panel and restrooms on the wide gravel path. Stroll through an oak-shaded picnic area to a junction at 50 yards. The Big Leaf Trail (Hike 54) goes to the right. Continue straight on the Ridge Trail, and cross a seasonal stream on the west edge of the park. Curve right and climb 150 yards to a posted junction with the Creekside Trail. Begin the loop on the right fork, staying on the Ridge Trail. Weave up the hillside through oaks and madrones to overlooks of the town of Windsor, the expansive Santa Rosa Plain, and the Mayacmas Mountains. Follow the ridge between two steep canyons, steadily gaining elevation. The trail tops out by power lines and descends 50 yards to a posted Y-fork. The South Ridge Trail veers off to the right (Hike 54). Curve left and slowly descend along the north-facing canyon wall. At the grassy valley floor is the Creekside Trail, our return route. For now, continue straight 100 yards and veer left on the Pond Trail. Follow the north side of the creek, surrounded by open, rolling hills. Loop around the pond and picnic site on the left. Join the Creekside Trail on the west end of the pond by the outlet stream. Go to the right and head down canyon along the south edge of the creek under pines and mossy oaks in a shaded, fern-filled glen. Traverse the narrow south canyon slope, and cross a bridge over a stream. Complete the loop 100 yards ahead at the Ridge Trail. Retrace your route straight ahead. ▪

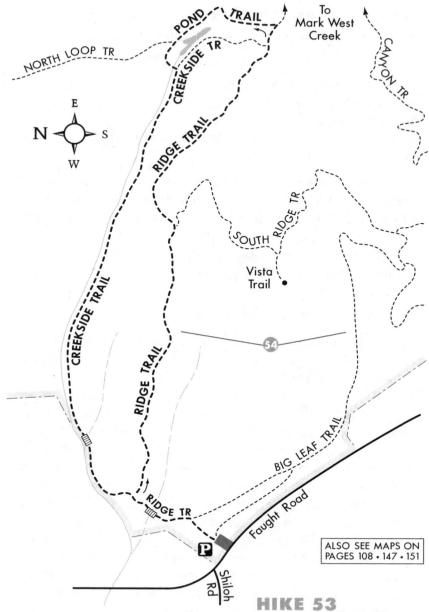

To Mark West Creek

POND TRAIL

NORTH LOOP TR

CREEKSIDE TR

CANYON TR

RIDGE TRAIL

E
N W S
W

SOUTH RIDGE TR

Vista Trail •

CREEKSIDE TRAIL

RIDGE TRAIL

54

BIG LEAF TRAIL

RIDGE TR

RIDGE TR

Faught Road

P

Shiloh Rd

ALSO SEE MAPS ON
PAGES 108 • 147 • 151

HIKE 53

Ridge Trail–Creekside Loop
SHILOH RANCH REGIONAL PARK

54. Big Leaf—South Ridge—Ridge Loop

SHILOH RANCH REGIONAL PARK
5750 Faught Road · Santa Rosa

Hiking distance: 3-mile loop
Hiking time: 2 hours
Elevation gain: 550 feet
Maps: U.S.G.S. Healdsburg and Mark West Springs
Shiloh Ranch Regional Park map

Summary of hike: This hike forms a loop in the south-central section of Shiloh Ranch Regional Park. The trail traverses lower hillside slopes through oak groves, then climbs the South Ridge Trail to a vista point with panoramic vistas of the Mayacmas Mountains, the expansive basin, and the north county. The hike returns along a ridge with gorgeous views across the Santa Rosa Plain.

Driving directions: Same as Hike 53.

Hiking directions: Walk past the trailhead map panel and restrooms on the wide gravel path. Stroll through an oak-shaded picnic area to a junction at 50 yards. Bear right on the Big Leaf Trail and begin the loop. Head southeast, traversing the hill parallel to Faught Road. Continue through oaks and manzanita with views of the vineyards on the valley floor. Pass a trail on the right coming up from the parking lot. Curve left, skirting a small vineyard on private land. Climb a short, forested slope, and continue at a level grade through majestic oaks, madrones, big leaf maple, and towering Douglas fir. Climb at a gentle grade. Make a U-shaped bend to an oak-studded grassland and a junction with the South Ridge Trail at an overlook with a bench of the Santa Rosa Plain. The right fork leads to a trailhead on Faught Road at the southwest corner of the park. Bear left and pass the Canyon Trail on the right. Cross a saddle with views of the Mayacmas Mountains and the town of Windsor. Weave a half mile up the mountain to the Vista Trail on the left by a power pole. Detour 100 yards left to an overlook with three benches and sweeping panoramic vistas. Return to the main trail, and continue to a signed junction with the Ridge Trail at 2 miles. Go to the left and follow the ridge downhill, overlooking the basin. Pass the Creekside Trail on the right (Hike 53). Cross a seasonal drainage and complete the loop, 50 yards shy of the trailhead. ■

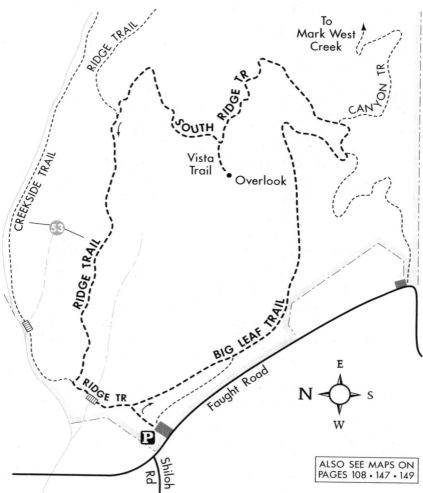

Big Leaf – South Ridge – Ridge Loop
SHILOH RANCH REGIONAL PARK

55. Stevenson Memorial Trail
ROBERT LOUIS STEVENSON STATE PARK

Hiking distance: 1.4 miles round trip or 2.2-mile loop
Hiking time: 1 hour
Elevation gain: 500 feet
Maps: U.S.G.S. Detert Reservoir
　　　　Bothe–Napa Valley and Robert Louis Stevenson State
　　　　Parks map

Summary of hike: Robert Louis Stevenson State Park encompasses 5,272 acres in the Mayacmas Mountains above Calistoga. The immense park straddles Sonoma, Napa, and Lake Counties. The centerpiece of the park is Mount Saint Helena, the highest peak in Sonoma County (Hike 56). This hike makes a loop along the lower portion of the trail to the Stevenson Memorial. In the summer of 1880, Robert Louis Stevenson, author of *Treasure Island* and *Kidnapped*, honeymooned for several months in an abandoned, two-story bunkhouse near the Silverado Mine. Stevenson wrote about this time in his book *Silverado Squatters*. A memorial marker identifies the site of the abandoned mine building. The memorial, unveiled in 1911, has a quartz base and an open, book-shaped Scotch granite cap inscribed with a Stevenson poem. This short loop hike zigzags up the hillside under the shade of Douglas fir, live oak, madrone, tanbark oak, and manzanita. Dogs are not allowed in the park.

Driving directions: Robert Louis Stevenson State Park is located in Napa Valley, northeast of Calistoga on Highway 29. Three main routes access Napa Valley from Sonoma County. FROM THE NORTH: Access is via Highway 128 out of Geyserville and Healdsburg. FROM SANTA ROSA: access is via Calistoga Road off of Highway 12. FROM THE SOUTH: Access is via Highway 12, south of the town of Sonoma.

　FROM HIGHWAY 29 AND LINCOLN AVENUE IN CALISTOGA: Drive 8.5 miles northeast on Lincoln Avenue (Highway 29), through town and up the winding mountain road. Park in the parking area

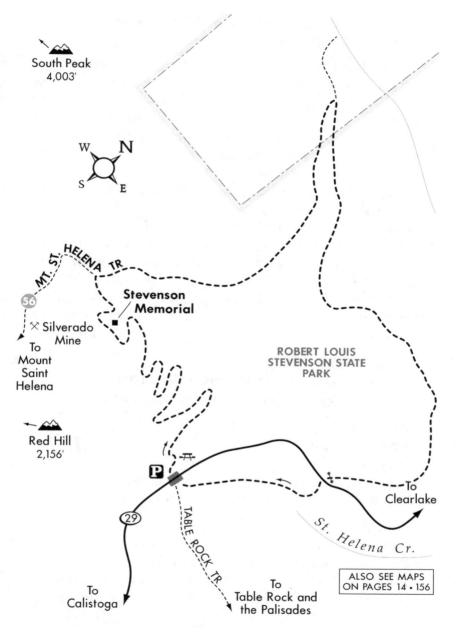

South Peak
4,003'

W N S E

MT. ST. HELENA TR.

56

✕ Silverado
Mine

To
Mount
Saint
Helena

**Stevenson
Memorial**

Red Hill
2,156'

ROBERT LOUIS
STEVENSON STATE
PARK

🅿

TABLE ROCK TR.

29

St. Helena Cr.

To
Clearlake

ALSO SEE MAPS
ON PAGES 14 • 156

To
Calistoga

To
Table Rock and
the Palisades

Stevenson Memorial Trail
ROBERT LOUIS STEVENSON STATE PARK

on the left at the road's summit. Additional parking is in a larger parking area directly across the road.

Hiking directions: Walk up the steps to a flat, grassy picnic area and posted trailhead. Head up the forested hillside on the rock-embedded path. Six switchbacks zigzag up the forested mountain. In a shady flat at 0.7 miles is the Stevenson Memorial, a stone monument by a mossy rock formation. This is the turn-around spot. For the 2.2-mile loop hike, climb two more switchbacks to the Mount Saint Helena Trail—a T-junction with a service road at 0.85 miles. The trail to Mount Saint Helena goes left and climbs 1,600 feet over the next 4.5 miles (Hike 56). For this hike, go to the right and steadily descend northward. Cross under power lines at a right U-bend and head southeast. Near Highway 29, pass through a metal gate to the road. Carefully cross the highway and descend 40 yards into the forest to a footpath. Bear right and climb 0.3 miles through the forest to the highway, directly across from the trailhead. Cautiously cross the road, completing the loop. ■

56. Mount Saint Helena Trail
ROBERT LOUIS STEVENSON STATE PARK

Hiking distance: 10.6 miles round trip
Hiking time: 5 to 6 hours
Elevation gain: 2,100 feet

map
page 156

Maps: U.S.G.S. Detert Reservoir and Mount Saint Helena
Bothe–Napa Valley and Robert Louis Stevenson State
Parks map

Summary of hike: Mount Saint Helena, in Robert Louis Stevenson State Park, is the tallest peak in Sonoma County at 4,339 feet. A 5.3-mile trail winds through the undeveloped park to the volcanic mountain's North Peak. It is a long, sinuous fire road on a south-facing slope, exposed to sun and wind. The popular hiking and biking route steadily climbs but is never steep.

The long distance and substantial elevation gain, however, make it a strenuous hike. Throughout the hike, the views are spectacular. From the summit are 360-degree vistas extending across Napa Valley to Mount Tamalpais, the twin peaks of Mount Diablo and San Francisco in the south, Mount Lassen and Snow Mountain in the north, the Vaca Mountains in the east, and the coastal ranges to the ocean in the west.

Driving directions: Same as Hike 55.

Hiking directions: Follow the hiking directions to Hike 55 to the T-junction with the service road at 0.8 miles, shortly after the Stevenson Memorial. The right fork weaves down the hillside back to Highway 29. For this hike, go to the left, as views open up of Napa Valley and the surrounding mountains. The trail passes above Silverado Mine, but it is not visible. At 1.6 miles, on a horseshoe right bend, is weather-chiseled Bubble Rock, a pock-marked igneous formation that is popular with rock climbers. Continue up the well-graded road cut into the chaparral-covered slope, with views across Napa County and Sonoma County. The exposed terrain is dotted with manzanita, small oaks, knobcone pines, bay laurel, and greasewood. Make a sweeping left bend at 2.25 miles, passing fractured rock columns. Cross under power lines and continue a half mile to a road junction on a saddle at 3.6 miles. The left branch leads 0.5 miles to 4,003-foot South Peak, the lower summit. Continue north—straight ahead—between North and South Peaks, with a view of Lake Berryessa on the right. Continue to a ridge at 4.5 miles. Veer left, entering Sonoma County, and head west toward the peak. Pass through groves of sugar pines and Douglas firs, then leave the forest for the final ascent. At the summit, pass a group of communication structures to the rocky north face above Rattlesnake and Bradford canyons. After savoring the views, return along the same route. ■

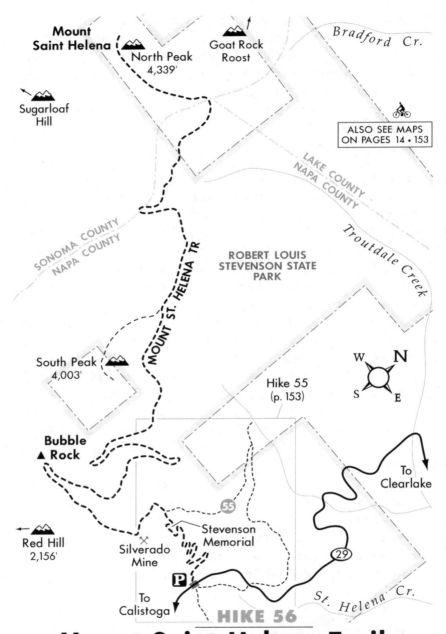

Mount
Saint Helena

North Peak
4,339'

Goat Rock
Roost

Bradford Cr.

Sugarloaf
Hill

ALSO SEE MAPS
ON PAGES 14 · 153

LAKE COUNTY
NAPA COUNTY

SONOMA COUNTY
NAPA COUNTY

MOUNT ST. HELENA TR

Troutdale Creek

ROBERT LOUIS
STEVENSON STATE
PARK

South Peak
4,003'

Hike 55
(p. 153)

W · N
S · E

Bubble
▲ Rock

To
Clearlake

Red Hill
2,156'

55

Silverado
Mine

Stevenson
Memorial

29

P

To
Calistoga

St. Helena Cr.

HIKE 56

Mount Saint Helena Trail
ROBERT LOUIS STEVENSON STATE PARK

57. Lower Ritchey Canyon Loop
Redwood—Ritchey Trails
BOTHE—NAPA VALLEY STATE PARK

Hiking distance: 3-mile loop

Hiking time: 1.5 hours

Elevation gain: 400 feet

Maps: U.S.G.S. Calistoga

Bothe—Napa Valley/Robert Louis Stevenson St. Pk. map

map page 160

Summary of hike: Bothe—Napa Valley State Park sits in the heart of Napa Valley between Calistoga and Saint Helena. The 1,900-acre park stretches along perennial Ritchey Creek and Mill Creek, reaching west into Sonoma County. The popular park offers camping, picnicking, swimming, horseback riding, and hiking, with more than 10 miles of trails. Hikes 57 and 58 follow the lush riparian habitat along Ritchey Creek, a tributary of the Napa River, in a redwood-lined drainage. This hike loops around the lower portion of the park and visits the old Hitchcock home site, dating back to the 1870s.

Driving directions: Bothe—Napa Valley State Park is located along Highway 29 between Calistoga and Saint Helena in Napa Valley. Three main routes access Napa Valley from Sonoma County. FROM THE NORTH: Access is via Highway 128 out of Geyserville and Healdsburg. FROM SANTA ROSA: Access is via Calistoga Road off of Highway 12. FROM THE SOUTH: Access is via Highway 12, south of the town of Sonoma.

FROM HIGHWAY 29 AND LINCOLN AVENUE IN CALISTOGA: Drive 3.5 miles south on Highway 29 to the posted state park entrance on the right. Turn right and drive 0.4 miles to the posted Ritchey Creek Trailhead and parking area on the right.

FROM HIGHWAY 29 IN SAINT HELENA: Drive 4.5 miles north on Highway 29 to the posted state park entrance on the left. Turn left and drive 0.4 miles to the posted Ritchey Creek Trailhead and parking area on the right.

Hiking directions: Pass the trailhead sign and enter the forest. Cross a service road to the banks of Ritchey Creek. Curve left, heading upstream, and follow the south side of the creek to a trail split at 0.4 miles. The Ritchey Canyon Trail crosses the creek to the right, our return route. Begin the loop to the left on the Redwood Trail, across the creek from the campground. Traverse the moist, north-facing slope to a second fork at 0.9 miles. The 1.5-mile Coyote Peak Trail veers left and climbs 700 feet through upland forest and chaparral to a 1,170-foot peak. Stay in the lush canyon on the Redwood Trail. Cross a tributary stream, and walk 100 yards to a third junction. An access to the Ritchey Canyon Trail crosses the creek to the right. Continue straight, staying on the hiking-only section of the Redwood Trail. Weave through the forest along the creek as the canyon narrows. The Redwood Trail ends in a shaded redwood forest. Rock hop over Ritchey Creek to a dirt road and a junction at 1.5 miles. To extend the hike, continue on the Hike 58 loop. For this shorter hike, bear right on the Vineyard Trail, and follow Ritchey Creek to a Y-fork. The Vineyard Trail veers left. Curve to the right on the Ritchey Canyon Trail, and follow the north side of the creek. Pass the creek crossing on the right that leads back to the Redwood Trail. Continue straight, reaching the Hitchcock home site on the right by a wood barn with a tin roof. Pass a campground access path on the left, and ford the creek to the right, completing the loop. Bear left and return 0.4 miles to the trailhead. ■

58. Upper Ritchey Canyon Loop
Redwood—Spring—Ritchey Trails
BOTHE—NAPA VALLEY STATE PARK

Hiking distance: 4.5-mile double loop

Hiking time: 2.5 hours

map
page 160

Elevation gain: 850 feet

Maps: U.S.G.S. Calistoga

Bothe—Napa Valley/Robert Louis Stevenson St. Pk. map

Summary of hike: Bothe—Napa Valley State Park lies along a rugged volcanic terrain. Within the park, the elevations range from 300 to 2,000 feet, producing diverse vegetation. The northern slopes and canyons are filled with an evergreen and deciduous forest, including redwoods, Douglas fir, tanbark oak, and blue oak. The southern, exposed slopes are covered with chaparral and brush. Ritchey Creek flows through the heart of the state park. A network of trails follows the riparian corridor through stands of coastal redwoods and ferns. This hike climbs into the secluded upper canyon and explores a sampling of the park's natural features.

Driving directions: Same as Hike 57.

Hiking directions: Take the Redwood Trail, following the hiking directions for Hike 57. Continue to the junction with the Spring Trail and Ritchey Canyon Trail at 1.5 miles. The Spring Trail goes left, our return route. Cross the road and take the posted Ritchey Canyon Trail. Climb the hillside and descend back to the creek. Rock hop over the creek, passing a cascading waterfall on the right. Climb again, cross three feeder streams, and pass a moss-covered rock cave. Climb steadily (with a few short, steep sections) to an open flat and a posted junction at 2.3 miles. Views of upper Ritchey Canyon and Diamond Mountain extend to the west. The right fork leads 1.2 miles into Upper Ritchey Canyon, continuing to a fruit orchard and meadow at the Traverso Homestead site from the 1880s. Take the Spring Trail straight ahead, and slowly descend through a mixed forest. Curve left on a dirt road among towering redwoods, and pass a junction with the South Fork Trail on a U-bend. Follow the serpentine road on a gentle but steady downhill grade. Cross a concrete spillway over the creek, completing the upper loop by the Redwood Trail. Continue straight ahead on the edge of the creek to a Y-fork. The Vineyard Trail veers left. Curve to the right on the Ritchey Canyon Trail, and follow the north side of the creek. Pass the creek crossing on the right leading to the Redwood Trail. Continue straight, reaching the Hitchcock home site on the right by the wood barn with a tin roof. Pass a campground access path on the left, and ford the creek to the right, completing the loop. Bear left and return 0.4 miles to the trailhead. ■

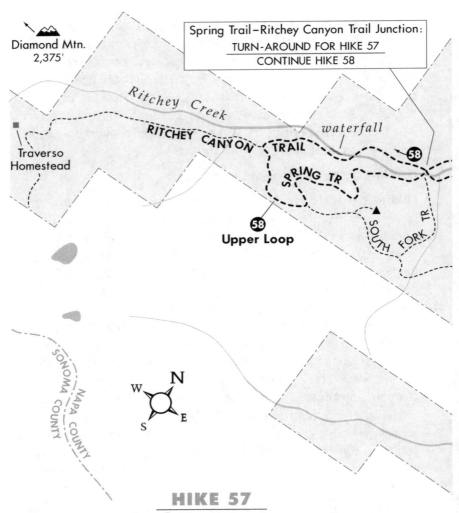

Diamond Mtn.
2,375'

Spring Trail–Ritchey Canyon Trail Junction:
TURN-AROUND FOR HIKE 57
CONTINUE HIKE 58

Ritchey Creek

RITCHEY CANYON TRAIL

waterfall

Traverso
Homestead

SPRING TR

58

58
Upper Loop

SOUTH FORK TR

N
W
E
S

SONOMA COUNTY

NAPA COUNTY

HIKE 57

Lower Ritchey Canyon Loop:
Redwood–Ritchey Trails

HIKE 58

Upper Ritchey Canyon Loop:
Redwood–Spring–Ritchey Trails

BOTHE–NAPA VALLEY STATE PARK

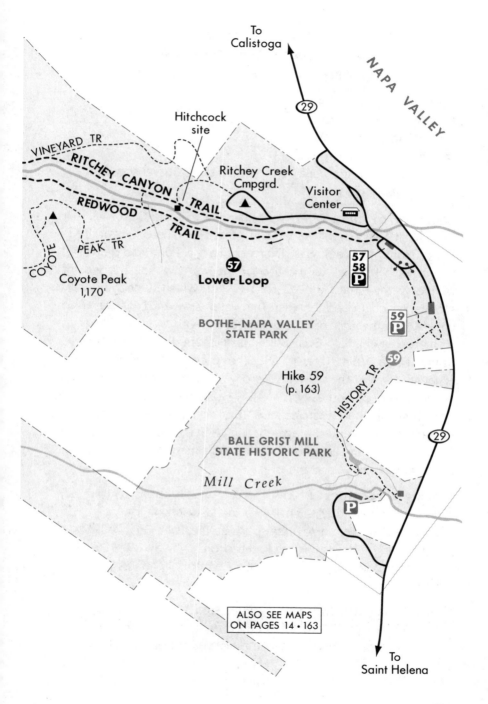

To
Calistoga

NAPA VALLEY

29

VINEYARD TR

RITCHEY CANYON TRAIL

Hitchcock
site

Ritchey Creek
Cmpgrd.

Visitor
Center

REDWOOD TRAIL

PEAK TR

COYOTE

Coyote Peak
1,170'

57 Lower Loop

57
58
P

59
P

59

BOTHE–NAPA VALLEY
STATE PARK

HISTORY TR

Hike 59
(p. 163)

BALE GRIST MILL
STATE HISTORIC PARK

29

Mill Creek

P

ALSO SEE MAPS
ON PAGES 14 • 163

To
Saint Helena

59. History Trail
BOTHE—NAPA VALLEY STATE PARK to
BALE GRIST MILL STATE HISTORIC PARK

Hiking distance: 2.4 miles round trip
Hiking time: 1.5 hours
Elevation gain: 200 feet
Maps: U.S.G.S. Calistoga
Bothe—Napa Valley and Robert Louis Stevenson State
Parks map

Summary of hike: Dr. Edward Bale had the Bale Grist Mill built in 1846. It was used for grinding grain (grist) into wheat flour. Water from Mill Creek was diverted into Mill Pond and delivered by redwood flumes to the top of the waterwheel. The weight of the water turned the 20-foot wheel, which turned the mill-stones, which ground the grist. The water-powered mill was used until 1905. The mill has been restored with a larger 36-foot diameter wheel. Bale Grist Mill State Historic Park is adjacent to Bothe—Napa Valley State Park. The parks are connected by Highway 29 and the 1.2-mile History Trail. This hike begins from the east end of Bothe—Napa Valley State Park and leads to the Bale Grist Mill State Historic Park. The trail passes an old pioneer cemetery with marked graves dating back to the mid-1800s. The hike climbs a ridge under a forest canopy, then descends into the Mill Creek drainage and the mill.

Driving directions: Follow the driving directions to Hike 57, then continue another 0.3 miles to the last parking lot.

To hike the trail in reverse, park at the Bale Grist Mill State Historic Park. The entrance is located on Highway 29—1.6 miles south of Bothe—Napa Valley State Park and 2.9 miles north of Saint Helena.

Hiking directions: From the picnic area, take the posted path south, parallel to Highway 29. Curve right, away from the high-way, to an open meadow and the historic White Church Ceme-tery. A side path on the left leads to the rock headstones. Back on the main trail, enter the forest of madrone, Douglas fir, and oaks. Climb the shaded hillside to the ridge. Follow the ridge, topping out in a half mile. The serpentine path slowly descends into the Mill Creek drainage to a tributary stream. Cross the stream and follow its west bank downstream to a posted junction at 0.9 miles. The left fork detours along the creek to the site of the old Mill Pond and the dam built in 1859. The History Trail crosses a wooden bridge over a seasonal stream to a trail split at Mill Creek. The left fork leads to the historic Grist Mill buildings. The right fork crosses a long wooden bridge over Mill Creek to the Bale Grist Mill parking lot. After exploring the mill and granary, return by retracing your steps. ■

P

BALE GRIST MILL STATE HISTORIC PARK

Mill Cr.

Mill

Bale Grist Mill and granary

Mill Pond

29

HISTORY TRAIL

White Church Cemetery

BOTHE—NAPA VALLEY STATE PARK

S

E ⊕ W

N

P

Hikes 57—58

57
58
P

ALSO SEE MAPS ON PAGES 14 · 161

History Trail
BOTHE—NAPA VALLEY STATE PARK
BALE GRIST MILL STATE HISTORIC PARK

To Hwy 29

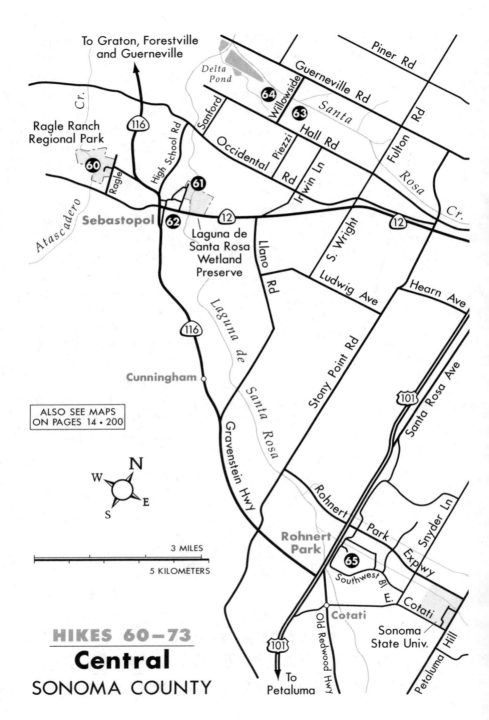

To Graton, Forestville and Guerneville

Delta Pond

Piner Rd

Guerneville Rd

Willowside

Santa

Fulton Rd

Ragle Ranch Regional Park

Sanford

Occidental

Piezzi

Hall Rd

Rosa

116

High School Rd

Rd

Irwin Ln

Cr.

60

Ragle

61

62

Sebastopol

12

Laguna de Santa Rosa Wetland Preserve

Llano Rd

S. Wright

12

Cr.

Atascadero

Ludwig Ave

Hearn Ave

116

Laguna de

Santa Rosa

Stony Point Rd

101

Santa Rosa Ave

Cunningham

ALSO SEE MAPS
ON PAGES 14 · 200

N

W   E

S

Gravenstein Hwy

Rohnert

Park

Expwy

Snyder Ln

3 MILES

5 KILOMETERS

Rohnert
Park

65

Southwest Bl

E.

Cotati

101

Old Redwood Hwy

Cotati

Sonoma
State Univ.

Petaluma Hill

To
Petaluma

HIKES 60–73
Central
SONOMA COUNTY

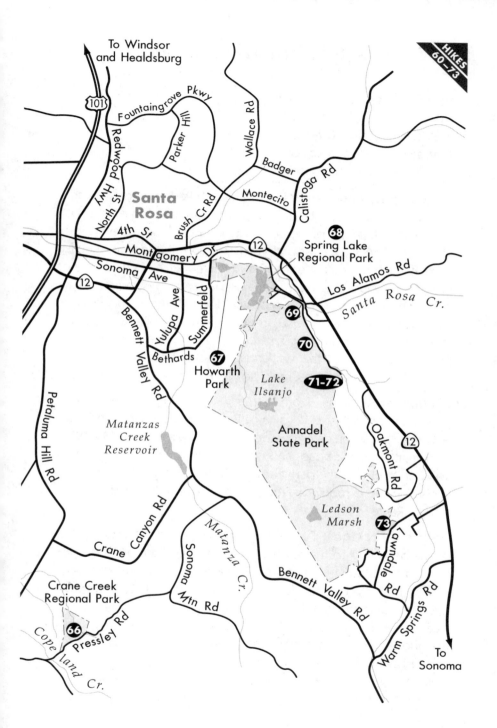

60. Ragle Ranch Regional Park

500 Ragle Road · Sebastopol

Hiking distance: 1.7-mile loop
Hiking time: 1 hour
Elevation gain: 50 feet
Maps: U.S.G.S. Sebastopol
Ragle Ranch Regional Park

Summary of hike: Ragle Ranch Regional Park covers 157 acres on the west side of Sebastopol. The eastern portion of the park has athletic fields, a playground, picnic areas, and a paved jogging path. The western portion of the park is the wild, natural side. It includes oak woodlands, a memorial redwood grove, open grasslands, and riparian wetlands overgrown with blackberry bushes. Atascadero Creek cuts through the scenic park. A multi-use hiking, biking, and equestrian trail loops around the undeveloped parkland. This hike circles the perimeter of the park on this trail through the wetlands, crossing bridges over small streams and Atascadero Creek. Dogs are allowed on the trails.

Driving directions: From Highway 101 in Santa Rosa, drive 7 miles west on Highway 12 to Ragle Road in Sebastopol. (En route, Highway 12 becomes Sebastopol Road, then Bodega Avenue.) Turn right on Ragle Road, and continue 0.5 miles to Ragle Ranch Road on the left—the park entrance. Turn left and enter the park. A parking fee is required. Free parking is available along the east side of Ragle Road.

Hiking directions: Follow the paved path along the west side of the park road to the gazebo picnic area and the posted junction for the Veteran's Memorial Grove. Head west and veer left, leaving the paved path. Continue on the dirt path 100 yards to the gated Blackberry Trail. Head down the hillside through an old pear orchard to bridge #4 and the Hilltop Trail on the right. Cross the bridge over the tributary stream, and quickly cross bridge #3 over Atascadero Creek. Enter the wetlands and pass the Thistle Trail, a cut-across route paralleling Atascadero Creek. Stroll through the riparian wetlands, passing large pockets of black-

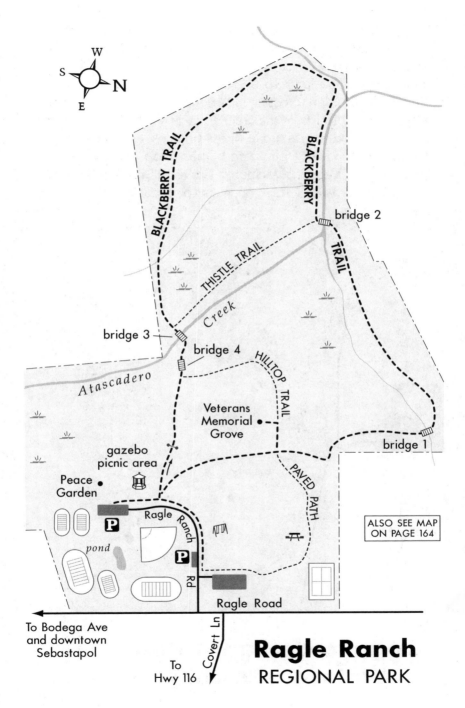

W N S E

BLACKBERRY TRAIL

BLACKBERRY TRAIL

bridge 2

THISTLE TRAIL

Creek

bridge 3

bridge 4

HILLTOP TRAIL

Atascadero

Veterans
Memorial
Grove

bridge 1

gazebo
picnic area

Peace
Garden

PAVED PATH

ALSO SEE MAP
ON PAGE 164

P

Ragle Ranch Rd

P

pond

Ragle Road

To Bodega Ave
and downtown
Sebastapol

Covert Ln

To
Hwy 116

Ragle Ranch
REGIONAL PARK

berry bushes while gradually gaining elevation from the basin. Loop around the perimeter of the wetland along the park's west boundary, passing black oak, willow, and ash groves. Skirt the north edge of the park to bridge #2 by the north end of the Thistle Trail. Bear left, crossing the bridge over Atascadero Creek. Parallel the north side of the creek through grasslands, a vineyard on the left, and an oak grove. Cross bridge #1 and head south. The dirt trail ends at a paved fork. The Hilltop Trail on the right leads to the Veteran's Memorial Grove, a planted redwood grove. The Blackberry Trail continues south back to the parking area. ■

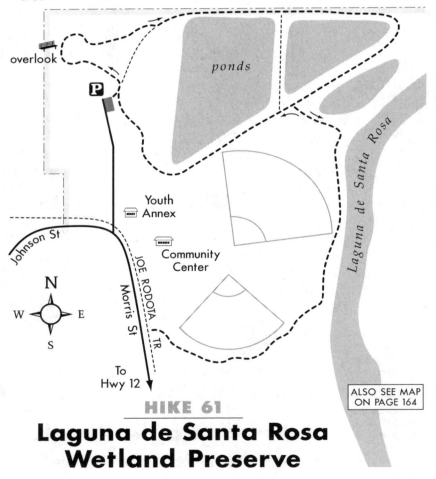

ALSO SEE MAP
ON PAGE 164

Laguna de Santa Rosa Wetland Preserve

61. Laguna de Santa Rosa Wetland Preserve

Hiking distance: 0.8-mile loop
Hiking time: 30 minutes
Elevation gain: Level
Maps: U.S.G.S. Sebastopol

map
page 168

Summary of hike: The Laguna de Santa Rosa waterway is the main artery in a 250-square-mile watershed between Sonoma Mountain and Sebastopol. It is the largest freshwater wetland on the northern California coast. The river is the largest and southernmost tributary of the Russian River. The sinuous Laguna de Santa Rosa stretches 14 miles from Windsor to Cotati in a 30,000-acre complex of creeks, pools, and oak woodlands. This area is prime bird habitat and an important stop for migrating waterfowl on the Pacific Flyway. The Laguna Wetlands Preserve in Sebastopol is among the best places to observe the laguna from the waterway itself. The trail is a raised gravel road that passes ponds, marshes, stands of valley oak, black walnuts, Oregon ash, and blackberries, with sweeping views of the expansive watershed. Dogs are allowed on the trails.

Driving directions: From Sebastopol Road (Highway 12) and Main Street in downtown Sebastopol, drive a quarter mile east on Sebastopol Road to Morris Street. Turn left and continue 0.4 miles, passing the community center and youth annex on the right. Turn right into the trailhead parking lot, just beyond the youth annex.

Hiking directions: At the trailhead arbor are three paths. Begin the loop on the left fork, and walk 100 yards to an overlook of the wetlands with a bench. Loop to the right and descend to a junction with the middle trail at a pond. The right fork leads back to the arbor. Bear left and skirt the edge of the pond on the right and open grasslands to the left. At the end of the first pond is a trail junction. The right fork cuts across between the two ponds. Continue straight on the left fork, skirting the north edge of the second pond. Curve right and head southwest between two ponds to another trail split by the left field of a baseball diamond. The right fork leads back to the trailhead by the youth annex, our return route. Detour on the left fork, and head south between the baseball field and lagoon. The trail ends on Morris Street by the community center. Return to the junction and complete the loop to the left.■

62. Joe Rodota Trail

Hiking distance: 1.5 miles round trip
Hiking time: 45 minutes
Elevation gain: Level
Maps: U.S.G.S. Sebastopol
West County & Rodota Trails map

Summary of hike: The Joe Rodota Trail is an abandoned railroad right-of-way that connects Santa Rosa with Sebastopol. The multi-use trail is named for the first director of the Sonoma County Regional Parks. The entire trail is 13 miles long. This hike follows the west portion of the trail in Sebastopol south of Highway 12. The trail leads through grasslands and a thick riparian forest in the Laguna de Santa Rosa wetlands under valley oak, willow, Oregon ash, and black walnut trees. Throughout the hike are sweeping views of dairy pastures, vineyards, creeks, and the Santa Rosa Plain. This is a popular trail for hiking, biking, jogging, and dog walking.

Driving directions: From Sebastopol Road (Highway 12) and Main Street in downtown Sebastopol, drive 0.1 mile south on Main Street to a parking lot on the left, south of Burnett Street.

Hiking directions: From the east end of the parking lot, cross Petaluma Avenue to the posted trailhead. Pass the map kiosk and head east on the paved path alongside oak and walnut trees. At 150 yards, pass a trail on the left that crosses two bridges over Calder Creek and leads to Highway 12, continuing to the Laguna de Santa Rosa Wetlands Preserve (Hike 61). Stay straight on the main trail, and cross a bridge over Laguna de Santa Rosa in a riparian habitat with willow trees and poison oak. Cross a second,

120-foot bridge over the Laguna Waterway. Follow the tree-lined path parallel to Highway 12, with views of the open, grassy wetlands. The trees soon give way to open meadows and a another bridge over a waterway. This is the turn-around spot.

To extend the hike, the trail continues 4.5 miles east, parallel to Highway 12, to downtown Santa Rosa by Railroad Square. ■

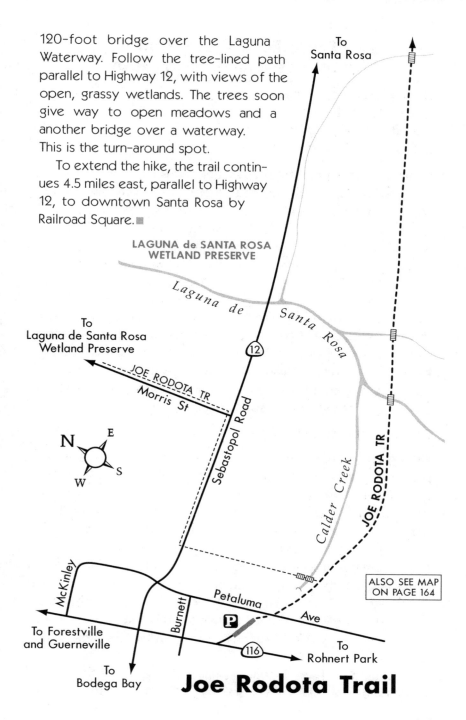

Joe Rodota Trail

63. Santa Rosa Creek Trail

WILLOWSIDE ROAD to FULTON ROAD

Hiking distance: 4 miles round trip
Hiking time: 2 hours
Elevation gain: Level
Maps: U.S.G.S. Sebastopol

Summary of hike: Santa Rosa Creek forms in the upper slopes of Red Hill between Sugarloaf Ridge State Park and Hood Mountain Regional Park. The creek flows through the heart of Santa Rosa and joins the Laguna de Santa Rosa north of Sebastopol. The Santa Rosa Creek Trail follows along the creek for 6.5 miles, from downtown Santa Rosa to Laguna de Santa Rosa by Delta Pond. Hikes 63 and 64 follow a section of the trail from Willowside Road between Santa Rosa and Sebastopol. This hike heads east along a raised gravel road on the south side of the Santa Rosa Creek Flood Channel. The trail runs under the shade of oak, black walnut, Oregon ash, and willow trees. It is a popular route for walkers, joggers, dog walkers, and bikers. A trail also follows the north side of the creek. On the north, however, there are no bridges over Abramson Creek or Peterson Creek.

Driving directions: Same as Hike 64.

Hiking directions: From the east side of Willowside Road, pass the trailhead posts, heading east. Follow the south side of Santa Rosa Creek upstream. The gravel path leads through the riparian corridor among oak, walnut, and willow trees. Pass Abramson Creek, a feeder stream joining Santa Rosa Creek from the north. Meander along a vineyard, then pass pastureland to the south. Continue atop the levee to a large pond on the right at 1.5 miles. Pass another vineyard straddling both sides of the trail. Curve right at the confluence with Piner Creek. Stroll between the creek and the backside of homes fronting Saddleback Court and Countryside Circle to Fulton Road at 2 miles. This is the turn-around spot.

To extend the hike, the trail continues 2.8 miles east to downtown Santa Rosa, where it becomes Prince Memorial Parkway. ■

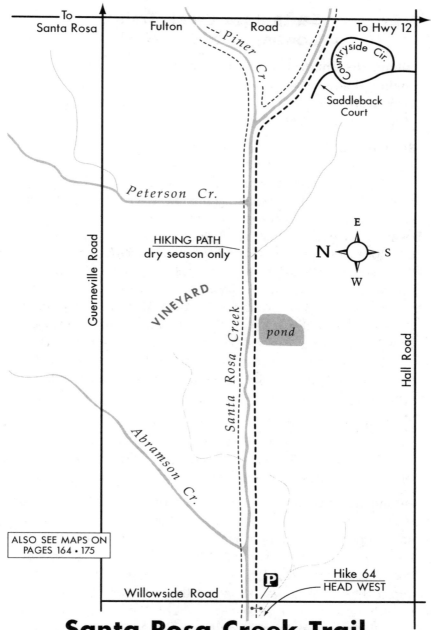

Santa Rosa Creek Trail
WILLOWSIDE ROAD to FULTON ROAD

64. Santa Rosa Creek Trail
WILLOWSIDE ROAD to DELTA POND

Hiking distance: 3 miles round trip
Hiking time: 1.5 hours
Elevation gain: Level
Maps: U.S.G.S. Sebastopol

Summary of hike: Delta Pond is a mile-long manmade pond along the Santa Rosa Creek Trail. It is an important stop for migrating waterfowl on the Pacific Flyway. It is also a thriving rookery for great blue herons, great egrets, and double-crested cormorants. The rookery is home to more than 150 nests. This hike heads west from Willowside Road, directly across from Hike 63. The trail begins on a gated gravel road maintained by the Sonoma County Water Agency. The trail follows the downstream course of Santa Rosa Creek under towering oaks, Oregon ash, black walnuts, and willows trees. The path skirts the north side of Delta Pond along the creek to the Laguna de Santa Rosa waterway. The pond is contained by a tall berm and is fenced. Public access up to the rim overlooking the pond is restricted. During the wet winter months, this path is muddy and it may be necessary to wade through large pools of water.

Driving directions: From Highway 101 in Santa Rosa, exit on Guerneville Road. Drive 4.5 miles west to Willowside Road and turn left. Continue 0.5 miles south to the trailhead on the south side of Santa Rosa Creek. Park on the narrow shoulder along the road.

Hiking directions: Pass the vehicle gate and head west on the gravel road. Follow the south edge of Santa Rosa Creek downstream through a lush, riparian corridor with walnut and willow trees. Walk through pastureland on the dirt path to the gated east end of Delta Pond at 0.7 miles. At the fence, leave the road and veer right on the grassy path. Skirt the north side of the pond between the berm and Santa Rosa Creek. The berm supporting Delta Pond prevents a view of the pond. At 1.5 miles, the trail ends by a gate at the far west end of Delta Pond, where the creek meets the Laguna Channel. Return along the same route. ∎

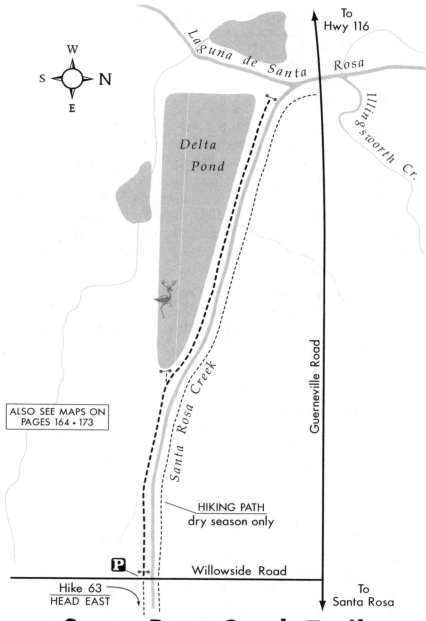

Santa Rosa Creek Trail
WILLOWSIDE ROAD to DELTA POND

65. Copeland Creek Trail

Hiking distance: 5 miles round trip
Hiking time: 2.5 hours
Elevation gain: Level
Maps: U.S.G.S. Cotati

Summary of hike: Copeland Creek originates on the steep slopes of Sonoma Mountain. It flows through Rohnert Park and Sonoma State University en route to the main channel of the Laguna de Santa Rosa. It is the southernmost tributary of the laguna. The Copeland Creek Trail is a wonderful creekside walk through Rohnert Park from Highway 101 to Sonoma State University. The level trail follows the tree-lined path, crosses bridges over waterways, and wanders through a butterfly garden, a native plant sanctuary, and campus lakes.

Driving directions: From Highway 101 in Rohnert Park, exit on the Rohnert Park Expressway. Drive one block east to Commerce Boulevard and turn right. Continue 0.5 miles to Avram Avenue. Turn left and quickly turn left again into the City of Rohnert Park Administrative Offices parking lot, located at 6750 Commerce Boulevard. The trailhead is at the north end of the parking lot.

Hiking directions: Head east along the south side of Copeland Creek. Follow the tree-lined, paved path upstream, passing a wooden footbridge that crosses over the creek at 0.15 miles. The level path passes a mix of riparian plants, including willows, bay, fir, oaks, and a few redwoods. Pass a second bridge over the creek, and walk 200 yards to Seedfarm Drive. Cross the road, railroad tracks, and a bridge over a water channel in rapid succession. Cross Country Club Drive at 0.7 miles, and continue east along the waterway, passing a third bridge over Copeland Creek to Snyder Lane at 1.3 miles. Cross Snyder Lane and skirt the edge of the athletic fields of Rancho Cotati High School. Enter Sonoma State University, passing a few school buildings and more redwood trees. The paved path soon ends and the dirt path begins. Walk past two large ponds and a grassy parkland on the right to a fourth bridge over the creek. Pass a native plant shade-house, an interpretive demonstration garden, and a bird and butterfly garden. A small nature trail loops around the main path. The trail ends at parking lot G in the university at 2.5 miles. ■

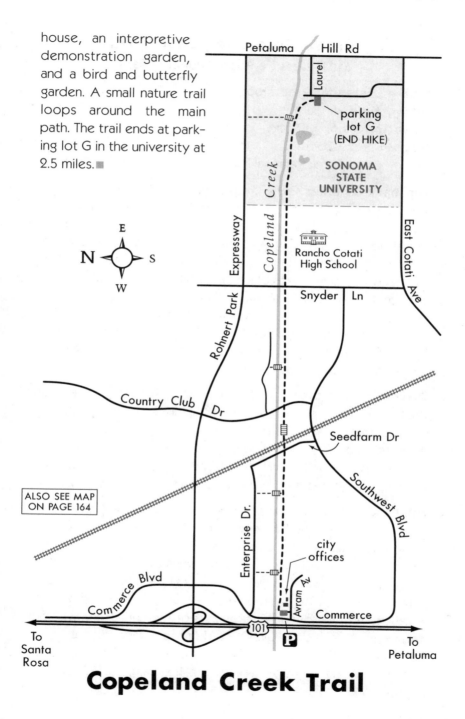

Copeland Creek Trail

66. Crane Creek Regional Park
6107 Pressley Road • Rohnert Park

Hiking distance: 2-mile loop
Hiking time: 1 hour
Elevation gain: 100 feet
Maps: U.S.G.S. Cotati
Crane Creek Regional Park map

Summary of hike: Crane Creek Regional Park encompasses 128 acres of rolling, grassy meadows on the east side of Rohnert Park. This diverse park contains oak savanna, riparian woodland, vernal pools, and bunchgrass meadows. Crane Creek and a seasonal stream flow through the wildflower-covered meadows. The park is bordered with black oak, white alder, California buckeye, and maple. Hiking, biking, and horse trails loop around the perimeter of the park. Several additional hiking-only trails explore the interior of the park. This hike leads to ridgetop overlooks of the park, then down to the bucolic setting along Crane Creek. Dogs are allowed on the trails.

Driving directions: From Highway 101 in Rohnert Park, exit on the Rohnert Park Expressway. Drive 2.7 miles east to a T-junction at Petaluma Hill Road. Turn right and head 1.2 miles south to Roberts Road. Turn left and continue 1.9 miles to the posted park entrance on the left. (En route, Roberts Road becomes Pressley Road.) Turn left and park in the lot. A parking fee is required.

Hiking directions: Three paths leave from the parking lot. Begin the loop on the Fiddleneck Trail to the west. Pass the map kiosk and head up the open, grassy slope to a junction. The Overlook Loop Trail veers left and rejoins the Fiddleneck Trail a short distance ahead. The Hawk Ridge Trail goes to the right. Stay on the Fiddleneck Trail, also on the right, and climb to a knoll with a bench. From the overlook are views of the entire park and the cattle-grazed hillsides. Follow the ridge to a second knoll and a junction with the Hawk Ridge Trail on the right at 0.3 miles. Detour right on the Hawk Ridge Trail to the Bowden Bluff Overlook.

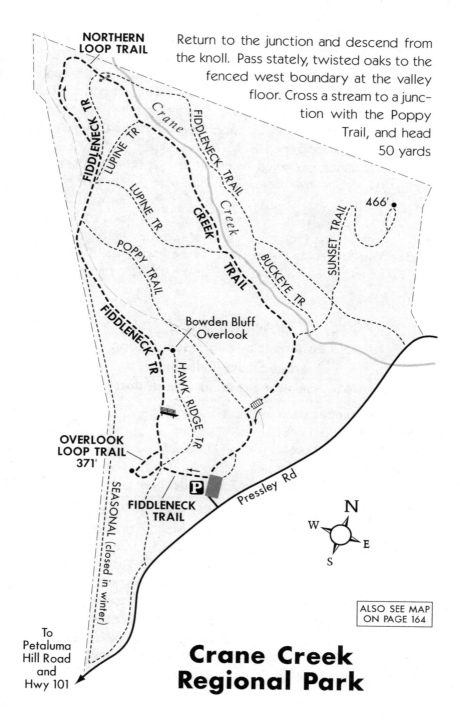

Return to the junction and descend from the knoll. Pass stately, twisted oaks to the fenced west boundary at the valley floor. Cross a stream to a junction with the Poppy Trail, and head 50 yards

NORTHERN LOOP TRAIL

FIDDLENECK TR

LUPINE TR

Crane

FIDDLENECK TRAIL

Creek

LUPINE TR

CREEK

TRAIL

POPPY TRAIL

466'

SUNSET TRAIL

BUCKEYE TR

Bowden Bluff
Overlook

FIDDLENECK TR

HAWK RIDGE TR

**OVERLOOK
LOOP TRAIL
371'**

SEASONAL (closed in winter)

P

**FIDDLENECK
TRAIL**

Pressley Rd

To
Petaluma
Hill Road
and
Hwy 101

N
W   E
S

ALSO SEE MAP
ON PAGE 164

Crane Creek
Regional Park

farther to the Lupine Trail. Stay on the Fiddleneck Trail to a junction with the Northern Loop Trail. Veer left on the Northern Loop, following the stream to the northwest corner of the park. Curve right along the north boundary to a 4-way junction at a gate. Cross the Fiddleneck Trail and pass through the gate on the Creek Trail. Stroll through the open meadow along the south edge of Crane Creek, lined with willows, alders, and bays. Pass mature bay laurels, buckeyes, and gnarled valley oaks to the east end of the Lupine Trail. Continue along Crane Creek, then curve away from the creek to a junction. The Sunset Trail crosses Crane Creek, links to the Buckeye Trail, and climbs 0.4 miles to a 466-foot overlook. The Creek Trail continues to the right, crossing a bridge over a steam to the east end of the Poppy Trail. Bear left, staying on the Creek Trail, and return to the trailhead parking lot. ■

67. Howarth Park
Old Fisherman's — Eagle Scout Loop
around Lake Ralphine
630 Summerfield Road • Santa Rosa

Hiking distance: 0.9-mile loop

Hiking time: 30 minutes

map
page 182

Elevation gain: Level

Maps: U.S.G.S. Santa Rosa

Howarth Park Map and Trail Guide

Summary of hike: Howarth Park lies adjacent to Spring Lake Regional Park on the east side of Santa Rosa. The diverse 152-acre community park is one of the city's oldest and largest parks. It includes tennis courts; a softball field; a climbing wall; an amusement area with a train, carousel, and animal barn; and a 25-acre lake with boat rentals. Hiking and biking trails surround Lake Ralphine in the center of the park. The trails connect with Spring Lake Regional Park (Hike 68) and continue into Annadel State Park (Hikes 69—73). This hike loops around Lake Ralphine under stands of oaks. Dogs are allowed on the trails.

Driving directions: From Highway 101 and Highway 12 in Santa Rosa, drive 1.5 miles west on Highway 12 to Farmers Lane. Turn left and drive 0.8 miles to Montgomery Drive, following the Highway 12 signs. Turn right and continue one mile to Summerfield Road. Turn right and go a quarter mile to the signed park entrance. Turn left into the park, and drive 0.2 miles to the parking lot at Lake Ralphine.

Hiking directions: From the south end of Lake Ralphine, take the paved Old Fisherman's Trail, a segment of the Bay Area Ridge Trail. Follow the east side of the lake to a fork at 0.1 mile. Curve left onto a dirt path. Meander through oak trees and a mixed riparian forest with willows, manzanita, and madrones. Pass short side paths leading to the lakeshore. At the north tip of the lake is a junction. The right fork leads 50 yards to the paved path and continues into Spring Lake Regional Park. Descend on the left fork—the Eagle Scout Trail—and cross a wooden bridge over the lake's inlet stream. Continue on the north side of the lake, staying close to the shoreline. Traverse the forested hillside above the lake toward the dam. Bear left and cross a bridge over the outlet stream channel. Walk across Lake Ralphine Dam, completing the loop.■

68. Spring Lake Regional Park
Spring Lake Loop
393 Violetti Road • Santa Rosa

Hiking distance: 2.6-mile loop
Hiking time: 1.5 hours
Elevation gain: 50 feet
Maps: U.S.G.S. Santa Rosa
      Spring Lake Regional Park map

map page 183

Summary of hike: Spring Lake Regional Park sits in the foothills of eastern Santa Rosa between Howarth Park (Hike 67) and Annadel State Park (Hikes 69—73). The 320-acre park is among the most popular parks in Santa Rosa. The centerpiece of the

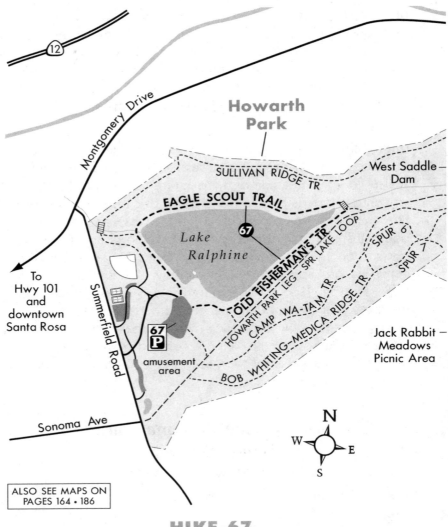

Howarth
Park

SULLIVAN RIDGE TR

West Saddle—
Dam

EAGLE SCOUT TRAIL

67

*Lake
Ralphine*

OLD FISHERMAN'S TR

HOWARTH PARK LEG – SPR. LAKE LOOP

SPUR 6

SPUR 7

CAMP WA-TAM TR.

HOWARTH WHITING-MEDICA RIDGE TR.

Montgomery Drive

12

To
Hwy 101
and
downtown
Santa Rosa

Summerfield Road

67
P

amusement
area

BOB WHITING-MEDICA RIDGE TR.

Jack Rabbit —
Meadows
Picnic Area

Sonoma Ave

N
W — E
S

ALSO SEE MAPS ON
PAGES 164 • 186

ALSO SEE MAPS ON
PAGES 164 • 186

HIKE 67
Howarth Park
LAKE RALPHINE LOOP

HIKE 68
Spring Lake Regional Park
SPRING LAKE LOOP

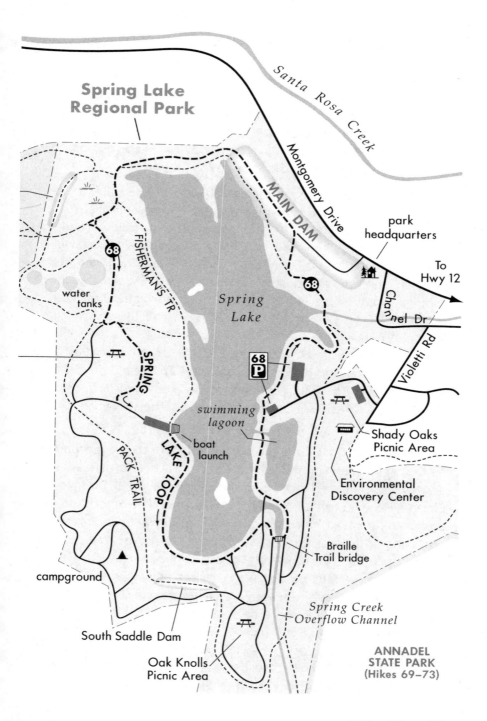

Spring Lake
Regional Park

Santa Rosa Creek

Montgomery Drive

MAIN DAM

park
headquarters

To
Hwy 12

68

FISHERMANS TR

Channel Dr

water
tanks

Spring
Lake

Violetti Rd

SPRING

68
P

swimming
lagoon

Shady Oaks
Picnic Area

boat
launch

LAKE LOOP

PACK TRAIL

Environmental
Discovery Center

Braille
Trail bridge

campground

Spring Creek
Overflow Channel

South Saddle Dam

ANNADEL
STATE PARK
(Hikes 69–73)

Oak Knolls
Picnic Area

park is Spring Lake, a 72-acre lake constructed in 1962 as a flood control reservoir. The lake is used for sailing, canoeing, and fishing (bass, bluegill, and trout). The expansive park also has a campground, picnic area, a 3-acre spring-fed swimming lagoon, and miles of multi-use trails. A paved biking path and a dirt equestrian trail intertwine around the lake. This hike circles the lake counterclockwise. Connector paths join the loop from numerous other locations. Bikes are allowed on this paved loop.

Driving directions: From Highway 101 and Highway 12 in Santa Rosa, drive 1.5 miles west on Highway 12 to Farmers Lane. Turn left and drive 0.8 miles to Montgomery Drive, following the Highway 12 signs. Turn right and continue 2.7 miles to Channel Drive. Turn right and go 0.2 miles to Violetti Road. Turn right and drive 0.2 miles to the posted park entrance on Violetti Road. Turn right, passing the entrance station, and drive straight ahead 0.2 miles to the parking lot at Spring Lake and the swimming lagoon. A parking fee is required.

From the town of Kenwood, drive 5.5 miles north on Highway 12 (Sonoma Highway) to Los Alamos Road. Turn left and drive 0.2 miles to Melita Road. Turn right and immediately veer left onto Montgomery Drive. Continue a half mile to Channel Drive and turn left. Continue with the directions above.

Hiking directions: From the parking lot, take the paved path to the right, following the edge of Spring Lake. Loop around a finger of the lake, and cross over the Santa Rosa Creek Diversion Channel. Head up to the top of the main dam, and walk northwest across the dam. After crossing, slowly descend, following the north end of the lake. Curve south through oak groves to a posted trail split. The right fork leads to Lake Ralphine in Howarth Park (Hike 67). Curve left, passing water storage tanks on the right. Weave into Jack Rabbit Meadows Picnic Area and down to the boat launch. Follow the shoreline south, and curve left along the south end of Spring Lake beneath South Saddle Dam. Continue along the shoreline. Cross the Braille Trail Bridge over the Spring Creek Overflow Channel. Skirt the west side of the swimming lagoon, completing the loop at the trailhead parking lot. ■

Annadel State Park

HIKES 69—73

6201 Channel Drive • Santa Rosa

map
page 186

Annadel State Park lies on the eastern edge of Santa Rosa at the north end of the Sonoma Mountains. The largely undeveloped park covers 5,000 pristine acres of oak woodlands, Douglas fir and redwood forests, and exposed chaparral slopes. The state park includes broad meadows, rolling hills, narrow ridges, stream-fed canyons, creeks, old cobblestone quarries, a 26-acre lake, and a wetland marsh. More than 35 miles of interconnecting hiking, jogging, biking, and horseback riding trails weave through the park's diverse habitats. Hikes 69—73 explore the wide range of terrain and landscape found at Annadel State Park.

69. Cobblestone—Orchard Loop
ANNADEL STATE PARK

Hiking distance: 4.7-mile loop
Hiking time: 2.5 hours
Elevation gain: 400 feet
Maps: U.S.G.S. Santa Rosa
       Annadel State Park map

map
page 188

Summary of hike: This hike forms a loop on the Cobblestone and Orchard Trails in Annadel State Park. The Cobblestone Trail is named for the basalt cobblestones that were mined out of the area's quarries. The stones were once used for paving roads. The old cobblestones can still be seen on the streets of San Francisco and Sacramento. The trail passes the Wymore Quarry, where a gravity-powered tram transported cobblestones to a railroad line at Channel Drive. The return route on the Orchard Trail runs through the remains of an old orchard. The loop travels through several diverse habitats and landscapes, including oak and manzanita savanna, open meadows, and a stream-fed draw. En route, the trail crosses a narrow ridge and leads to vistas of upper Sonoma Valley and the Santa Rosa Plain.

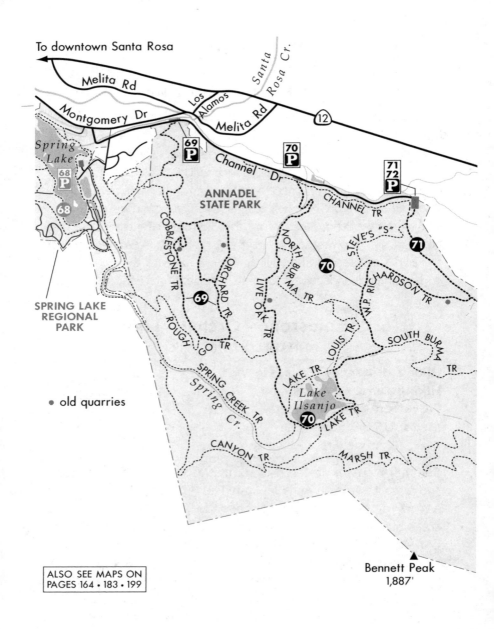

To downtown Santa Rosa

Melita Rd

Montgomery Dr

Los Alamos

Melita Rd

Santa Rosa Cr.

Channel Dr

12

69 P

70 P

71 72 P

Spring Lake

68 P

68

ANNADEL STATE PARK

COBBLESTONE TR

ORCHARD TR

ROUGH GO TR

LIVE OAK TR

NORTH BURMA TR

70

CHANNEL TR

STEVE'S "S"

71

W.P. RICHARDSON TR

SPRING LAKE REGIONAL PARK

69

SPRING CREEK TR

Spring Cr.

LAKE TR

LOUIS TR

SOUTH BURMA TR

• old quarries

Lake Ilsanjo

70

LAKE TR

CANYON TR

MARSH TR

Bennett Peak
1,887'

ALSO SEE MAPS ON
PAGES 164 • 183 • 199

HIKES 69–73
Annadel State Park

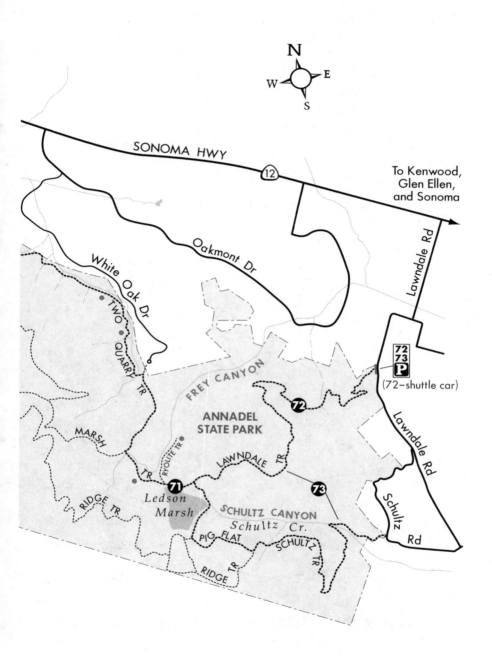

Driving directions: From Highway 101 and Highway 12 in Santa Rosa, drive 1.5 miles west on Highway 12 to Farmers Lane. Turn left and drive 0.8 miles to Montgomery Drive, following the Highway 12 signs. Turn right and continue 2.7 miles to Channel Drive. Turn right and go 0.6 miles to the posted Cobblestone Trail on the right. Park in the pullout on the left.

From the town of Kenwood, drive 5.5 miles north on Highway 12 (Sonoma Highway) to Los Alamos Road. Turn left and drive 0.2 miles to Melita Road. Turn right and immediately veer left onto Montgomery Drive. Drive a half mile to Channel Drive and turn left. Continue with the directions above.

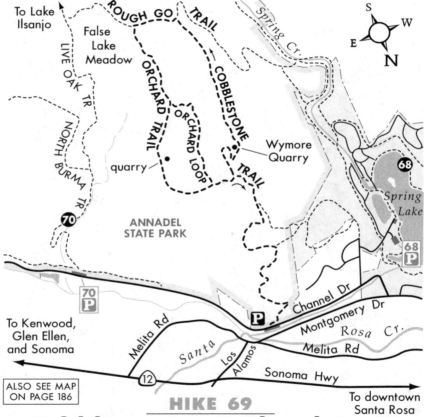

ALSO SEE MAP
ON PAGE 186

ALSO SEE MAP ON PAGE 186

HIKE 69

Cobblestone – Orchard Loop
ANNADEL STATE PARK

Hiking directions: Walk past the map kiosk on the Cobblestone Trail, entering the shady forest with moss-covered rocks. Pass through an oak and manzanita grassland, and weave up the north-facing hillside. Head up a draw and level out in a wide, open meadow. Skirt the west edge of the meadow, then curve left and cross through the grassland to a junction at 0.7 miles. The right fork leads to Spring Lake Regional Park (Hike 68). Stay left and reenter the mixed forest. Continue climbing to a sitting bench and an overlook of upper Sonoma Valley. Cross a minor ridge to a second junction with a path that leads to Spring Lake Regional Park. A short distance ahead is a junction with the Orchard Trail at 1.2 miles. Begin the loop to the right, staying on the Cobblestone Trail. Cross the narrow ridge, with two steep dropoffs. Make a sweeping right bend, then a left bend, passing the Wymore Quarry on the left. Traverse the hillside, with views west across the Santa Rosa Plain, to a posted T-junction at 2.2 miles. Bear left on the Rough Go Trail. Walk 0.2 miles, passing an open meadow rimmed with oaks, to a junction with the Orchard Trail. The right fork leads to Lake Ilsanjo (Hike 70). Bear left on the Orchard Trail, and follow the west edge of False Lake Meadow to a junction. The two paths form a loop around the knoll just ahead, rejoining in a half mile. The left fork is slightly shorter. The right fork passes an old quarry. Both paths rejoin at 3.4 miles and lead a short distance to the Cobblestone Trail, completing the loop. Return 1.2 miles to the right. ∎

70. Lake Ilsanjo
ANNADEL STATE PARK

Hiking distance: 6.2-mile loop
Hiking time: 3.5 hours
Elevation gain: 600 feet
Maps: U.S.G.S. Santa Rosa and Kenwood
  Annadel State Park map

map
page 191

Summary of hike: In the 1930s, Joe Coney bought the land that is now Annadel State Park. In the 1950s he built Lake Ilsanjo on Spring Creek and named it after himself and his wife Ilse. Joe used the 26-acre lake as a hunting and fishing retreat for his friends. Lake Ilsanjo is now the heart of the park, popular with picnickers, cyclists, joggers, equestrians, hikers, and anglers hoping to catch bluegill and bass. This hike leads to Lake Ilsanjo, surrounded by meadows filled with wildflowers. The trail skirts the lakeshore and returns via the Richardson Trail, an old ranch road shaded by redwoods and mixed oak woodlands.

Driving directions: From Highway 101 and Highway 12 in Santa Rosa, drive 1.5 miles west on Highway 12 to Farmers Lane. Turn left and drive 0.8 miles to Montgomery Drive, following the Highway 12 signs. Turn right and continue 2.7 miles to Channel Drive. Turn right and go 1.5 miles to the posted North Burma Trail and Channel Trail. Park along the right side of the road. A parking fee is required.

From the town of Kenwood, drive 5.5 miles north on Highway 12 (Sonoma Highway) to Los Alamos Road. Turn left and drive 0.2 miles to Melita Road. Turn right and immediately veer left onto Montgomery Drive. Drive a half mile to Channel Drive and turn left. Continue with the directions above.

Hiking directions: Head up the forested slope on the North Burma Trail. Follow the west side of a stream, originating from False Lake Meadow. Rock-hop over the creek and climb two switchbacks. Pass a 15-foot cataract, reaching a posted trail split on a flat at 0.7 miles. The North Burma Trail goes left. Stay straight on the Live Oak Trail and traverse the hillside, skirting the east side of grassy False Lake Meadow. At the summit, pass the site of an old quarry on the left. Gradually descend and cross a small bridge, emerging from the shady oak forest into False Lake Meadow. Cross the tree-rimmed grasslands to a junction with the Rough Go Trail at 1.6 miles. Follow the Rough Go Trail straight ahead through the rocky grassland. At just over 2 miles, the Rough Go Trail ends at a junction with the Lake Trail on the west side of Lake Ilsanjo. Both directions circle the lake. For this hike, curve right, crossing the dam and spillway. Loop around the south and east sides of the picturesque lake. Cross two of the lake's feeder streams and a picnic area with a side loop on the left. At the

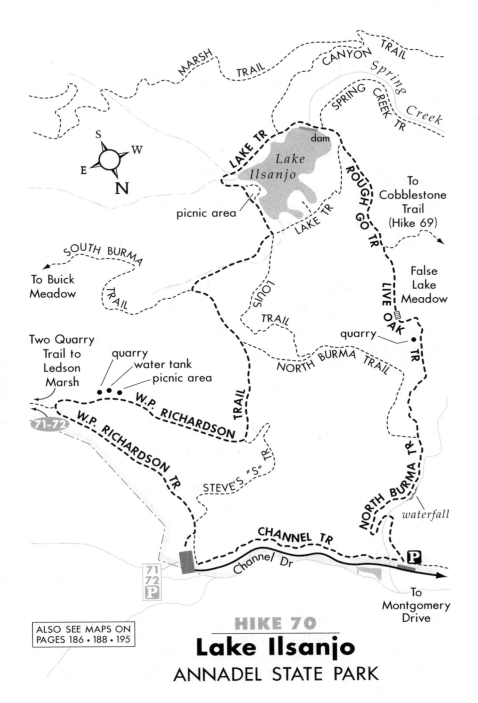

MARSH TRAIL

CANYON TRAIL

Spring Creek

SPRING CREEK TR

S
W
E
N

dam

Lake Ilsanjo

LAKE TR

ROUGH GO TR

To Cobblestone Trail (Hike 69)

picnic area

LAKE TR

LIVE OAK TR

False Lake Meadow

SOUTH BURMA

To Buick Meadow

TRAIL

LOUIS TRAIL

quarry

Two Quarry Trail to Ledson Marsh

quarry
water tank
picnic area

71-72

W.P. RICHARDSON TRAIL

NORTH BURMA TRAIL

W.P. RICHARDSON TR

STEVE'S "S" TR

NORTH BURMA TR

waterfall

71
72
P

CHANNEL TR

Channel Dr

P

To Montgomery Drive

ALSO SEE MAPS ON PAGES 186 • 188 • 195

HIKE 70

Lake Ilsanjo
ANNADEL STATE PARK

north end of the lake is a 4-way junction at 3 miles. The left fork loops back to the Rough Go Trail. The Louis Trail continues straight ahead for a shorter 5.1-mile hike. For this hike, bear right on the W.P. Richardson Trail, an old ranch road. Head up the dirt road, staying left past a junction with the South Burma Trail. Traverse the hill, passing the North Burma Trail. Begin an easy descent through a forest of redwoods, Douglas fir, and coast live oak, passing Steve's "S" Trail at 3.9 miles. Pass a picnic area, water tank, and wood steps to a quarry site, all on the right. At 4.6 miles, pass the Two Quarry Trail (Hike 71) on a horseshoe left bend. Continue down to the parking lot at the east end of Channel Drive at 5.5 miles. Head left and walk 0.7 miles on forested Channel Drive or the Channel Trail back to the trailhead. ∎

71. Two Quarry Trail to Ledson Marsh
ANNADEL STATE PARK

Hiking distance: 7 miles round trip
Hiking time: 4 hours
Elevation gain: 800 feet
Maps: U.S.G.S. Kenwood
       Annadel State Park map

map
page 194

Summary of hike: Ledson Marsh sits in a large 1,100-foot-high circular depression on the quieter, southeast side of the park. The marsh was built as a reservoir to water eucalyptus trees. It is now overgrown with cattails, tules, and native grasses. It is a popular bird observation site with more than 100 species of birds. The Two Quarry Trail, named for two basalt quarry sites along the trail, leads into the eastern portion of the park to Ledson Marsh. The hike begins on the Warren Richardson Trail at the east end of Channel Drive and joins with the Two Quarry Trail. This hike may be combined with Hike 72 for a 6.4-mile shuttle hike.

Driving directions: From Highway 101 and Highway 12 in Santa Rosa, drive 1.5 miles west on Highway 12 to Farmers Lane. Turn left and drive 0.8 miles to Montgomery Drive, following the Highway 12 signs. Turn right and continue 2.7 miles to Channel

Drive. Turn right and go 2.2 miles to the large parking lot at the end of the road. A parking fee is required.

From the town of Kenwood, drive 5.5 miles north on Highway 12 (Sonoma Highway) to Los Alamos Road. Turn left and drive 0.2 miles to Melita Road. Turn right and immediately veer left onto Montgomery Drive. Drive a half mile to Channel Drive and turn left. Continue with the directions above.

Hiking directions: From the far end of the parking lot, take the hikers-only footpath to the W.P. Richardson Trail, a wide dirt road. Bear left and head up the old boulder-studded ranch road to an oak-rimmed meadow with a view of Sugarloaf Ridge. At 0.9 miles, on a horseshoe right bend, is a picnic area and junction. Leave the road and take the Two Quarry Trail to the left. Cross a stream and head east on the footpath through bay laurel and towering Douglas fir trees. Traverse the hillside, parallel to the creek on the left, and cross three small feeder streams. Pass a rock quarry on the right, where the trail begins to climb. Head up the lush canyon, rising above, then returning to the creek. Pass a second distinct quarry on the right, and curve away from the creek. Stroll through the quiet forest, cross another tributary stream, and return to the creek by a series of small waterfalls and pools. Hop over the creek to a T-junction at 2.4 miles. The left fork leaves the park to White Oak Drive, a private road. Go to the right, staying on the Two Quarry Trail, which is now a dirt road. Steadily gain elevation through the dense forest, weaving along the contours of the canyon wall. Leave the canyon to an expansive meadow with a picnic area and posted junction. Bear left on the Marsh Trail, crossing a stream. Pass remnants of another quarry on the right to the northwest corner of Ledson Marsh at 3.3 miles. Follow the north edge of the reed-covered marsh a quarter mile to a junction with the Lawndale Trail, the turn-around point for this hike. The Marsh Trail continues to the right along the east side of Ledson Marsh. Straight ahead—Hike 72—leads nearly 3 miles down to Lawndale Road at the northeast corner of Annadel State Park. For the 6.4-mile shuttle hike to Lawndale Road, continue with Hike 72. ■

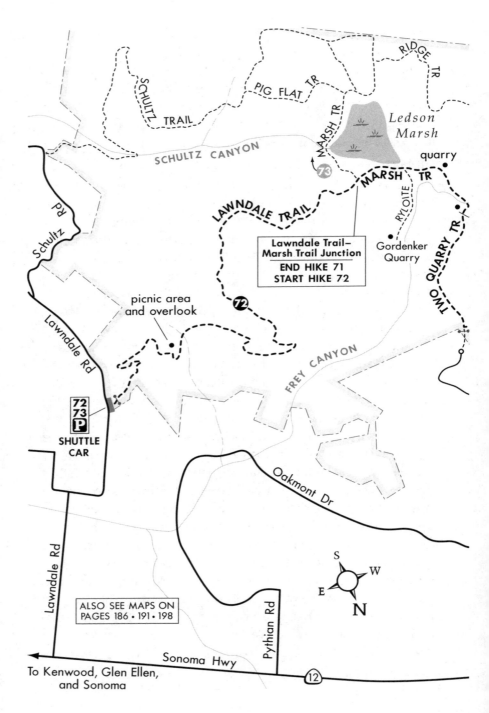

SCHULTZ TRAIL

PIG FLAT TR

RIDGE TR

MARSH TR

Ledson Marsh

quarry

SCHULTZ CANYON

MARSH TR

RYLOITE

TWO QUARRY TR

LAWNDALE TRAIL

Gordenker Quarry

Schultz Rd

Lawndale Trail–Marsh Trail Junction
END HIKE 71
START HIKE 72

Lawndale Rd

picnic area and overlook

72

FREY CANYON

73

72
73
P

SHUTTLE CAR

Oakmont Dr

Lawndale Rd

ALSO SEE MAPS ON
PAGES 186 • 191 • 198

Pythian Rd

S W
E N

Sonoma Hwy

12

To Kenwood, Glen Ellen,
and Sonoma

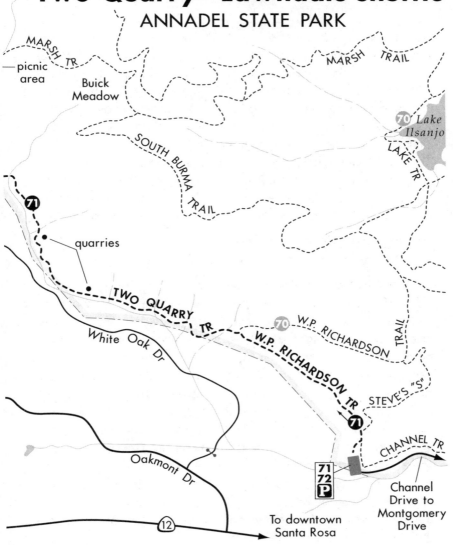

HIKE 71
Two Quarry Trail to Ledson Marsh
HIKE 72
Two Quarry–Lawndale shuttle
ANNADEL STATE PARK

MARSH TR.

picnic area

Buick Meadow

MARSH TRAIL

70 Lake Ilsanjo

SOUTH BURMA TRAIL

LAKE TR

71

quarries

TWO QUARRY TR

White Oak Dr

70 W.P. RICHARDSON

W.P. RICHARDSON TR

TRAIL

STEVE'S "S"

71

Oakmont Dr

CHANNEL TR

71 72 P

Channel Drive to Montgomery Drive

To downtown Santa Rosa

12

72. Two Quarry—Lawndale Shuttle
ANNADEL STATE PARK

Hiking distance: 6.4-mile one-way shuttle
Hiking time: 3.5 hours
Elevation gain: 800 feet
Maps: U.S.G.S. Kenwood
Annadel State Park map

**map
page 194**

Summary of hike: Between 1870 and 1920, Italian stone-cutters worked in the basalt quarries of present-day Annadel State Park. The cobblestones were used for paving streets throughout northern California. The Two Quarry Trail leads into the quieter eastern portion of the park towards Ledson Marsh, joining with the Marsh Trail and the Lawndale Trail. This hike continues from Hike 71, utilizing a shuttle car at the Lawndale Trailhead. After passing the quarries, the hike descends from Ledson Marsh to Lawndale Road, weaving through redwood and Douglas fir forests to vistas of Sonoma Valley and the surrounding mountains. The quarries have since been reclaimed by moss.

Driving directions: Same as Hike 71.
SHUTTLE CAR: Same Hike 73 (Lawndale Trailhead).

Hiking directions: Begin at the end of Hike 71—on the north edge of Ledson Marsh at the Lawndale Trail—Marsh Trail junction. The Marsh Trail follows the east side of Ledson Marsh. For this hike, continue straight ahead on the Lawndale Trail at a level grade. Descend through oak trees into the canyon. Traverse the canyon walls under a forest canopy of firs and redwoods. Head downhill to a right bend under powerlines. The vistas extend across Sonoma Valley to Sugarloaf Ridge, Bald Mountain, and Red Mountain. Continue traversing the steep hillside and make a sharp left bend, crossing over a seasonal drainage. Emerge from the forest to a grassy knoll and picnic area overlooking Sonoma Valley. Loop around the knoll and curve left over another drainage. Zigzag down two switchbacks, crossing a drainage on the second bend. Wind down to the base of the mountain and the trailhead on Lawndale Road. ■

73. Lawndale Trail— Schultz Canyon Loop

ANNADEL STATE PARK

Hiking distance: 7-mile loop
Hiking time: 4 hours
Elevation gain: 700 feet
Maps: U.S.G.S. Kenwood
Annadel State Park map

map
page 198

Summary of hike: The Lawndale Trail begins at the eastern end of Annadel State Park in Sonoma Valley. The trail is an old road once used by stonecutters working in the basalt quarries. The road follows a stream drainage, climbs to knolls with overlooks, weaves under a canopy of redwoods and Douglas firs, and emerges at Ledson Marsh above 1,100 feet. The water collected in Ledson Marsh overflows into Schultz Canyon. The hike returns down the remote canyon, following the forested watercourse.

Driving directions: From Highway 101 and Highway 12 in Santa Rosa, drive 1.5 miles west on Highway 12 to Farmers Lane. Turn left and drive one mile to 4th Street, following the Highway 12 signs. Turn right and continue 8.4 miles to Lawndale Road. Turn right and go 1.1 mile to the trailhead parking lot on the right at the base of the mountains.

From the town of Kenwood, drive 2 miles north on Highway 12 (Sonoma Highway) to Lawndale Road. Turn left and continue with the directions above.

Hiking directions: Walk past the trailhead gate, and head up the grassy slope dotted with oak, madrone, and buckeye trees. Loop around a lush, stream-fed canyon and continue up the hillside through moss-covered valley oaks and manzanita. Curve right, crossing the drainage, and emerge to a grassy knoll with a picnic area and open vistas. The views extend across Sonoma Valley to Sugarloaf Ridge, Hood Mountain, Bald Mountain, and Red Mountain. Loop left around the knoll, and reenter a cool Douglas fir and redwood forest with several species of ferns

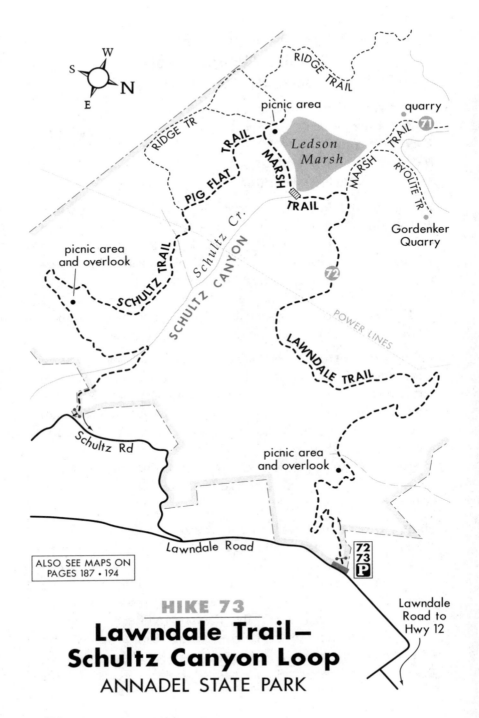

ALSO SEE MAPS ON
PAGES 187 • 194

HIKE 73
Lawndale Trail–
Schultz Canyon Loop
ANNADEL STATE PARK

198 - Day Hikes Around Sonoma County

covering the forest floor. Cross two more seasonal drainages, steadily climbing on a gentle grade. After gaining 500 feet in elevation, the trail switchbacks to the left beneath power lines. Top a minor ridge and slowly curve right around a hill. Cross under the power lines, where the trail levels out. Continue to a junction with the Marsh Trail at 2.9 miles. Bear left on the Marsh Trail, and cross a bridge over Schultz Creek, the outlet steam of Ledson Marsh. Skirt the east edge of the reed-filled marsh to a signed junction with a picnic area overlooking the wetland at 3.3 miles. Bear left on the Pig Flat Trail, and cross the flat through oaks and manzanita to a staggered junction at 3.8 miles. To the right is the Ridge Trail. Twenty yards ahead, bear left and head east on the Schultz Trail. Cross a tributary of Schultz Creek, and meander through the forest down the south wall of Schultz Canyon. Curve out of the canyon and switchback left to vistas down Sonoma Valley. Pass a picnic area and overlook on the left, and return into Schultz Canyon. At the canyon floor, follow the creek downstream 150 yards and hop over the creek. Traverse the hill to the east edge of Annadel State Park, reaching the gate at Schultz Road. Bear left on Schultz Road, and climb 0.8 miles up the narrow, winding road to Lawndale Road. Go to the left and continue a half mile downhill to the trailhead at the base of the mountain. ■

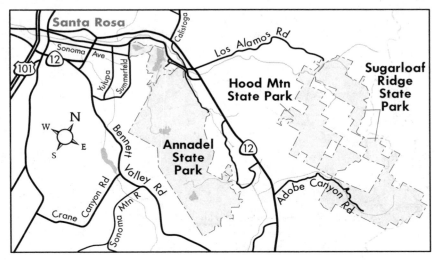

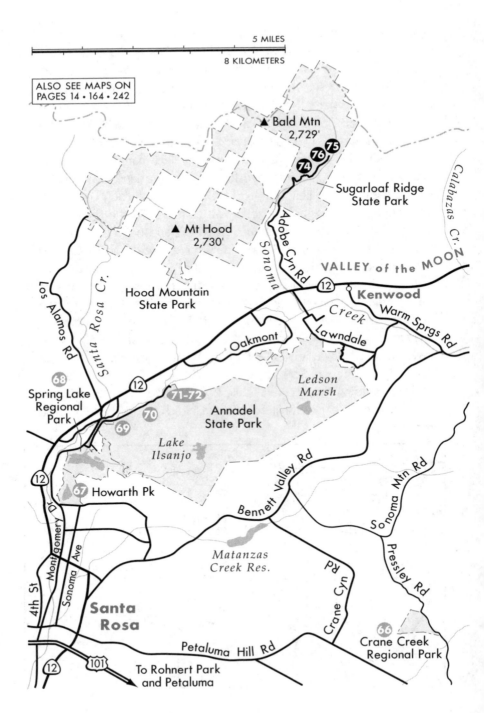

5 MILES

8 KILOMETERS

ALSO SEE MAPS ON
PAGES 14 • 164 • 242

▲ Bald Mtn
2,729'

75
76
74

Sugarloaf Ridge
State Park

Calabazas Cr.

▲ Mt Hood
2,730'

Adobe Cyn Rd

Sonoma

VALLEY of the MOON

Hood Mountain
State Park

Los Alamos Rd

Santa Rosa Cr.

12

Kenwood

Creek

Warm Sprgs Rd

Lawndale

Oakmont

68

Ledson
Marsh

Spring Lake
Regional
Park

12

71-72

70

69

Annadel
State Park

12

Lake
Ilsanjo

67

Howarth Pk

Bennett Valley Rd

Sonoma Mtn Rd

Montgomery Dr

Sonoma Ave

4th St

Matanzas
Creek Res.

Santa
Rosa

Crane Cyn Rd

Pressley Rd

66

Crane Creek
Regional Park

12

101

Petaluma Hill Rd

To Rohnert Park
and Petaluma

200 - Day Hikes Around Sonoma County

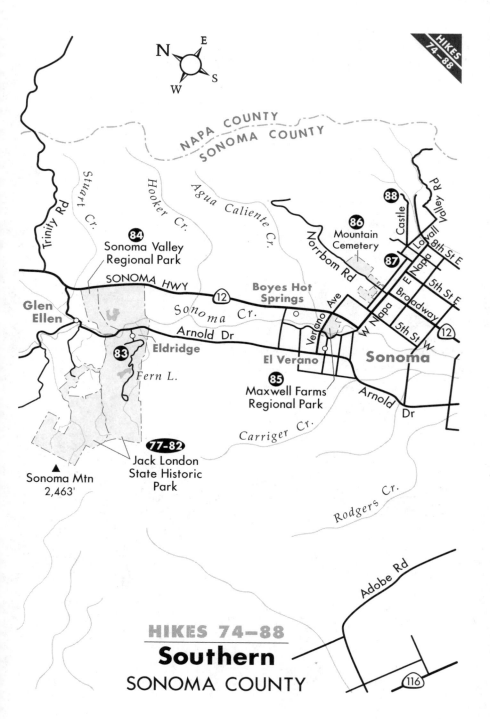

N E
S
W

NAPA COUNTY
SONOMA COUNTY

Trinity Rd

Stuart Cr.

Hooker Cr.

Agua Caliente Cr.

Norrbom Rd

84 Sonoma Valley Regional Park

86 Mountain Cemetery

88

Castle

Lovall Valley Rd

8th St E

87

El Napa

5th St E

SONOMA HWY

12

Boyes Hot Springs

Verano Ave

Broadway

Glen Ellen

Sonoma Cr.

Arnold Dr

W Napa

5th St W

83 Eldridge

El Verano

Sonoma

12

Fern L.

85 Maxwell Farms Regional Park

Arnold

Dr

Carriger Cr.

▲ Sonoma Mtn 2,463'

77-82 Jack London State Historic Park

Rodgers Cr.

Adobe Rd

HIKES 74–88
Southern
SONOMA COUNTY

116

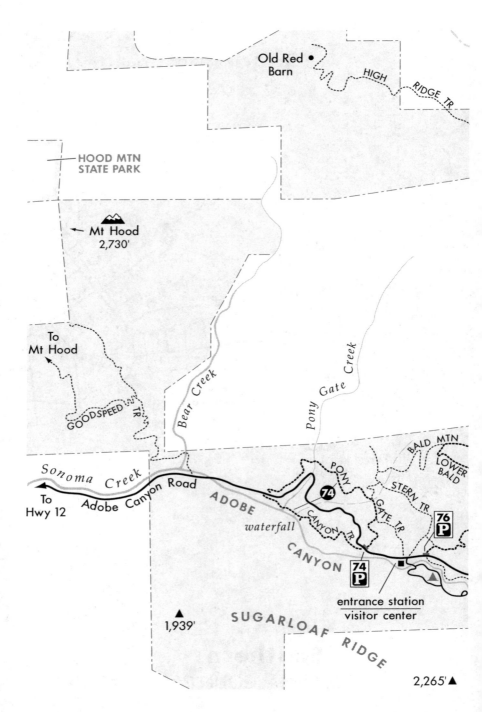

Old Red Barn

HIGH RIDGE TR

HOOD MTN STATE PARK

Mt Hood 2,730'

To Mt Hood

Pony Gate Creek

Bear Creek

GOODSPEED TR

Sonoma Creek

To Hwy 12

Adobe Canyon Road

BALD MTN

LOWER BALD

PONY

STERN TR

GATE TR

74

CANYON TR

ADOBE

waterfall

76 P

CANYON

74 P

SUGARLOAF

entrance station
visitor center

1,939'

RIDGE

2,265' ▲

Sugarloaf Ridge
State Park

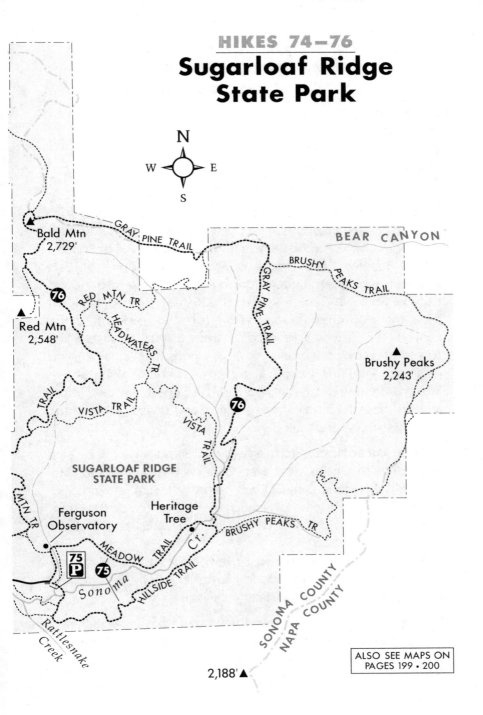

N
W   E
S

GRAY PINE TRAIL

BEAR CANYON

Bald Mtn
2,729'

BRUSHY PEAKS TRAIL

76

RED MTN TR

GRAY PINE TRAIL

▲ Red Mtn
2,548'

HEADWATERS TR

TRAIL

▲ Brushy Peaks
2,243'

VISTA TRAIL

76

VISTA TRAIL

SUGARLOAF RIDGE
STATE PARK

Ferguson
Observatory

Heritage
Tree

MTN TR

MEADOW TRAIL

Cr.

BRUSHY PEAKS TR

75
P

75

HILLSIDE TRAIL

Sonoma

SONOMA COUNTY

NAPA COUNTY

Rattlesnake

Creek

2,188' ▲

ALSO SEE MAPS ON
PAGES 199 • 200

74. Pony Gate—Canyon Loop
SUGARLOAF RIDGE STATE PARK
2605 Adobe Canyon Road • Kenwood

Hiking distance: 1.7-mile loop
Hiking time: 1 hour
Elevation gain: 450 feet
Maps: U.S.G.S. Kenwood
Sugarloaf Ridge State Park map

Summary of hike: Sugarloaf Ridge State Park is named for its distinct conical-shaped ridge of volcanic rock. The 2,200-foot ridge rises above Adobe Canyon from the south edge of Sonoma Creek. Sonoma Creek forms on the upper slopes of Bald Mountain and flows through the grassy meadow into Adobe Canyon. Sonoma Creek Falls plunges 25 feet over a jumble of huge, moss-covered boulders in the forested shade of Adobe Canyon. The Canyon Trail leads to the waterfall through a lush forest of redwoods, oaks, bay, sycamore, maple, alder, and madrone. The Pony Gate Trail traverses a grassy slope above Sonoma Creek through a mixed forest of coast live oak, laurel, and fir. These two trails form a scenic and diverse loop in the lower west corner of the park.

Driving directions: From Highway 101 and Highway 12 in Santa Rosa, drive 11.4 miles west and south on Highway 12 (Sonoma Highway) to Adobe Canyon Road on the left. Turn left and continue 3.2 miles up the winding mountain road to the posted trailhead parking area on the left. It is located 0.2 miles shy of the park entrance station.

From the town of Kenwood, drive 0.9 miles north on Highway 12 (Sonoma Highway) to Adobe Canyon Road on the right. Turn right and continue with the directions above.

Hiking directions: Take the posted trail from the upper east end of the parking area, and head up the forested hillside. The vistas extend across Adobe Canyon to the forested wall of Sugarloaf Ridge and across Sonoma Valley to Sonoma Mountain.

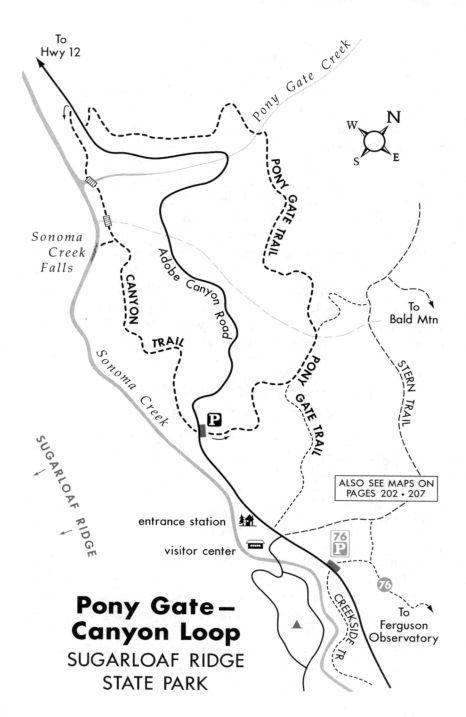

To
Hwy 12

Pony Gate Creek

N
W   E
S

PONY GATE TRAIL

Sonoma
Creek
Falls

CANYON

Adobe Canyon Road

TRAIL

To
Bald Mtn

Sonoma Creek

PONY GATE TRAIL

STERN TRAIL

SUGARLOAF RIDGE

P

ALSO SEE MAPS ON
PAGES 202 • 207

entrance station

76
P

visitor center

CREEKSIDE TR

76

To
Ferguson
Observatory

Pony Gate–
Canyon Loop
SUGARLOAF RIDGE
STATE PARK

Traverse the hillside to a junction with the Pony Gate Trail at 0.2 miles. Bear left and cross a tributary of Sonoma Creek to a Y-fork. Stay to the left and descend under a canopy of oaks, pines, and madrones to Pony Gate Creek. Follow the cascading creek 20 yards downstream, and rock-hop across the gulch. Climb up the hill and weave through the shady forest. Steadily descend to Adobe Canyon Road at 1.1 mile. Cautiously walk 50 yards down the road to the posted Canyon Trail on the left. Descend steps into a redwood, oak, and fern-filled forest. Head southeast in lush Adobe Canyon above Sonoma Creek. Follow the creek upstream, and cross a wooden footbridge over Pony Gate Creek. Cross a second bridge over the tributary stream to a junction at 1.3 miles. Detour 50 yards to the right to Sonoma Creek Falls, tumbling through a rocky ravine amid redwoods, Douglas firs, and moss-covered boulders. After enjoying the falls, return to the main trail. Climb steps, steadily gaining elevation through the dense forest. Emerge from the forest at Adobe Canyon Road across from the trailhead, completing the loop.■

75. Meadow—Hillside Loop
SUGARLOAF RIDGE STATE PARK
2605 Adobe Canyon Road • Kenwood

Hiking distance: 2.2-mile loop
Hiking time: 1 hour
Elevation gain: 250 feet
Maps: U.S.G.S. Kenwood and Rutherford
      Sugarloaf Ridge State Park map

Summary of hike: Sugarloaf Ridge State Park encompasses 2,700 acres of steep, rugged hills ranging in elevation from 600 to 2,729 feet. The park includes a campground, primitive campsites, picnic areas, rolling meadows, an observatory with three telescopes, and 25 miles of hiking and equestrian trails. The Meadow Trail strolls along the north side of Sonoma Creek in a scenic, grassy meadow. The path leads to Heritage Tree, a

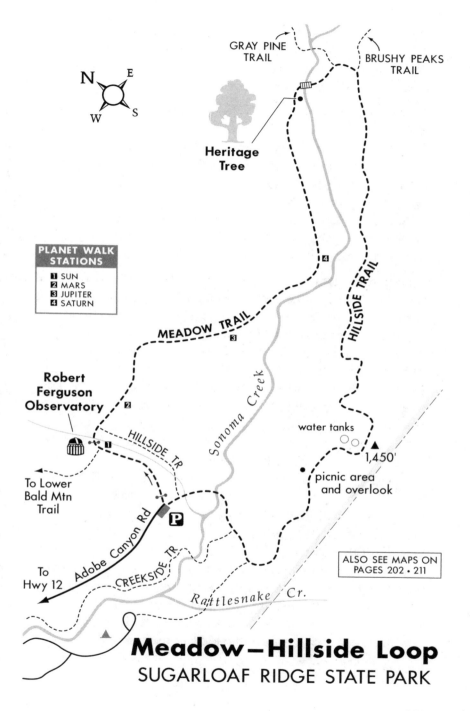

GRAY PINE
TRAIL

BRUSHY PEAKS
TRAIL

Heritage
Tree

N E
W S

**PLANET WALK
STATIONS**

1 SUN
2 MARS
3 JUPITER
4 SATURN

4

HILLSIDE TRAIL

MEADOW TRAIL

3

**Robert
Ferguson
Observatory**

2

Sonoma Creek

HILLSIDE TR

1

water tanks

▲
1,450'

To Lower
Bald Mtn
Trail

picnic area
and overlook

Adobe Canyon Rd

P

CREEKSIDE TR

To
Hwy 12

ALSO SEE MAPS ON
PAGES 202 · 211

Rattlesnake Cr.

▲

Meadow—Hillside Loop
SUGARLOAF RIDGE STATE PARK

massive big-leaf maple tree in a creekside picnic area. The Hillside Trail traverses the forested hills on the opposite side of Sonoma Creek at the foot of Sugarloaf Ridge. These two trails form an easy loop in the heart of the park.

Driving directions: From Highway 101 and Highway 12 in Santa Rosa, drive 11.4 miles west and south on Highway 12 (Sonoma Highway) to Adobe Canyon Road on the left. Turn left and continue 3.8 miles up the winding mountain road to the end of the road, 0.4 miles past the park entrance station. The posted trailhead parking area is on the right. A parking fee is required.

From the town of Kenwood, drive 0.9 miles north on Highway 12 (Sonoma Highway) to Adobe Canyon Road on the right. Turn right and continue with the directions above.

Hiking directions: Walk past the vehicle gate and observatory sign, following the wide gravel road along a stream. Pass the Robert Ferguson Observatory on its right, and walk through the trail gate. Cross over the stream and pass the Hillside Trail. Skirt the north edge of the large meadow to Sonoma Creek at a half mile. En route, interpretive signs about the sun, Mars, Jupiter, and Saturn line the trail. Follow the creek upstream through towering oaks and bay laurel. At 0.9 miles, pass the sprawling Heritage Tree in a picnic area on the banks of Sonoma Creek. Cross the wood bridge over the creek to a junction with Gray Pine Trail on the left (Hike 77), then the Brushy Peaks Trail on the left. Stay to the right both times, and head southwest on the Hillside Trail along the edge of the meadow. Gradually climb the hillside toward Sugarloaf Ridge. Traverse the slope through grasslands and a forest of Douglas fir, California bay, and coast live oak. Weave up the hill to 1,450 feet, the trail's highest point. Head downhill past two wooden water tanks and a picnic area overlook to a posted junction with the Creekside Nature Trail. Bear right, staying on the Hillside Trail, and continue downhill. Pass a second junction with the Creekside Nature Trail. Hop over Sonoma Creek and complete the loop at the trailhead. ■

76. Bald Mountain—Gray Pine Loop
SUGARLOAF RIDGE STATE PARK
2605 Adobe Canyon Road • Kenwood

Hiking distance: 7-mile loop
Hiking time: 4 hours
Elevation gain: 1,600 feet
Maps: U.S.G.S. Kenwood and Rutherford
Sugarloaf Ridge State Park map

map
page 211

Summary of hike: Sugarloaf Ridge State Park is located in the heart of the Mayacmas Mountains high above the town of Kenwood. Towering Bald Mountain, the park's highest peak at 2,729 feet, straddles the county line between Sonoma and Napa Counties. This hike forms a loop from the lower sloping meadow to the Bald Mountain summit. At the summit are 360-degree views, from the Sierra Nevada Range to the San Francisco skyline and the Golden Gate Bridge. Two illustrated panels point out more than 30 of the surrounding peaks, towns, and valleys. The Gray Pine Trail, the return route, follows the isolated Sugarloaf Ridge for over a mile along the county border, then descends along the headwaters of Sonoma Creek.

Driving directions: From Highway 101 and Highway 12 in Santa Rosa, drive 11.4 miles west and south on Highway 12 (Sonoma Highway) to Adobe Canyon Road on the left. Turn left and continue 3.5 miles up the winding mountain road to the large trailhead parking area on the left. It is located 0.1 mile past the park entrance station. A parking fee is required.

From the town of Kenwood, drive 0.9 miles north on Highway 12 (Sonoma Highway) to Adobe Canyon Road on the right. Turn right and continue with the directions above.

Hiking directions: Walk past the trailhead map and head up the grassy slope. Weave through an oak grove to a meadow and a triangle junction. The right fork leads to the observatory on the Meadow Trail. Go to the left on the Lower Bald Mountain Trail, beginning the loop. Climb to the upper end of the meadow, and enter an oak grove with manzanita and madrone. At one mile the trail reaches the Bald Mountain Trail, a paved fire road. Bear right and head up the narrow road to sweeping views of Sonoma Valley and the surrounding mountains. Pass the Vista Trail at 1.2 miles on a U-shaped bend. For a shorter 4.5 mile loop, take the Vista Trail to the right. For this hike, continue straight, weaving up the contours of the forested mountain. Pass a couple of stream-fed gullies and overlooks. At 2 miles, the Red Mountain Trail cut-across breaks off to the right. Continue 0.4 miles to a road on the left leading up to the top of Red Mountain. This short quarter-mile paved road leads up to the microwave tower at the 2,548-foot summit. The road ends at a gate before reaching the tower. Back on the main trail, weave up the dirt road on the upper mountain slope to amazing vistas. The final ascent curves clockwise to a junction with the High Ridge Trail. Bear right and walk 80 yards to the Gray Pine Trail on the left, just shy of the summit. Detour right to the 2,729-foot bald summit with a bench, 360-degree vistas, and two interpretive maps. After resting and savoring the views, return 20 yards to the Gray Pine Trail. Descend along the rolling grassy ridge, which follows the Napa-Sonoma county line. The views extend down both valleys from the ridge. Enter a mixed forest and continue east, staying on the ridge to the east end of Red Mountain Trail and a picnic bench at 3.6 miles. At just under 4 miles, curve right, leaving the ridge, and head south to a signed junction with the Brushy Peak Trail. Bend right, staying on the Gray Pine Trail, and steadily descend on the wide dirt trail. At 4.8 miles, curve left and follow a branch of Sonoma Creek in an oak grove. Make an S-bend and cross another feeder creek. Parallel and hop over Sonoma Creek to a junction with the Vista Trail at 5.3 miles. Ford the creek again, reaching a T-junction with the Meadow Trail. Bear right and cross a wood bridge over Sonoma Creek to Heritage Tree, a massive big-leaf maple tree on the banks of Sonoma Creek. Stroll through the open meadow along Sonoma Creek to the Ferguson Observatory at 6.4 miles. Leave the road and take the Meadow Trail to the right. Walk up the slope and veer left at the triangle junction, completing the loop at 6.6 miles. Retrace your steps 0.4 miles to the left.■

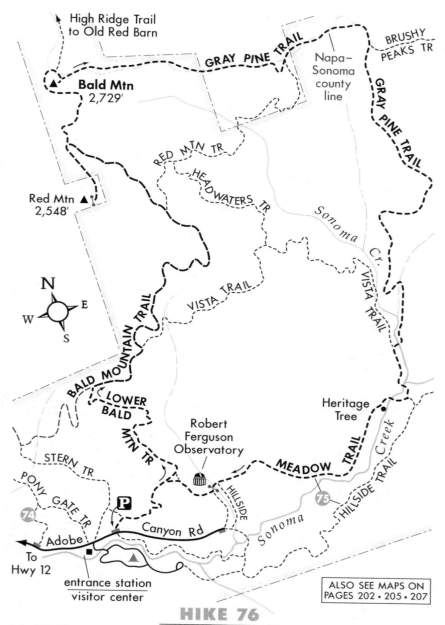

High Ridge Trail
to Old Red Barn

GRAY PINE TRAIL

BRUSHY PEAKS TR

Napa–
Sonoma
county
line

GRAY PINE TRAIL

▲ Bald Mtn
2,729'

RED MTN TR

HEADWATERS TR

Sonoma Cr.

Red Mtn ▲
2,548'

VISTA TRAIL

VISTA TRAIL

N
W E
S

BALD MOUNTAIN TRAIL

LOWER
BALD
MTN TR

STERN TR

PONY GATE TR

Robert
Ferguson
Observatory

Heritage
Tree

MEADOW TRAIL

Creek

HILLSIDE

HILLSIDE TRAIL

Sonoma

75

74

P

Canyon Rd

Adobe

To
Hwy 12

entrance station
visitor center

ALSO SEE MAPS ON
PAGES 202 • 205 • 207

HIKE 76

Bald Mountain–Gray Pine Loop
SUGARLOAF RIDGE STATE PARK

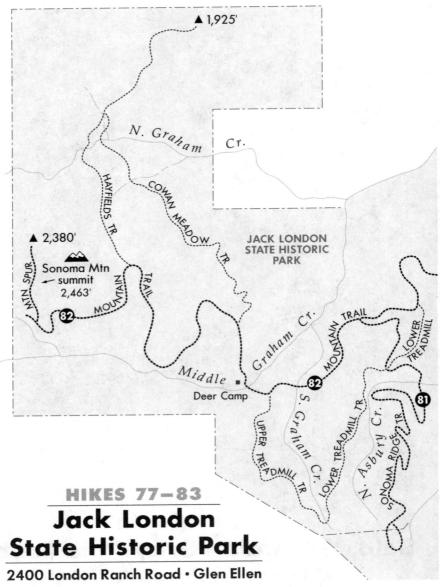

▲ 1,925'

N. Graham Cr.

HAYFIELDS TR.

COWAN MEADOW TR.

JACK LONDON
STATE HISTORIC
PARK

▲ 2,380'

Sonoma Mtn
← summit
2,463'

MTN. SPUR

MOUNTAIN TRAIL

MOUNTAIN

82

Graham Cr.

MOUNTAIN TRAIL

LOWER TREADMILL

Middle

Deer Camp

82

S. Graham Cr.

UPPER TREADMILL TR.

LOWER TREADMILL TR.

N. Asbury Cr.

SONOMA RIDGE TR.

81

HIKES 77–83
Jack London
State Historic Park
2400 London Ranch Road · Glen Ellen

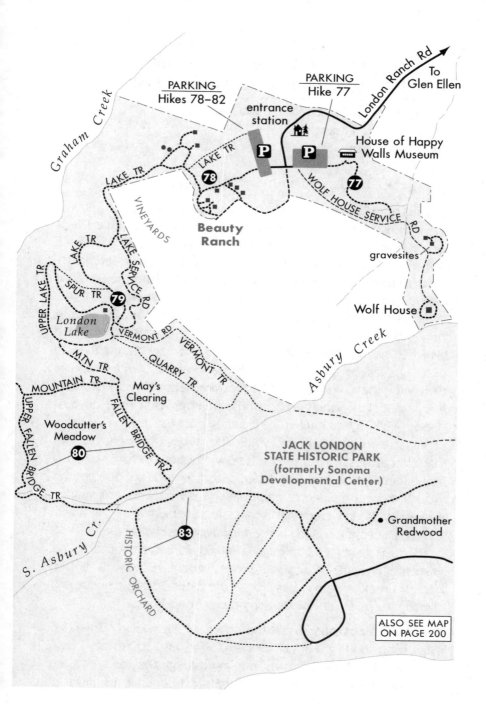

PARKING
Hikes 78–82

PARKING
Hike 77

London Ranch Rd

To
Glen Ellen

entrance
station

Graham Creek

LAKE TR

LAKE TR

78

VINEYARDS

Beauty
Ranch

House of Happy
Walls Museum

WOLF HOUSE SERVICE RD

77

gravesites

LAKE TR

LAKE SERVICE RD

SPUR TR

79

UPPER LAKE TR

London
Lake

VERMONT RD

VERMONT TR

QUARRY TR

Wolf House

Asbury Creek

MTN TR

MOUNTAIN TR

UPPER FALLEN BRIDGE TR

May's
Clearing

Woodcutter's
Meadow

80

FALLEN BRIDGE TR

JACK LONDON
STATE HISTORIC PARK
(formerly Sonoma
Developmental Center)

S. Asbury Cr.

HISTORIC ORCHARD

83

• Grandmother
Redwood

ALSO SEE MAP
ON PAGE 200

77. Wolf House Ruins
and Jack London's Grave
JACK LONDON STATE HISTORIC PARK

Hiking distance: 1.5 miles round trip
Hiking time: 1 hour
Elevation gain: 150 feet
Maps: U.S.G.S. Glen Ellen
Jack London State Historic Park map

Summary of hike: The Wolf House was Jack London's 26-room mansion built from locally quarried stone, unpeeled redwood logs, and Spanish tiles. The massive four-level, lava-rock house encompassed 15,000 square feet and had nine fireplaces. His dream house burned down in 1913, days before the Londons planned to move in. The stonework and walls remain.

Jack London's grave sits on a quiet knoll in a grove of oaks. A large block of red lava from the Wolf House rests atop Jack's and his wife Charmian's ashes. Adjacent to the boulder are the marked older graves of two pioneer children named David and Lillie Greenlaw. Their wooden headstones are dated November 1876, the year Jack London was born. The trail begins at The House of Happy Walls, a beautiful stone building built by London's widow Charmian between 1919 and 1922. The two-story structure was modeled after the Wolf House. It now functions as a museum and visitor center. The building is dedicated to Jack London and his work. It houses mementos and collections from London's worldwide travels and personal possessions, including his writings, letters, photographs, art, home furnishings, and clothes.

This trail takes you through a mixed forest en route to his gravesite and the Wolf House ruins in the redwoods above Asbury Creek. A path loops around the exterior of the house and climbs to a platform overlooking the second floor.

Driving directions: From the town of Kenwood, drive 3.6 miles south on Highway 12 (Sonoma Highway) to Arnold Drive. Turn right and drive 0.9 miles, passing through the town of Glen Ellen, to London Ranch Road. Turn right and continue 1.3 miles up

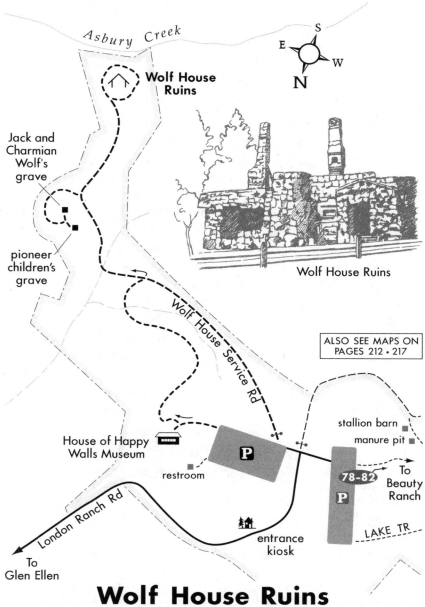

Asbury Creek

S
E — N — W

Wolf House Ruins

Jack and Charmian Wolf's grave

pioneer children's grave

Wolf House Service Rd

Wolf House Ruins

ALSO SEE MAPS ON
PAGES 212 • 217

stallion barn
manure pit

House of Happy Walls Museum

restroom

P

P

78-82

To Beauty Ranch

London Ranch Rd

entrance kiosk

LAKE TR

To Glen Ellen

Wolf House Ruins
Jack London's grave
JACK LONDON STATE HISTORIC PARK

the hill to the park entrance station. From the kiosk, turn left and drive 0.1 mile to the museum parking lot. A parking fee is required.

From West Napa Street in Sonoma, drive 5.9 miles north on Highway 12 (Sonoma Highway) to Arnold Drive and turn left. Continue with the directions above.

Hiking directions: From the far end of the parking lot, walk up the paved path to the House of Happy Walls Museum, a field-stone structure with Spanish roof tiles. After visiting the museum and the exhibits, take the signed trail from the southeast corner of the building. Gently descend on the forested dirt path through bay laurel, madrone, and oaks. Cross a stream, reaching the Wolf House Service Road at 0.3 miles. Bear left on the narrow road, parallel to the creek on the left. Cross over the creek and head uphill to a road fork. Detour left and wind around about 110 yards to Jack London's gravesite on a knoll. On the left are the graves of Jack and his wife Charmian, dated 11-26-16. A lava boulder from the house ruins sits atop their ashes. To the right are the graves of the two pioneer children. Return to the main trail and continue 0.15 miles to the Wolf House in a redwood grove. A path circle the ruins, with views of the gorgeous lava rock arches and fireplaces. A raised platform overlooks the pool and the house. Return on the same trail. ■

78. Beauty Ranch
JACK LONDON STATE HISTORIC PARK

Hiking distance: 0.75 miles round trip
Hiking time: 1 hour
Elevation gain: 50 feet
Maps: U.S.G.S. Glen Ellen
Jack London State Historic Park map

Summary of hike: Jack London's Beauty Ranch is tucked into the foothills of Sonoma Mountain above the town of Glen Ellen. The experimental ranch, part of the state historic park, still contains the original structures. The wood-framed cottage is where

London lived and wrote many of his books from 1905 until his death in 1916. Over the course of 16 prolific years, Jack London wrote 51 books and nearly 200 short stories, including *Call of the Wild* and *The Sea Wolf*. Sonoma Valley became known as *Valley of the Moon*, from London's 1913 novel by the same name. There are several unique structures included amongst the ranch buildings. The innovative Pig Palace is a circular piggery with a central feeding and round storage tower designed by London. Two 40-foot-high silos were built in 1914, the first cement silos in California. A rock sherry barn, part of the old Kohler–Frohling winery, was built by Chinese laborers in 1884, then converted into a stable for London's English shire horses. London hired Italian

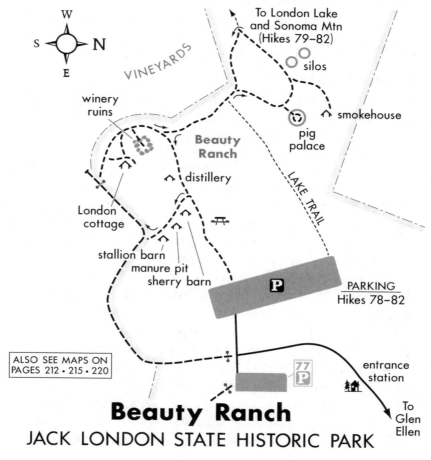

Beauty Ranch

JACK LONDON STATE HISTORIC PARK

masons to build an additional stallion barn and a rock manure pit. A distillery building from the old winery still exists, as well as other ruins from the 1880s winery damaged by the 1906 earthquake. This interpretive hike loops through the grounds of the historic former ranch.

Driving directions: From the town of Kenwood, drive 3.6 miles south on Highway 12 (Sonoma Highway) to Arnold Drive. Turn right and drive 0.9 miles, passing through the town of Glen Ellen, to London Ranch Road. Turn right and continue 1.3 miles up the hill to the park entrance station. From the kiosk, turn right and drive 0.1 mile to the trailhead parking lot. A parking fee is required.

From West Napa Street in Sonoma, drive 5.9 miles north on Highway 12 (Sonoma Highway) to Arnold Drive and turn left. Continue with the directions above.

Hiking directions: At the trailhead, directly across from the road to the parking lot, take the posted Beauty Ranch–Mountain Trails path. Walk through a eucalyptus grove and picnic area to a T-junction by the sherry barn on the left. Bear left past the barn to the rock-walled manure pit and stallion barn. Curve right on the paved service road. Continue along the edge of a vineyard on the left to the Jack London Cottage on the right and a view of the terraced hillside. Curve right, passing the cottage to the rock-wall ruins of the historic winery. Stroll past the rock walls or enter the open structure. Curve left, staying on the edge of the vineyard toward the two 40-foot silos erected between 1912 and 1915. As the gravel road curves left (before reaching the silos) veer to the right on the grassy path. Climb to the circular rock-walled Pig Palace in an oak grove. Loop around the central feed tower and the ring of 17 pig pens. Continue to the cement-block silos and a junction. A side path goes right to a rock smokehouse behind the Pig Palace. Return to the main road. The right fork on the Lake Trail leads to the lake and bathhouse (Hike 79). Instead, bear left and return to the trail split by the winery ruins. Curve left, passing the distillery building constructed in 1888. Complete the loop at the sherry barn. Return to the left. ■

79. Lake Trail Loop
JACK LONDON STATE HISTORIC PARK

Hiking distance: 2.5-mile double loop
Hiking time: 1.5 hours
Elevation gain: 400 feet
Maps: U.S.G.S. Glen Ellen
      Jack London State Historic Park map

map page 220

Summary of hike: London Lake sits at the foot of Sonoma Mountain surrounded by redwood groves. Jack London originally built the lake in 1915 as a five-acre irrigation reservoir. It quickly became a swimming hole and entertainment area for the Londons and their guests. The redwood bathhouse on the northeast shore and the curved stone dam to the south were also built by London. Encroaching vegetation and sediment have reduced the lake's size in half. Cattails rim the shore and redwoods cover the mountain slope. This trail strolls through Beauty Ranch (Hike 78), then loops around the lake to vista points and overlooks.

Driving directions: Same as Hike 78.

Hiking directions: At the trailhead, directly across from the road to the parking lot, take the posted Beauty Ranch–Mountain Trails path. Walk through a eucalyptus grove and picnic area to a T-junction by the sherry barn on the left. Go to the right, passing the distillery and winery ruins to a trail split. Veer to the right, skirting the Jack London Vineyard, and curve left, passing the 40-foot silos on the right. Leave Beauty Ranch on the Lake Trail, with close-up views of Sonoma Mountain. Follow the dirt road through oak groves, pines, and madrones to a posted junction with a pipe gate across the road. Leave the road and begin the loop on the Lake Trail to the right, a hiking-only trail. Walk through the dense forest with redwoods and bay laurel, and rejoin the Lake Service Road at one mile. Continue 20 yards to the right, and veer right on the footpath, located to the east side of London Lake by the redwood bathhouse and the stone dam. Take the Upper Lake Trail, passing the old log bathhouse, and follow the north side of the lake. Pass the Lake Spur Trail on the right. Make a U-shaped left bend, and traverse the hillside to an overlook of the lake. Descend to the Mountain Trail Road on a horseshoe bend. The right fork heads up to Sonoma Ridge and the summit of Sonoma Mountain (Hike 82). For this hike, go to the left and cross the lake's inlet stream. Follow the south side of London Lake to a T-junction. To the right is the Vineyard Trail. Bear left along the rock dam, completing the loop. Follow the winding dirt service road downhill back to Jack London's Vineyard, completing the second loop. Return to Beauty Ranch and the trailhead.■

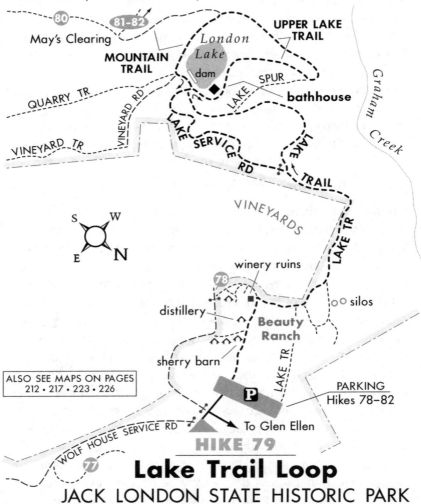

ALSO SEE MAPS ON PAGES
212 • 217 • 223 • 226

HIKE 79

Lake Trail Loop
JACK LONDON STATE HISTORIC PARK

80. Woodcutter's Meadow
Fallen Bridge—Upper Fallen Bridge Loop
JACK LONDON STATE HISTORIC PARK

Hiking distance: 4.5 miles round trip with a loop
Hiking time: 3 hours
Elevation gain: 700 feet
Maps: U.S.G.S. Glen Ellen
       Jack London State Historic Park map

*map
page 223*

Summary of hike: The Fallen Bridge Trail begins at May's Clearing, an open grassy slope above London Lake at the north end of Woodcutter's Meadow. At the meadow is a vista point with views down Sonoma Valley to San Pablo Bay and across the valley to the Mayacmas Mountains. The Upper Fallen Bridge Trail loops around Woodcutter's Meadow on the forested slope of Sonoma Mountain. The two trails form a loop through a dense forest of redwoods, crossing two bridges over cascading North Asbury Creek. Access to the loop is from the Lake Trail and Mountain Trail (Hike 79). En route, the trail weaves through the historic buildings of Beauty Ranch and passes London Lake.

Driving directions: Same as Hike 78.

Hiking directions: At the trailhead, directly across from the road to the parking lot, take the posted Beauty Ranch—Mountain Trails path. Walk through a eucalyptus grove and picnic area to a T-junction by the sherry barn on the left. Go to the right, passing the distillery and winery ruins to a trail split. Veer to the right, skirting the Jack London Vineyard, and curve left, passing the 40-foot silos on the right. Leave Beauty Ranch on the Lake Trail. Follow the dirt road through oak groves, pines, and madrones to a posted junction. Continue straight, passing through the vehicle gate on the dirt road. Follow the edge of the Jack London Vineyard on the left. Weave up the road to the southeast corner of London Lake. Walk along the base of the rock-walled dam to a signed junction. Go to the right on the Mountain Trail, and follow the south side of London Lake to a horseshoe left bend and a junction. The Upper Lake Trail (Hike 79) goes to the right. Stay on the road to the left, and climb to a clearing with a bench and junction. This point overlooks May's Clearing, a large grassy meadow.

The Fallen Bridge Trail, our return route, goes to the left. Begin the loop to the right, staying on the Mountain Trail. Enter a lush forest with redwoods, madrones, bay laurel, and ferns. Climb 0.2 miles to a signed junction with the Upper Fallen Bridge Trail. Leave the road and head 0.3 miles south through Woodcutter's Meadow to North Asbury Creek. Cross a bridge over the cascading creek and curve left. Descend along the stair-stepping creek under the shade of towering redwoods to the lower bridge and junction. The trail straight ahead enters the newly acquired land of Jack London State Historic Park, leading to a historic orchard and Grandmother Redwood (Hike 83). Bear left and cross the bridge over North Asbury Creek. Curve away from the creek on the cliffside path. Cross a tributary stream and head up to May's Clearing on the right. Complete the loop at the vista point. Return 1.4 miles to the right, retracing your route.■

81. Sonoma Ridge Trail
JACK LONDON STATE HISTORIC PARK

Hiking distance: 9.5 miles round trip
Hiking time: 6 hours
Elevation gain: 1,300 feet
Maps: U.S.G.S. Glen Ellen
       Jack London State Historic Park map

map
page 226

Summary of hike: Sonoma Mountain has a long forested ridge running north and south that forms the backbone of Jack London State Historic Park. The Sonoma Ridge Trail follows the east side of the ridge through the 1,400-acre state park, climbing steadily south. The hike begins at Beauty Ranch and climbs up the forested slope beyond London Lake. The trail passes through deep woods, redwood groves, and open meadows, offering sweeping vistas down Sonoma Valley to San Pablo Bay and across to the Mayacmas Mountains. The trail ends at a small loop by the fenced south park boundary.

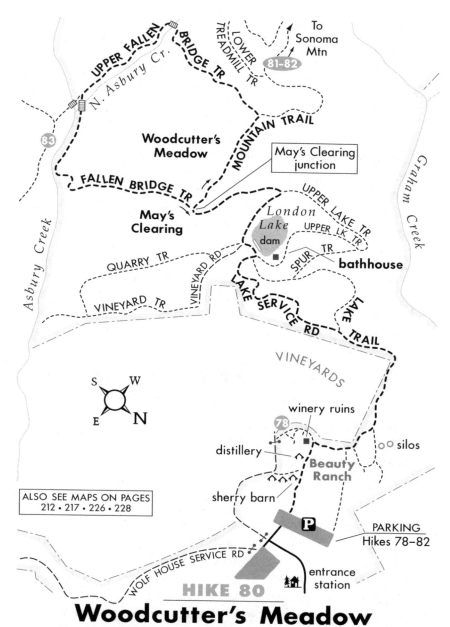

UPPER FALLEN

BRIDGE TR

LOWER TREADMILL TR

To Sonoma Mtn

81-82

N. Asbury Cr.

83

MOUNTAIN TRAIL

Woodcutter's Meadow

May's Clearing junction

FALLEN BRIDGE TR

May's Clearing

London Lake

dam

UPPER LAKE TR

UPPER LK TR

bathhouse

Asbury Creek

Graham Creek

QUARRY TR

VINEYARD RD

VINEYARD TR

LAKE SERVICE RD

SPUR TR

LAKE TRAIL

VINEYARDS

S W
E N

winery ruins

78

silos

distillery

Beauty Ranch

sherry barn

ALSO SEE MAPS ON PAGES
212 • 217 • 226 • 228

P

PARKING
Hikes 78–82

WOLF HOUSE SERVICE RD

HIKE 80

entrance station

Woodcutter's Meadow
Fallen Bridge–Upper Fallen Bridge
JACK LONDON STATE HISTORIC PARK

Driving directions: Same as Hike 78.

Hiking directions: Follow the hiking directions for Hike 80 to the junction at May's Clearing. The Fallen Bridge Trail veers off to the left (south) to North Asbury Creek. Continue straight on the Mountain Trail. Enter a lush forest with redwoods, bay laurel, tanbark oaks, and ferns. Traverse Woodcutter's Meadow on the left, passing the Upper Fallen Bridge Trail. Pass Pine Tree Meadows, a small glade on the right, and make a horseshoe left bend to the Lower Treadmill Road on the right. A short distance ahead is the Sonoma Ridge Trail by a map kiosk at 2.2 miles.

Bear left on the Sonoma Ridge Trail, and angle up the side of the mountain. Cross the Lower Treadmill Trail through a forest of Douglas fir, madrone, and bay to rocky North Asbury Creek in a redwood grove. Cross over to the south side of the creek, and zigzag up switchbacks at an easy grade. The far-reaching vistas extend to a grassy slope below the ridgeline at 2,100 feet. At 5.3 miles is a road split, forming a 0.3-mile loop. Circle the loop at the park boundary and retrace your steps. ∎

82. Sonoma Mountain Trail to Summit
JACK LONDON STATE HISTORIC PARK

Hiking distance: 8 miles round trip
Hiking time: 5 hours
Elevation gain: 1,800 feet
Maps: U.S.G.S. Glen Ellen
      Jack London State Historic Park map

map
page 226

Summary of hike: The Sonoma Mountains stretch from Santa Rosa to Sonoma. The volcanic range forms the western rim of 17-mile-long Sonoma Valley, known as the Valley of the Moon. The Mountain Trail, a fire road, climbs along Sonoma Mountain through Jack London State Historic Park. The trail leads through unspoiled forests with redwoods, big-leaf maple, redwood, black oak, buckeye, bay, and madrone to the park summit, a short distance east of the 2,463-foot summit of Sonoma Mountain. The actual summit sits just outside the park boundary on private land.

Driving directions: Same as Hike 78.

Hiking directions: Follow the hiking directions for Hike 80 to the junction at May's Clearing. The Fallen Bridge Trail veers off to the left (south) to North Asbury Creek. Continue straight on the Mountain Trail, and enter a lush forest with redwoods, bay laurel, tanbark oaks, and ferns. Traverse Woodcutter's Meadow on the left, passing the Upper Fallen Bridge Trail. Pass Pine Tree Meadows, a small glade on the right, and make a horseshoe left bend to the Lower Treadmill Road on the right. A short distance ahead is the Sonoma Ridge Trail by a map kiosk at 2.2 miles. Hike 81 heads left (south) on the Sonoma Ridge Trail.

For this hike, continue straight ahead through the forest, crossing South Graham Creek to Upper Treadmill Road on the left. Continue on the Mountain Trail. Cross Middle Graham Creek to the Deer Camp rest area in a redwood grove on the north side of the creek, once a camping site for Jack London and his guests. Climb through a meadow, with views of Sonoma Valley and the Mayacmas Mountains, to the Cowan Meadow Trail on the right. Stay left, continually climbing to the north canyon wall above Middle Graham Creek. Climb through meadows and oak forests to the Hayfields Trail, breaking off to the right en route to the park's north boundary. Stay to the left, contouring through a large meadow to the north branch of the Middle Graham Creek headwaters. Climb along the creek to the west boundary of the park. Curve right and climb a quarter mile to the 2,380-foot park summit, a short distance from, and 80 feet lower than, the privately owned Sonoma Mountain summit. Return along the same route. ■

83. Fern Lake, Historic Orchard, and Grandmother Redwood
JACK LONDON STATE HISTORIC PARK

Hiking distance: 4.5 miles round trip
Hiking time: 2.5 hours
Elevation gain: 650 feet
Maps: U.S.G.S. Glen Ellen

map
page 228

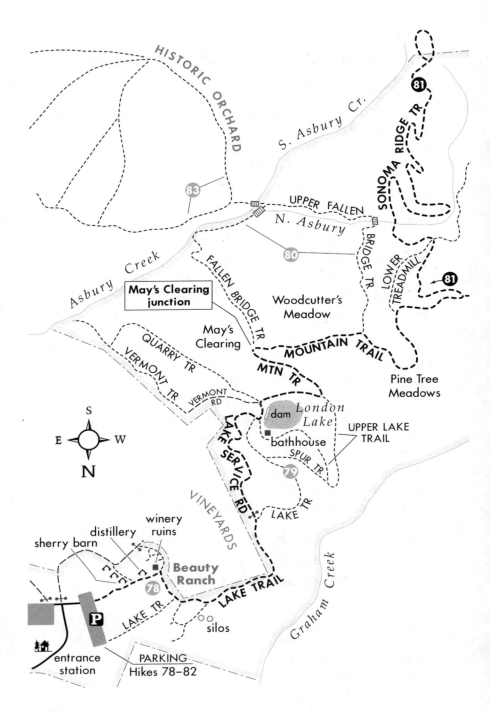

HISTORIC ORCHARD

S. Asbury Cr.

81

SONOMA RIDGE TR.

83

UPPER FALLEN

N. Asbury

BRIDGE TR.

LOWER TREADMILL

81

80

Asbury Creek

FALLEN BRIDGE TR.

May's Clearing junction

May's Clearing

Woodcutter's Meadow

MOUNTAIN TRAIL

MTN TR.

Pine Tree Meadows

QUARRY TR.

VERMONT TR.

VERMONT RD.

LAKE SERVICE RD.

dam

London Lake

bathhouse

UPPER LAKE TRAIL

SPUR TR.

79

LAKE TR.

S

E — W

N

VINEYARDS

distillery

winery ruins

sherry barn

Beauty Ranch

78

LAKE TR.

LAKE TRAIL

Graham Creek

silos

P

entrance station

PARKING
Hikes 78–82

HIKE 81
Sonoma Ridge Trail
HIKE 82
Sonoma Mountain Trail to summit
JACK LONDON STATE HISTORIC PARK

LOWER TREADMILL

UPPER TREADMILL

S. Graham

MOUNTAIN

▲ Deer Camp

TRAIL

Middle Graham Creek

MOUNTAIN

82

82

TRAIL

MTN SPUR

Sonoma Mountain summit 2,463'

▲ 2,380'

COWAN MEADOW TR

HAYFIELDS TR

North Graham Creek

1,925' ▲

ALSO SEE MAPS ON PAGES
212 • 215 • 217 • 223

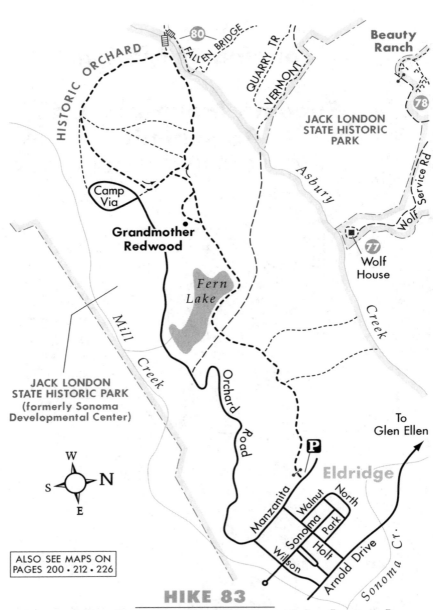

HIKE 83

Fern Lake • Historic Orchard
Grandmother Redwood
JACK LONDON STATE HISTORIC PARK

Summary of hike: In 1991, land was transferred from the Sonoma Developmental Center to Jack London State Historic Park. The Sonoma Developmental Center is a state-owned facility for the mentally and physically impaired. The 1,600-acre facility is part of the small town called Eldridge, with its own post office and fire department. The orchard was planted in the early 1900s as a way for the residents to have meaningful work growing and selling fruit. The historic orchard encompasses 400 acres, with apple, peach, plum, pear, prune, apricot, and cherry trees. Most of the original orchard remains today. Fern Lake was used for irrigating the orchard. An ancient redwood tree known as Grandmother Redwood is an enormous first growth redwood in a quiet grove along the trail to the orchard. The giant tree has a huge girth but the top of the tree is gone, either snapped off by the 1906 earthquake or from fire. Owls are frequently spotted in the tree. This hike begins from the small town of Eldridge, located just south of Glen Ellen. The hike leads to Fern Lake and Grandmother Redwood, then circles the historic orchard. A side path crosses a bridge over Asbury Creek and enters the original section of Jack London State Historic Park. A trail system for the new tract of land is in the planning stage but has not yet been fully realized.

Driving directions: From the town of Kenwood, drive 3.6 miles south on Highway 12 (Sonoma Highway) to Arnold Drive. Turn right and drive 2.2 miles, passing through the town of Glen Ellen, to Holt Street. Turn right and continue a quarter mile to Manzanita at a T-intersection. Turn right and go 0.15 miles to a parking pullout on the left.

From West Napa Street in Sonoma, drive 5.9 miles north on Highway 12 (Sonoma Highway) to Arnold Drive and turn left. Continue with the directions above.

Hiking directions: Pass the chained entrance and head west on the grassy path. Walk through a grove of gnarled oaks with lace lichen draped from the branches. Cross two draws and continue through the rolling hills, gaining elevation. Merge with an old dirt road in a pocket of bay laurel trees. Stay left at an unsigned fork, where views open up of Sonoma Valley, Sugarloaf Ridge, and the towers atop Sonoma Mountain. At 0.8 miles, the trail reaches a road. The left fork returns to the town of Eldridge via Orchard Road. Cross the road and continue on the footpath straight ahead to an overlook of Fern Lake. Skirt the northeast side of the lake, and descend to the northern tip. Cross the outlet stream and climb the forested hillside. The path levels out and enters a redwood forest. Stroll through the shady grove, passing circular stands of redwoods. Watch on the left for a side path. Bear left 30 yards into a hollow. Grandmother Redwood stands on the left. After marveling at the details of the ancient tree, continue past the tree and loop back to the main trail. Bear left and walk a short distance to a trail split. The left fork leads to Camp Via. Begin the loop to the right, passing a couple of trail forks. Stay to the right, entering an open expanse. Circle the perimeter of the meadow above Asbury Creek to a trail fork. The right fork leads 30 yards to the creek and enters the original tract of Jack London State Historic Park. Curve left and walk to an overlook of Camp Via and the historic orchard. Traverse the hillside above the orchard to a T-junction by a wire fence. The right fork enters the camp. Bear left 200 yards, completing the loop. Retrace your steps back to the trailhead. ▪

84. Sonoma Valley Regional Park
13630 Sonoma Highway 12 • Glen Ellen

Hiking distance: 2.5-mile loop
Hiking time: 1.5 hours
Elevation gain: 225 feet
Maps: U.S.G.S. Glen Ellen
      Sonoma Valley Regional Park map

Summary of hike: Sonoma Valley Regional Park is tucked into the base of the Sonoma Mountains along the verdant valley floor. The park sits on the west edge of the wide valley, just south of the creekside town of Glen Ellen and six miles north of Sonoma. The 162-acre park is filled with rolling oak woodlands and grassy meadows and is known for its beautiful displays of California

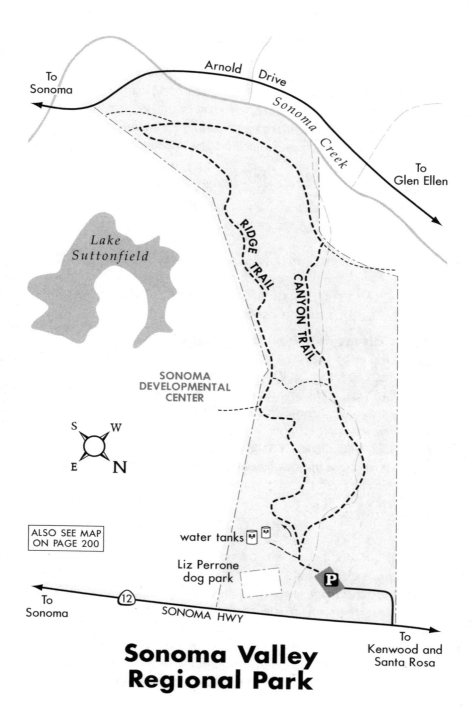

To
Sonoma

Arnold Drive

Sonoma Creek

To
Glen Ellen

*Lake
Suttonfield*

RIDGE TRAIL

CANYON TRAIL

SONOMA
DEVELOPMENTAL
CENTER

S W
E N

ALSO SEE MAP
ON PAGE 200

water tanks

Liz Perrone
dog park

P

To
Sonoma

12

SONOMA HWY

To
Kenwood and
Santa Rosa

Sonoma Valley
Regional Park

poppies, wild irises, and lupines. The park has picnic areas and the Liz Perrone Dog Park, a one-acre fenced grassland for off-leash canines. Dirt and paved trails used for hiking, biking, and horseback riding weave through the streamside corridor. This hike stays on the wide main route, climbing the rolling hillside to the picturesque ridge and returning through the stream-fed meadow with gorgeous blue oaks. Dogs are allowed on the trails.

Driving directions: From the town of Kenwood, drive 4 miles south on Highway 12 (Sonoma Highway) to the posted park entrance. (It is located 0.4 miles south of Arnold Drive.) Turn right and drive 0.2 miles to the trailhead parking lot. A parking fee is required.

From East Napa Street in Sonoma, drive 5.5 miles north on Highway 12 (Sonoma Highway) to the park entrance on the left. (It is located 1.8 miles north of Madrone Road.) Turn left and drive 0.2 miles to the trailhead parking lot.

Hiking directions: From the far end of the parking lot, take the paved path. Curve to the right, passing a road to the water tanks, to a trail fork at 100 yards. Begin the loop to the left on the Ridge Trail, and climb up to the ridge. Curve to the right and follow the grassy ridge dotted with oaks to an overlook with sitting benches. The views include the Sonoma Mountains, the Mayacmas Mountains, Sonoma Valley, and Lake Suttonfield. Continue through the oak savanna, passing a series of side paths that veer off from the main route. Stay on the wider, main route to a fenceline. The trail beyond the fence enters the Sonoma Developmental Center. Bear right, keeping the fence to your left, and descend 40 yards to a junction. Go to the left and traverse the hillside along the park boundary through a forest of oak, madrone, and manzanita. Curve right and weave down the hillside to the open rolling grasslands on the valley floor near Arnold Drive. Take the Canyon Trail to the right, and parallel a seasonal tributary of Sonoma Creek. Meander through the stream-fed meadow. Blue oaks draped with strands of lace lichen dot the meadow. Cross over the seasonal creek seven times, completing the loop. Stay to the left, returning to the trailhead. ■

85. Maxwell Farms Regional Park
Three Meadow—Back Meadow—Bay Tree Loop
100 Verano Avenue • Sonoma

Hiking distance: 1-mile loop
Hiking time: 35 minutes
Elevation gain: Level
Maps: U.S.G.S. Sonoma
       Maxwell Farms Regional Park map

map
page 234

Summary of hike: Maxwell Farms Regional Park is located at the northwest end of Sonoma just south of Boyes Hot Springs. The 85-acre park borders Sonoma Creek in a lush riparian corridor. The park has two distinct personalities. The developed northeast portion of the park includes picnic areas, athletic fields, a playground, and a Boys and Girls Club. The southwest half of the park is a natural 40-acre oasis with woodlands that are dominated by immense California bays and lush grassland meadows. The Maxwell family lived on this land from 1859 to 1968. They planted plum and apricot orchards in the late 1800s, which are still productive. This hike loops around the natural area and follows the watercourse of Sonoma Creek. Dogs are allowed on the trails.

Driving directions: From Sonoma Plaza in downtown Sonoma, drive 1 mile west on West Napa Street to Highway 12 (Sonoma Highway). Turn right and continue 0.6 miles to Verano Avenue. Turn left and go 0.1 mile to the posted park entrance on the left. Turn left and park in the lot. A parking fee is required.

From the town of Kenwood, drive 8 miles south on Highway 12 (Sonoma Highway) to Verano Avenue and turn right. Continue with the directions above.

Hiking directions: From the far, southeast end of the parking lot, walk down the service road past the Valley of the Moon Boys and Girls Club. Curve right to the group picnic area on the left and a posted junction. Continue straight ahead on the Three Meadow Trail—a dirt footpath—to a 4-way junction. Begin the loop to the left on the Bay Tree Trail through oaks, bay laurels, and blackberry bushes to the south park boundary and another junction. The left fork loops back to the ranger residence and returns to the group picnic area. Curve to right on the Back Meadow Trail, skirting the south end of the park. The trail merges with the Three Meadow Trail and continues along the park boundary 20 feet above Sonoma Creek. Follow the creek upstream, heading north to the west end of the Bay Tree Trail. Bear right on the Bay Tree Trail, and stroll through an amazing tunnel of massive bay laurels. Complete the loop at the junction with the Three Meadows Trail. Return left to the parking lot. ■

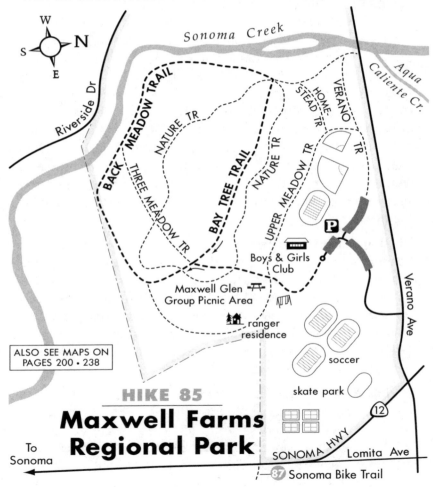

ALSO SEE MAPS ON
PAGES 200 • 238

HIKE 85

Maxwell Farms Regional Park

To
Sonoma

86. Sonoma Overlook Trail

Hiking distance: 3 miles round trip
Hiking time: 1.5 hours
Elevation gain: 400 feet
Maps: U.S.G.S. Sonoma
Sonoma Overlook Trail map

map
page 236

Summary of hike: The Sonoma Overlook Trail is a gorgeous hike that is a short half mile from the Sonoma Plaza in downtown Sonoma. The trail traverses the hillside above the north end of town to a grassy plateau below the summit of Schocken Hill. The hike begins at Mountain Cemetery and leads to the plateau through a mixed woodland forest. A short trail loops around the plateau to a memorial bench with a bird's-eye view of Sonoma, the sloping ridge of Sonoma Mountain, and vistas across Sonoma Valley to San Pablo Bay.

Driving directions: From West Napa Street by the Sonoma Plaza in downtown Sonoma, drive 0.5 miles north on First Street West (along the west edge of the plaza) to the posted Mountain Cemetery on the right. It is across the street from Depot Park and just before the hill. Turn right and park by the signed trailhead.

Hiking directions: Pass the trailhead panel and walk up the grassy slope, skirting the west edge of the cemetery. Cross a seasonal stream in a small canyon, and zigzag up the hillside in a grove of oaks and California bays. Pass a moss-covered lava rock and an old rock wall. Emerge from the forest to a clearing in a sloping meadow and a Y-fork with a vista of Sonoma and the surrounding mountains. The Toyon Trail veers right and descends to Toyon Road at the upper end of Mountain Cemetery. This trail can be used on the return route by winding down the cemetery roads to the entrance and trailhead. For now, continue straight on the left fork. Steadily gain elevation through manzanita and majestic, twisted valley oaks. Switchback to the left, and gently climb to a junction at the Upper Meadow at 1.25 miles. Begin the loop around the meadow to the right. Pass basalt outcroppings en route to sweeping vistas, including the sloping ridge of

Sonoma Mountain. At the south end of the loop is a memorial stone bench. Just beyond the bench is a trail split. The right fork curves to the upper end of the meadow and ends at the fenced boundary. The main trail stays on the plateau to the left and completes the loop. Return on the same trail, or use the alternative Toyon Trail.■

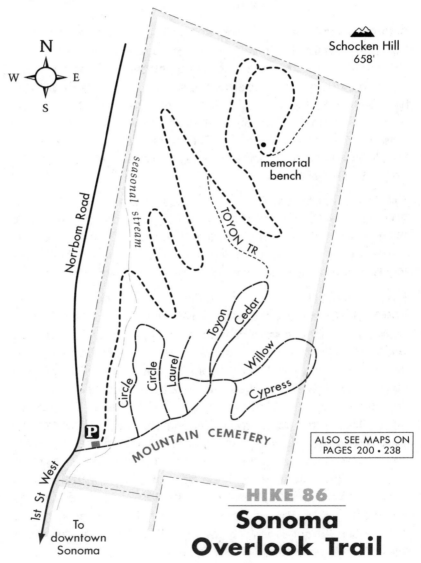

Schocken Hill
658'

memorial
bench

TOYON TR

seasonal stream

Norrbom Road

Toyon

Cedar

Willow

Cypress

Circle

Circle

Laurel

P

MOUNTAIN CEMETERY

1st St West

To
downtown
Sonoma

ALSO SEE MAPS ON
PAGES 200 • 238

HIKE 86
Sonoma
Overlook Trail

87. Sonoma Bike Path

Hiking distance: 3 miles round trip
Hiking time: 1.5 hours
Elevation gain: Level
Maps: U.S.G.S. Sonoma
Sonoma State Historic Park map

map
page 238

Summary of hike: The Sonoma Bike Path is a hiking, biking, and jogging trail that crosses through the heart of Sonoma just north of Sonoma Plaza. The path stretches from Fourth Street East, by Sebastiani Vineyards and Winery, to the Sonoma Highway across from Maxwell Farms Regional Park (Hike 85). The dog friendly path passes through vineyards, Depot Park, the Sonoma Depot Museum (built as a replica of the Sonoma's first train depot of 1880), Sonoma State Historic Park, and the open grasslands around General Vallejo's gothic Victorian home. The trail is popular with locals as well as visitors.

Driving directions: From East Napa Street by the Sonoma Plaza in downtown Sonoma, drive 0.5 miles east on East Napa Street to Fourth Street East. Turn left and continue a quarter mile to the posted trail across from Lovall Valley Road by the Sebastiani Vineyards. Park along either side of the street.

Hiking directions: From Fourth Street East at the west end of Lovall Valley Road, head west on the paved path through the Sebastiani Vineyards. Cross Second Street East, and continue through a landscaped greenbelt to First Street East at 0.35 miles. Cross the street and enter Depot Park, with a eucalyptus grove, historical museum, and train cars on the left. Athletic fields are on the right. A side path circles the museum and train cars. At a half mile is First Street West and the historic Depot Hotel, built in 1870 and closed in 1923. Cross through the vast grasslands of Sonoma State Historic Park to Third Street West. To the right, the forested road leads to General Mariano Vallejo's home, dating back to the 1850s. Continue straight ahead through the open meadow to Fourth Street West. Cross the street, leaving the state park, and pass through a greenbelt corridor between homes. Cross Fifth

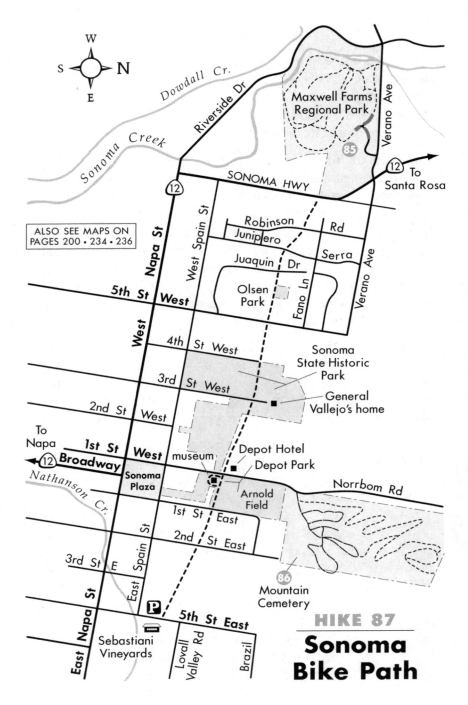

W N S E

Dowdall Cr.

Riverside Dr

Sonoma Creek

Maxwell Farms Regional Park

Verano Ave

85

12 To Santa Rosa

SONOMA HWY

Napa St

West Spain St

ALSO SEE MAPS ON PAGES 200 • 234 • 236

Robinson Rd

Juniper

Juaquin Dr

Serra

Olsen Park

Fano Ln

Verano Ave

5th St West

West

4th St West

3rd St West

2nd St West

Sonoma State Historic Park

General Vallejo's home

To Napa

1st St West

12 Broadway

Nathanson Cr.

museum

Depot Hotel Depot Park

Norrbom Rd

Sonoma Plaza

Arnold Field

1st St East

2nd St East

Spain St

3rd St E

East Spain St

East Napa St

P

Sebastiani Vineyards

Lovall Valley Rd

Brazil

5th St East

86

Mountain Cemetery

HIKE 87
Sonoma Bike Path

Street West at just over one mile, and continue through the corridor. Pass Olsen Park, Juaquin Drive, Junipero Serra Drive, and Robinson Road to the end of the trail at the Sonoma Highway (Highway 12). Across the highway is Maxwell Farms Regional Park (Hike 85). Return by retracing your steps. ■

88. Bartholomew Memorial Park
Grape Stomp—You-Walk Miwok Trail Loop
1695 Castle Road (Closed from January 1 to April 1)

Hiking distance: 2.4-mile loop
Hiking time: 1.5 hours
Elevation gain: 450 feet
Maps: U.S.G.S. Sonoma
         Bartholomew Foundation Trail Map

map
page 241

Summary of hike: Bartholomew Memorial Park is a little known gem tucked into the hills less than two miles northeast of Sonoma. The 375-acre park leases part of its diverse land to Bartholomew Winery. This hike is not a meandering stroll through a winery, it only begins and ends there. The trail is a backcountry hike winding through oak-covered mountain slopes and redwood groves. The hike follows portions of Arroyo Seco and the South Fork of Arroyo Seco to a pond, lake, cave, and two awesome overlooks. Dogs are allowed on the trail

Driving directions: From East Napa Street by the Sonoma Plaza in downtown Sonoma, drive one mile east on East Napa Street to 7th Street East. Turn left and continue 0.3 miles to Castle Road. Turn right and drive a 0.4 miles to the Bartholomew Park Winery entrance. Enter the winery grounds and go a quarter mile to a road fork. The right fork leads to the tasting room. Veer left 0.1 mile to the trailhead parking lot.

A second trailhead is located off of Old Winery Road. From East Napa Street, just east of 8th Street East, turn north on Old Winery Road. Drive 0.75 miles to the posted trailhead parking area on the left.

Hiking directions: From the north end of the parking lot, follow the posted trail 40 yards to Duck Pond. Curve right along the east side of the pond to a trail gate. Pass through the gate and cross a stream in an oak, manzanita, and madrone forest. Climb the hill on the Grape Stomp Trail and traverse the slope, parallel to the stream. Head up the shaded draw and recross the stream. Climb steps and zigzag up the hill to Grape Stomp Bench and an overlook of Sonoma and San Pablo Bay. Weave along the contours of the hills with small dips and rises. Descend to a fork of Arroyo Seco Creek by a private road. Rock-hop over the creek and cross the road. Climb eight steps and head up the forested hillside. Follow the north side of Arroyo Seco Creek, passing above Benicia's Lake. Descend steps and hop over the creek upstream of the lake. Enter a redwood grove with Douglas fir and continue climbing. A side path on the right leads to the east shore of the lake. The main trail continues to a posted junction at one mile. Angel's Flight Trail descends to the right for a slightly shorter and easier loop. Bear left on the You-Walk Miwok Trail, climbing to the 640-foot summit that is just past a bench. On clear days, the vistas extend as far as the Golden Gate Bridge. Descend from the upper slope with the aid of dirt and log steps to the Shortcut Trail on the right. Stay straight 20 yards to a side path on the right to Szeptaj Point Bench, with beautiful views of Sonoma from under a canopy of oaks. Continue downhill on the main trail to a posted junction. Detour to the left 80 yards. Follow the South Fork of Arroyo Seco upstream, passing small waterfalls. Continue over mossy boulders to Solano's Hideaway, a massive rock formation with caves. Solano was an Indian chief of the Suisun Tribe and a friend of General Vallejo. Return to the junction and continue west, passing a junction with the lower south end of Angel's Flight Trail. Pass through a trail gate and skirt the backside of the Buena Vista Winery. Pass through a second gate to a narrow paved road by a gazebo on the left. Cross a rock bridge over Arroyo Seco Stream and follow the path on the right side of the road. Cross Castle Road and complete the loop at the trailhead parking lot. ■

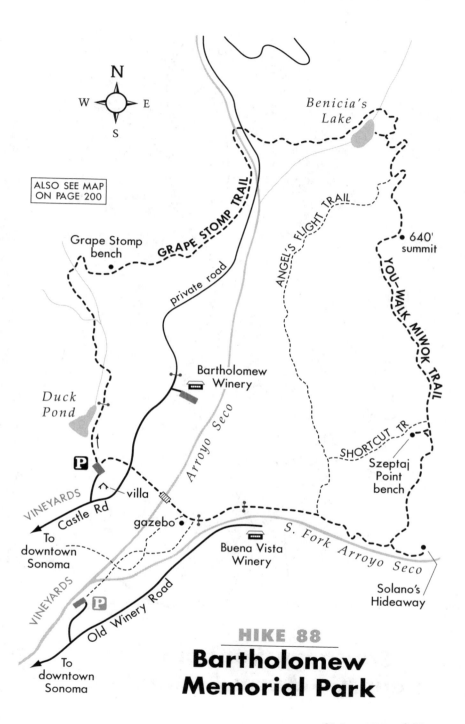

N
W E
S

Benicia's Lake

ALSO SEE MAP ON PAGE 200

Grape Stomp bench

GRAPE STOMP TRAIL

private road

ANGEL'S FLIGHT TRAIL

640' summit

YOU-WALK MIWOK TRAIL

Duck Pond

Bartholomew Winery

Arroyo Seco

SHORTCUT TR.

Szeptaj Point bench

P

villa

VINEYARDS

Castle Rd

gazebo

To downtown Sonoma

S. Fork Arroyo Seco

Buena Vista Winery

VINEYARDS

P

Old Winery Road

Solano's Hideaway

To downtown Sonoma

HIKE 88

Bartholomew Memorial Park

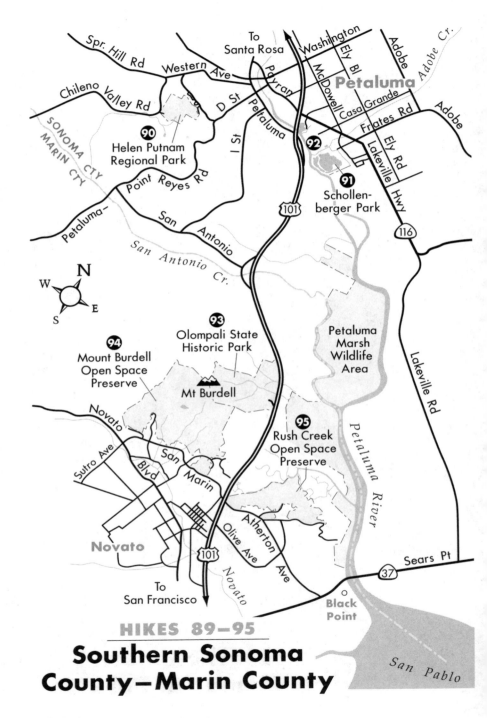

HIKES 89–95

Southern Sonoma
County–Marin County

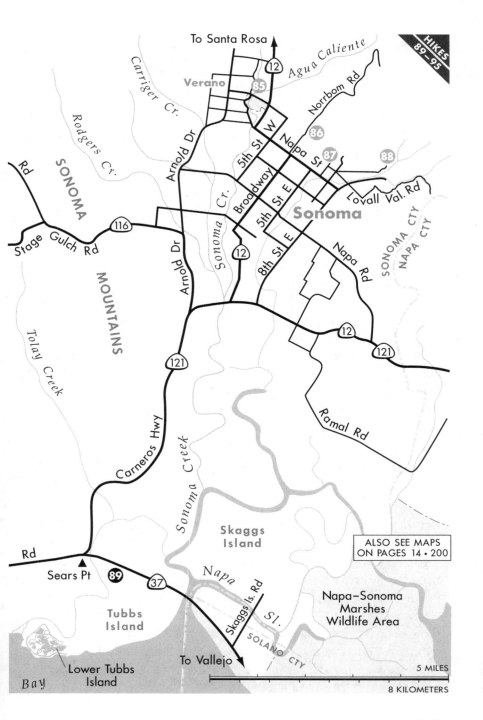

To Santa Rosa

Agua Caliente

12

Verano

85

Norrbom Rd

Carriger Cr.

Rodgers Cr.

86

5th St W

Napa St

87

88

Rd

SONOMA

Arnold Dr

Broadway

St E

Lovall Val. Rd

Sonoma

116

Sonoma Cr.

5th St E

SONOMA CTY

NAPA CTY

Stage Gulch Rd

Arnold Dr

12

8th St E

Napa Rd

MOUNTAINS

Tolay Creek

121

12

121

Carneros Hwy

Ramal Rd

Sonoma Creek

Skaggs
Island

ALSO SEE MAPS
ON PAGES 14 • 200

Rd

Sears Pt

89

37

Napa

Skaggs Is. Rd

St.

Napa–Sonoma
Marshes
Wildlife Area

Tubbs
Island

SOLANO CTY

Lower Tubbs
Island

To Vallejo

5 MILES

Bay

8 KILOMETERS

89. San Pablo Bay National Wildlife Refuge
Lower Tubbs Island • Tolay Creek

Hiking distance: 5.5 to 8 miles round trip
Hiking time: 3 to 5 hours
Elevation gain: Level
Maps: U.S.G.S. Sears Point and Petaluma Point

Summary of hike: San Pablo Bay National Wildlife Refuge lies along San Pablo Bay at the northern reaches of San Francisco Bay. The wildlife refuge encompasses 13,000 acres between the mouth of the Petaluma River and Mare Island by Vallejo. The refuge includes tidal wetlands, mud flats, salt marshes, and open water. Numerous waterways drain through the surrounding terrain, including the Napa River, Petaluma River, Sonoma Creek, Tolay Creek, and many sloughs. The waterways are interspersed with grasslands, oak woodlands, and agricultural fields. The Lower Tubbs Island, near Tolay Creek, is the most accessible portion of the national wildlife refuge, luring bird watchers, wildlife photographers, and hikers. Lower Tubbs Island Bird Sanctuary is a 332-acre preserve within the refuge. It is a sanctuary for migrating birds, waterfowl, and shorebirds. This trail follows a dirt levee 2.75 miles to the bird sanctuary on Lower Tubbs Island, then continues another 1.5 miles to Midshipman Point at the tip of the open waters. The terrain is flat, exposed, and windswept with wide open vistas.

Driving directions: From Napa Street by the Sonoma Plaza in downtown Sonoma, drive 3.7 miles south on Broadway (Highway 12) to Highway 121 (Freemont Drive). Veer to the right and continue 0.7 miles to a 4-way stop at Highways 116 and 121 (Arnold Drive). Turn left and go 6.6 miles south on Highway 121 to Highway 37 (Sears Point Road). Turn left and drive 0.7 miles, crossing over Tolay Creek and skirting the lagoon, to the first right turn. Turn right and park on the right at the posted trailhead.

To leave, it is not possible to turn left onto Highway 37. Out of the parking lot, turn right and drive 3 miles east, crossing the

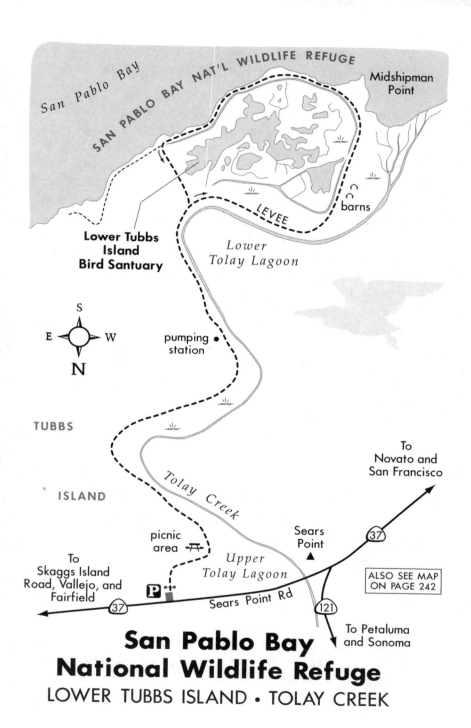

San Pablo Bay

SAN PABLO BAY NAT'L WILDLIFE REFUGE

Midshipman Point

Lower Tubbs Island Bird Santuary

LEVEE

barns

Lower Tolay Lagoon

S

E — W

N

pumping station

TUBBS

ISLAND

Tolay Creek

To Novato and San Francisco

picnic area

Sears Point

37

Upper Tolay Lagoon

ALSO SEE MAP ON PAGE 242

To Skaggs Island Road, Vallejo, and Fairfield

P

37

Sears Point Rd

121

To Petaluma and Sonoma

San Pablo Bay National Wildlife Refuge

LOWER TUBBS ISLAND • TOLAY CREEK

arched bridge over Sonoma Creek, to posted Skaggs Island. Turn left on Skaggs Island Road, and turn around in the dirt pullout on the right. Return to the west.

Hiking directions: Pass the trailhead gate and map panel on the dirt road. Follow the levee of Tolay Creek south along the edge of the wetlands and agricultural fields. At 0.4 miles curve left, passing a picnic area with an information map on the left. (Dogs are not allowed past the picnic area.) Continue southeast and bend right, with views of Mount Tamalpais and Mount Diablo in the distance. A parallel path follows the top of the levee on the right overlooking the Tolay Creek Lagoon. At 1.6 miles, veer left and pass a metal pumping station on the left. Continue southeast to a trail split at 2.3 miles by an information kiosk, the viewing area, and the entrance into the Lower Tubbs Island Bird Sanctuary. Begin the loop to the right between Lower Tolay Lagoon and Lower Tubbs Island, surrounded by tidal sloughs and salt marshes. Pass a group of red barns on the right, and curve left to the mouth of Tolay Creek. Follow the edge of San Pablo Bay on the levee road, where there is a view of Midshipman Point (the obvious promontory) and the mouth of the Petaluma River. At the east end of Lower Tubbs Island is a road split. Stay to the left along the Tubbs Island setback and complete the loop. Return to the right.■

90. Helen Putnam Regional Park
411 Chileno Valley Road • Petaluma

Hiking distance: 2.2-mile loop
Hiking time: 1.5 hours
Elevation gain: 300 feet
Maps: U.S.G.S. Petaluma
　　　Helen Putnam Regional Park map

Summary of hike: Helen Putnam Regional Park is located in the Petaluma countryside two miles southwest of downtown. The 216-acre park lies across rolling open meadows punctuated by mature oak savannah. The park also includes a shaded picnic area,

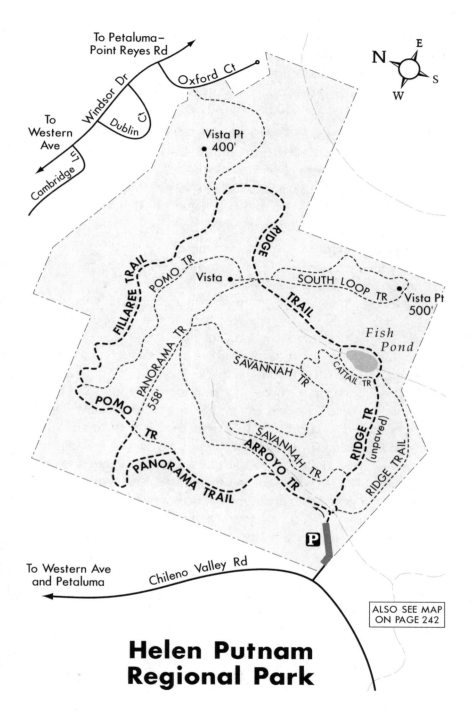

To Petaluma–
Point Reyes Rd

Oxford Ct

Windsor Dr

Dublin Ct

To
Western
Ave

Cambridge Ln

N
E
S
W

Vista Pt
● 400'

FILLAREE TRAIL

POMO TR

Vista ●

RIDGE

SOUTH LOOP TR

● Vista Pt
500'

TRAIL

Fish
Pond

PANORAMA TR

558'

SAVANNAH TR

CATTAIL TR

POMO

TR

SAVANNAH TR

ARROYO TR

RIDGE TR
(unpaved)

RIDGE TRAIL

PANORAMA TRAIL

P

To Western Ave
and Petaluma

Chileno Valley Rd

ALSO SEE MAP
ON PAGE 242

Helen Putnam
Regional Park

playground, and a fishing pond. Hiking, biking, and equestrian trails wind through the hills, with panoramic vistas of southern Sonoma County and northern Marin County. Eight well-marked trails wind through the park. This route follows the park's perimeter and visits Fish Pond. Dogs are allowed on the trails.

Driving directions: From Highway 101 in Petaluma, exit on Washington Street. Drive one mile southwest to Petaluma Boulevard. Turn left and go one block to Western Avenue. Turn right and continue 1.8 miles to Chileno Valley Road. Turn left and drive 0.8 miles to the posted park entrance. Turn left into the parking lot. A parking fee is required.

Hiking directions: From the far end of the parking lot, bear left by the map kiosk on the Arroyo Trail. Walk 0.1 mile to a junction. Go to the left on the Panorama Trail and climb the grassy hill. At the ridge is an overlook of the rolling pastureland with pockets of oaks. A bench sits next to a sprawling, majestic coast live oak. Top the slope to a junction with the Pomo Trail at 0.4 miles. Bear left, staying on the Panorama Trail, and descend on the gentle slope. Head uphill to the oak grove and horse pasture at the west park boundary. Continue on the upper ridge east, and bear left on the Pomo Trail. Descend into a shaded oak woodland and follow the ridge. Loop right to a posted fork at 0.9 miles. Bear left on the Fillaree Trail. Meander through the oaks to a T-junction with the paved Ridge Trail at 1.3 miles, located at an overlook of Petaluma, the Chileno Valley, and the coastal hills. Take the right fork up the gentle grade, passing the Pomo Trail on the right and the South Loop Trail on the left. (The loop trail leads to a 500-foot vista point.) Sheltered by hills on three sides, descend parallel to a small seasonal creek to Fish Pond at 1.9 miles. Curve around the east shore of the oval pond to a junction. Leave the paved Ridge Trail, and veer right along the south end of the pond to the water tank. Go to the left on the Ridge Trail and traverse the hillside. Pass the Savannah Trail on the right, returning to the parking lot. ▪

91. Schollenberger Park

Hiking distance: 2-mile loop
Hiking time: 1 hour
Elevation gain: level
Maps: U.S.G.S. Petaluma River
     Schollenberger Park Self-Guided Tour map

**map
page 250**

Summary of hike: Schollenberger Park resides in southern Petaluma alongside the Petaluma River. The river is actually a 14-mile tidal slough stretching from Petaluma to San Pablo Bay. The 240-acre city park, created in 1995, was the site for materials dredged from the bottom of the shallow Petaluma River, allowing river navigation. A circular two-mile path loops around the dredge ponds overlooking the preserved wildlife sanctuary, the wetlands, tidal marsh, and open fields. It is prime bird habitat for shorebirds and migrating waterfowl. The trail is popular for dog walking, jogging, bird watching, wildlife photography, and nature study, with sweeping vistas of southern Sonoma County and northern Marin County. Trail brochures are available at the trailhead for the self-guided interpretive trail.

Driving directions: From Highway 101 in Petaluma, exit on Lakeville Highway (Highway 116). Drive one mile east to South McDowell Boulevard and turn right. Continue 0.3 miles to Cader Lane on the left. Turn right into the posted park entrance and parking lot.

Hiking directions: Follow the paved path south past the restrooms and map kiosk to a junction. Pick up the interpretive trail guide, which corresponds with 15 numbered learning stations. Begin the loop on the right fork, and head southwest along Adobe Creek on the right. Just before reaching viewing station 5 is a junction. The Alman Marsh Trail (Hike 92) crosses a bridge over the creek and follows the wetlands one mile to the Petaluma River and marina. Continue straight on the west side of the dredge spoils ponds. The south end of the far pond parallels the serpentine Petaluma River, while the east side overlooks the wetlands. As you continue around the ponds, use the guide to

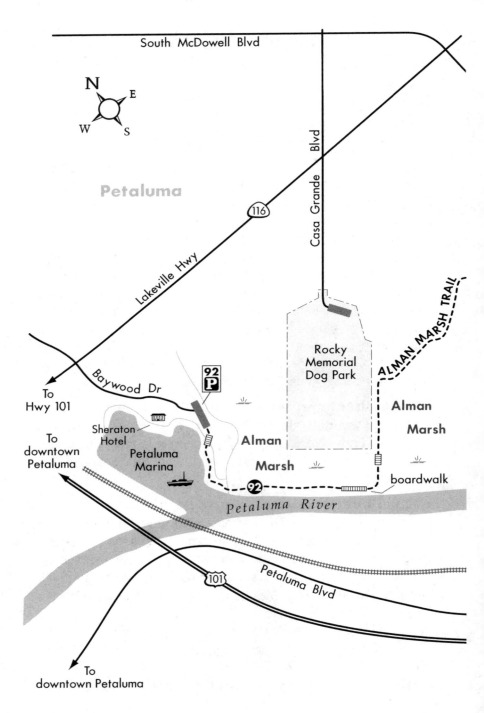

South McDowell Blvd

N
E
W
S

Petaluma

Casa Grande Blvd

116

Lakeville Hwy

Rocky
Memorial
Dog Park

ALMAN MARSH TRAIL

Baywood Dr

To
Hwy 101

92
P

Alman

Marsh

Alman

Marsh

Sheraton
Hotel

To
downtown
Petaluma

Petaluma
Marina

92

boardwalk

Petaluma River

101

Petaluma Blvd

To
downtown Petaluma

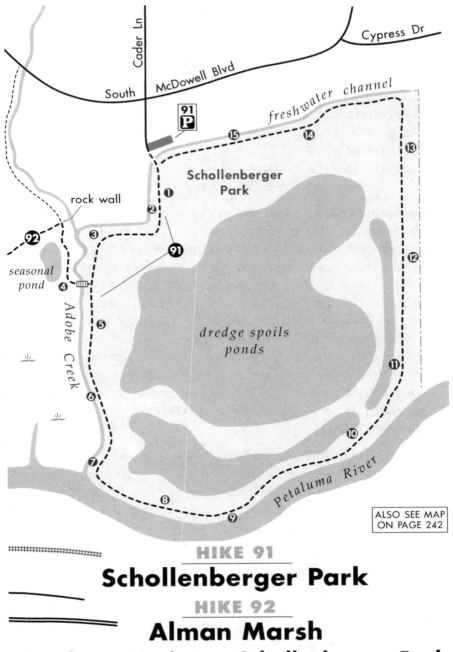

South McDowell Blvd

Cader Ln

Cypress Dr

freshwater channel

91 P

rock wall

92

seasonal pond

Adobe Creek

Schollenberger Park

91

dredge spoils ponds

Petaluma River

ALSO SEE MAP
ON PAGE 242

HIKE 91
Schollenberger Park
HIKE 92
Alman Marsh
Petaluma Marina to Schollenberger Park

learn about the history, geology, restoration, ponds, animals, birds, and wetland ecology of the immediate area. ∎

92. Alman Marsh
Petaluma Marina to Schollenberger Park

Hiking distance: 2 miles round trip
Hiking time: 1 hour
Elevation gain: Level
Maps: U.S.G.S. Petaluma River
      Schollenberger Park Self-Guided Tour map

map
page 250

Summary of hike: Alman Marsh lies on the land between Schollenberger Park and the Petaluma River. The Alman Marsh Trail is a one-mile trail linking the Petaluma River by the Petaluma Marina with Schollenberger Park. The trail follows a short portion of the Petaluma River, where bass and sturgeon fishing is a popular pasttime along the riverbank. After cutting away from the river, the path meanders through scenic and fertile tidal marsh, wetlands, open fields with freshwater channels, and around a seasonal pond. En route to the dredge ponds at Schollenberger Park, the trail skirts Rocky Memorial Dog Park, a nine-acre grassland bordering Alman Marsh. The park sits on the site of the old city landfill and is accessed from Casa Grande Road. Dogs are allowed on the trail.

Driving directions: From Highway 101 in Petaluma, exit on Lakeville Highway (Highway 116). Drive 0.1 mile east to Baywood Drive and turn right. Continue 0.2 miles to the far end of the parking lot, passing the Sheraton Hotel to the posted trailhead. Park in the spaces near the footbridge.

Hiking directions: Cross the footbridge over the freshwater channel into the wetland. Head south to the Petaluma River and curve left, following the river downstream. Cross a 120-foot boardwalk over the wetland and curve inland, away from the river. Cross a bridge over another water channel and skirt the east side of Rocky Memorial Dog Park, an off-leash grassland. Zigzag northeast, passing a seasonal pond on the right to a metal bridge.

Cross the pedestrian bridge over Adobe Creek to a T-junction with the Shollenberger Park Trail at the dredge spoils ponds, just north of viewing station 5 (Hike 91). Return by retracing your route, or continue around the ponds for an additional 2 miles. ■

93. Olompali State Historic Park

Hiking distance: 2.7-mile loop
Hiking time: 2 hours
Elevation gain: 750 feet
Maps: U.S.G.S. Petaluma River
　　　Olompali State Historic Park map

map
page 255

Summary of hike: Olompali State Historic Park is located a few miles north of Novato on the northeast slope of Burdell Mountain, facing San Antonio Creek and the Petaluma River Marsh Wildlife Area. The name comes from the Coast Miwok language meaning *southern village* or *southern people*. The 700-acre park has a colorful and varied past, including being the site of Marin County's largest Miwok Indian village from about 500 A.D. and a major Miwok trading center. In the mid 1800s Galen and Mary Burdell owned the land. They built an ornate 26-room mansion with a Victorian formal garden, brick-lined walkways, gazebos, exotic plants, fountains, and a lily pond. The Burdell mansion burned down in 1969, but the old adobe walls still remain. In the 1940s it was a Jesuit seminary. In 1966 it was home to the Grateful Dead band. A picture of the band relaxing on the Olompali hillside is on the back cover of their *American Beauty* album. In 1967 it was a hippy commune for a group known as *The Chosen Family*. It became a state park in 1982. This loop hike climbs the east-facing mountain slope, passing several historic ranch buildings and an interpretive Miwok village, which has been reconstructed with the assistance of Coast Miwok descendants. The path leads through rolling grasslands with majestic gnarled oaks and stream-fed ravines. The hike includes vistas of the coastal mountain ranges, the Petaluma River estuary, and San Pablo Bay. Olompali State Historic Park connects with the Mount Burdell Open Space Preserve (Hike 94) at the ridge.

Driving directions: The park entrance is accessible only from southbound traffic on Highway 101. From Highway 101 in Petaluma, drive 8 miles south to the posted Olompali Park exit on the north end of Novato. (The turnoff is 2.4 miles south of San Antonio Road.) Drive 0.3 miles into the trailhead parking lot. A parking fee is required.

To leave the park and head back towards Petaluma, drive 2.2 miles south on Highway 101 to the San Marin Drive/Atherton Avenue exit in Novato. Turn left, crossing over the highway, and turn left again, heading north on Highway 101.

Hiking directions: This hike makes a loop along the lower slopes of Burdell Mountain and around the reconstructed Miwok village. The posted trailhead is at the far west end of the parking lot. Head up the grassy slope along a row of oak trees. Pass the historic Burdell Ranch buildings on the right to a posted junction. Begin the loop to the right, and cross the wooden bridge over a seasonal creek. Pass the Burdell Barns on the right, dating back to the 1880s, and follow the gravel road to the left. Meander through oaks to the site of the Coast Miwok village at 0.35 miles. Stroll through the village with interpretive panels, a roundhouse, a native plant garden, an acorn granary, and a redwood bark *kotcha* (dwelling). Continue past the village through towering bay laurels, and parallel a stream in a deep ravine on the right. Enter a tree-shaded glen, passing an old ranch reservoir on the right, formed in the creek from a wooden spillway. Continue upstream on the south canyon wall. At 0.8 miles leave the stream and canyon on a switchback to the left. Weave through the oak forest, and cross a minor ridge to a posted junction at 1.1 mile. The Upper Mount Burdell Trail (the right fork) climbs 3.3 miles to the summit of Burdell Mountain and Mount Burdell Open Space Preserve, connecting to Hike 94. Take the left fork on the Lower Mount Burdell Trail and traverse the mountain slope, overlooking the Petaluma River basin. Gently descend with the aid of a couple switchbacks, and enter an oak-studded grassland with overlooks of the Miwok Village and the Burdell Ranch. Complete the loop at the bridge and return to the right. ∎

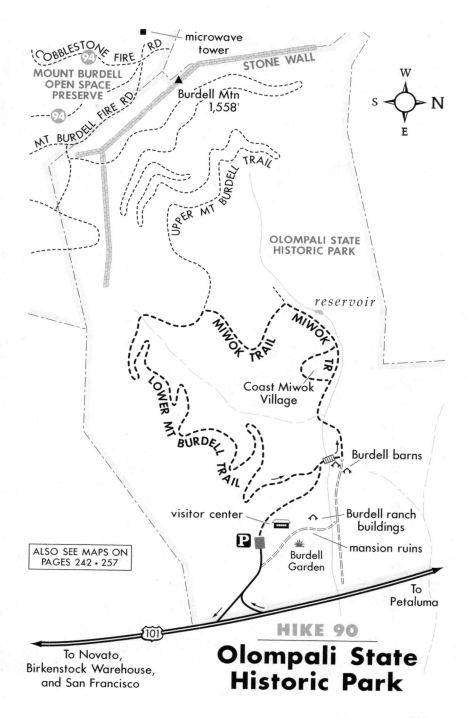

microwave tower

COBBLESTONE FIRE RD

MOUNT BURDELL
OPEN SPACE
PRESERVE

MT BURDELL FIRE RD.

STONE WALL

Burdell Mtn
1,558'

W N S E

UPPER MT BURDELL TRAIL

OLOMPALI STATE
HISTORIC PARK

reservoir

MIWOK TRAIL

MIWOK TR

LOWER MT BURDELL TRAIL

Coast Miwok
Village

Burdell barns

visitor center

Burdell ranch
buildings

mansion ruins

P

Burdell
Garden

To
Petaluma

ALSO SEE MAPS ON
PAGES 242 • 257

101

To Novato,
Birkenstock Warehouse,
and San Francisco

HIKE 90

Olompali State
Historic Park

94. Mount Burdell Open Space Preserve

Hiking distance: 4.8-mile loop
Hiking time: 2.5 hours
Elevation gain: 1,150 feet
Maps: U.S.G.S. Petaluma River and Novato
Mt. Burdell Open Space Preserve map

Summary of hike: Burdell Mountain rises 1,558 feet from the Novato Valley floor on the northeast corner of Marin County. The serpentine slopes are covered with rolling grasslands and groves of live oak, bay laurel, and buckeye. Two major parks reside on Burdell Mountain: Olompali State Historic Park (Hike 93) occupies 700 acres on the northeast face, while Mount Burdell Open Space Preserve occupies 1,600 acres on the

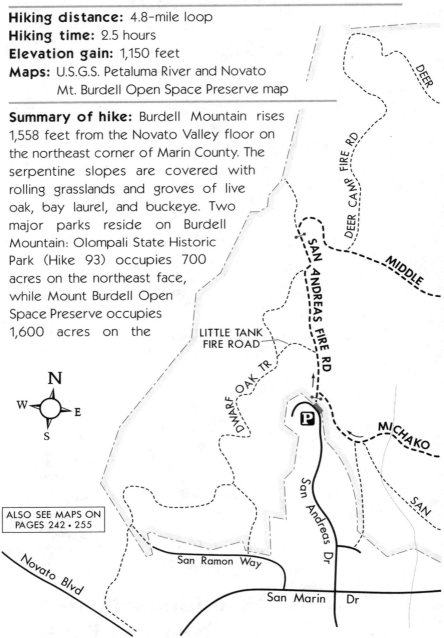

ALSO SEE MAPS ON
PAGES 242 • 255

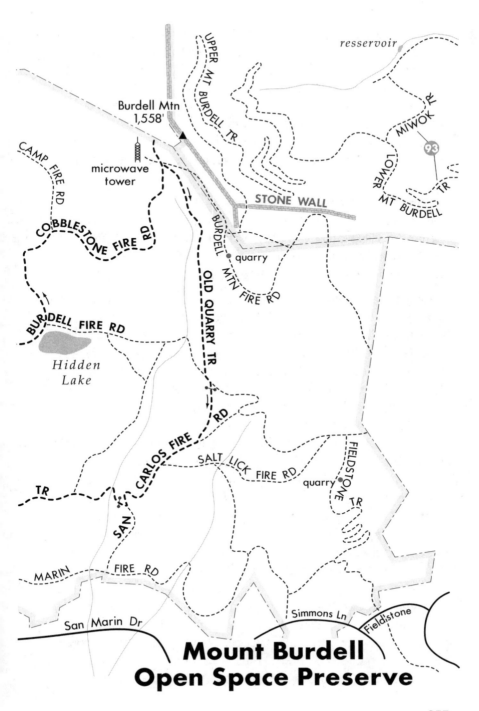

resservoir

UPPER MT BURDELL TR

Burdell Mtn
1,558'

MIWOK TR

93

LOWER MT BURDELL

CAMP FIRE RD

microwave
tower

STONE WALL

BURDELL MTN FIRE RD

COBBLESTONE FIRE RD

quarry

BURDELL FIRE RD

OLD QUARRY TR

Hidden Lake

RD

FIELDSTONE TR

SAN CARLOS FIRE

SALT LICK FIRE RD

quarry

TR

MARIN FIRE RD

Simmons Ln

Fieldstone

San Marin Dr

Mount Burdell
Open Space Preserve

southwest slope. This hike forms a loop on the southwest flank of the mountain, from the lower meadows to the ridge separating the two parks. At the summit are sweeping vistas, from Mount Saint Helena to Mount Diablo and San Francisco. En route, the hike visits Hidden Lake, a seasonal pond midway to the summit; an old stone wall built by Chinese laborers in the late 1800s; and remnants of old rock quarries once used for the streets in San Francisco. The trails are open to hikers, cyclists, equestrians, and dogs.

Driving directions: From Highway 101 in Petaluma, drive 10 miles south to the San Marin Drive/Atherton Avenue exit on the north end of Novato. Drive 2.2 miles west on San Marin Drive to San Andreas Drive and turn right. Continue 0.6 miles to the signed entrance gate. Park along San Andreas Drive.

Hiking directions: From the trailhead gate and map board, begin the loop on the left fork. Climb up the San Andreas Fire Road through an oak savannah with California bay, passing the Little Tank Fire Road on the left. Pass through a cattle gate, and crest the hill to a large bowl-shaped meadow. Curve right and climb through the sloping meadow dotted with valley oak to a Y-fork with the Deer Camp Fire Road. Continue straight on the Middle Burdell Fire Road, with a view of Novato and the bay. Top the slope to the northwest edge of Hidden Lake and a junction at 1.5 miles. The right fork stays on the Middle Burdell Fire Road and eliminates 1.2 miles of the hike for a shorter and much easier loop. For this hike, bear left on the Cobblestone Fire Road to another Y-fork with the Deer Camp Fire Road at 1.9 miles. Veer to the right, staying on the Cobblestone Fire Road, and keep climbing toward the summit. The remains of a rock quarry site can be spotted on the right. At 2.5 miles, the trail tops out just below the ridge at a 5-way junction. The left fork leads to the microwave tower. The sharp right fork—the Old Quarry Trail—is our return route. The Burdell Mountain Fire Road heads southeast on the 90-degree right fork. It connects with the Upper Mount Burdell Trail in Olompali State Historic Park and descends on the northeast slope of the mountain. Detour on the unmarked trail straight ahead about 200 yards to the rounded rock wall built without mortar at the ridge and park boundary. This old stone wall was built by Chinese laborers. From the ridge are vistas across the Petaluma River Marshes and Upper San Pablo Bay. Return to the junction and take the Old Quarry Trail. Steeply descend the stone-embedded path in the small canyon. Use careful footing, as the trail drops 700 feet in just over a half mile and is littered with loose rock. The path soon levels out and traverses a grassy meadow to a T-junction with the Middle Burdell Fire Road at 3.3 miles. Bear left 100 yards and pick up the posted Quarry Trail on the right. Go through a cattle gate and continue downhill. Merge with the San Carlos Fire Road and curve right. Weave down the oak-dotted hill and bear right on Michako Trail at 3.9 miles. Walk through another cattle gate and cross the rolling hills, completing the loop at the trailhead.■

95. Rush Creek Open Space Preserve

Hiking distance: 5.5 miles round trip
Hiking time: 2.5 hours
Elevation gain: 70 feet

**map
page 261**

Maps: U.S.G.S. Novato and Petaluma River
      Rush Creek Open Space Preserve map

Summary of hike: Stretching along the banks of the Petaluma River is a flat fertile region with coastal salt marshes and diked farmland. Rush Creek Open Space Preserve is adjacent to a vast wetland area along the Petaluma River, but is surrounded by oak woodlands. The preserve lies between Burdell Mountain and the Petaluma River delta. The 528-acre open space is a resting and nesting site for thousands of migrating and resident waterfowl. Within the preserve is Rush Creek Marsh; Pinheiro Ridge, a low 200-foot hill; and Cemetery Marsh, named for the adjacent Valley Memorial Park Cemetery. The trail follows the Pinheiro Ridge Fire Road (an old ranch road) along the base of Pinheiro Ridge. The hike skirts the south edge of Rush Creek, then loops around Cemetery Marsh to Black John Slough, a unit of the

Petaluma River Marsh. Throughout the hike are vistas of the expansive tidal wetlands and Burdell Mountain (Hike 94).

Driving directions: From Highway 101 in Petaluma, drive 10 miles south to the San Marin Drive/Atherton Avenue exit on the north end of Novato. Turn left on Atherton Avenue, crossing over the freeway, and quickly turn left on Binford Road. Drive one block to the signed trailhead on the right. Park on the shoulder of the road.

Hiking directions: At the trailhead are two trails. The right fork follows Atherton Avenue and Bugeia Lane before curving north, away from the road and into the open space to Cemetery Marsh. To enter the quiet of the open space, take the left fork straight ahead on the Pinheiro Ridge Fire Road. Follow the base of Pinheiro Ridge along the edge of the vast Rush Creek Marsh. Stroll through the hills covered with oak and bay trees. Curve over the rolling hills, staying on the edge of the wetland. Enter the shade of the forest, and descend to a junction at 1.3 miles. The left fork is our return route. Begin the loop to the right, emerging from the forest to the open west edge of Cemetery Marsh. Continue to the south end of the brackish marsh and a junction with trail bridges in each direction at 1.9 miles. The Pinheiro Ridge Fire Road continues on the right fork, passing the cemetery and leading out of the preserve to Bugeia Lane. Stay straight on the left fork and cross the bridge. Curve left on the Rush Creek Fire Road, skirting the east edge of Cemetery Marsh on the fire road. Follow the base of Bahia Ridge along the cove, with a view of Burdell Mountain. At 2.6 miles is a 3-way trail split. The left fork is the return route. The right fork climbs through an oak and bay laurel forest to the ridge. Take the middle fork, rising gently up the hill and curving right. Stroll through the forest to Black John Slough and the vast wetlands. Follow the curving contours of the hills, choosing your own turn-around spot.

To return, head back to the 3-way trail split at the north end of Cemetery Marsh. Take the lower fork to a berm. Bear left and cross the head of Cemetery Marsh on the narrow, raised trail, completing the loop. Return 1.3 miles to the trailhead. ■

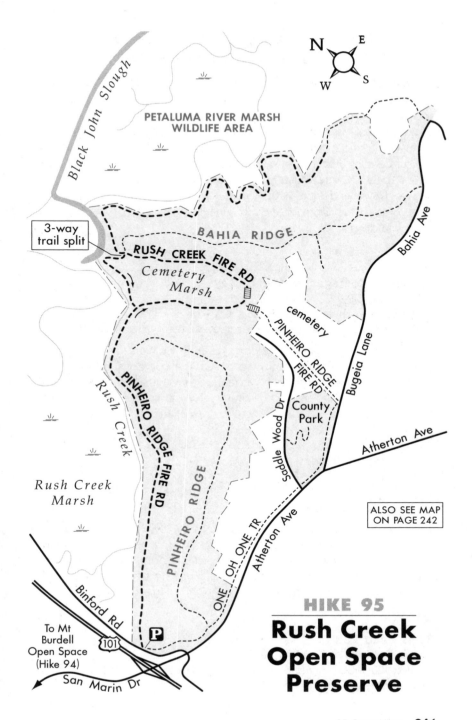

N
E
W
S

Black John Slough

PETALUMA RIVER MARSH
WILDLIFE AREA

3-way
trail split

BAHIA RIDGE

RUSH CREEK FIRE RD

Cemetery
Marsh

cemetery

PINHEIRO RIDGE
FIRE RD

Bahia Ave

Bugeia Lane

Rush Creek

PINHEIRO RIDGE FIRE RD

PINHEIRO RIDGE

Saddle Wood Dr

County
Park

Atherton Ave

Rush Creek
Marsh

ALSO SEE MAP
ON PAGE 242

ONE OH ONE TR.

Atherton Ave

To Mt
Burdell
Open Space
(Hike 94)

Binford Rd

101

P

San Marin Dr

Rush Creek
Open Space
Preserve

Sonoma County Accommodations
Author Recommendations

Sonoma County has a wide variety of accommodations. The following recommendations are places I stayed while hiking, writing about, and enjoying Sonoma County.

All of the 13 accommodations listed below are clean and comfortable with friendly, helpful staffs. Their locations offer easy access to the surrounding area. I look forward to returning to many or all of these hotels, bed and breakfasts, or resorts. My wife, Linda, and I nearly always travel and hike with Kofax, our yellow labrador. With the exception of the Santa Rosa Hyatt Vineyard Creek, all of the lodgings welcome dogs.

Anchor Bay

Mar Vista Cottages at Anchor Bay
(877) 855-3522 · (707) 884-3522
35101 South Highway One · Gualala, CA 95445
www.marvistamendocino.com · reservations@marvistamendocino.com

The Mar Vista Cottages are 12 cottages with kitchens nestled on nine acres across the highway from the ocean. The gorgeous grounds have an organic fruit and vegetable garden, egg-laying hens, and a hot tub. The garden and eggs are complimentary for the guests to harvest and enjoy.

Cloverdale

KOA Camping Resort
(800) 368-4558 · (707) 894-3337
1166 Asti Ridge Road · PO Box 600 · Cloverdale, CA 95425
www.winecountrykoa.com

The Cloverdale KOA is the most gorgeous and well maintained KOA I have ever seen. The 60-acre campground sits on a hill among oaks and pines overlooking Alexander Valley. There is a pool, a fish pond, and camping cabins with private bathrooms. A hiking trail leads from the campground down to Crocker Creek.

Gualala · The Sea Ranch

Rams Head Realty
(800) 785-3455 · (707) 785-2427
PO Box 123 · 1000 Annapolis Road · The Sea Ranch, CA 95497
www.ramshead.com

Rams Head Realty and Rentals has the largest selection of rental homes at Sea Ranch, with more than 120 homes to choose from. The homes are completely furnished and many have private hot tubs. You can choose locations from the ocean bluffs to the redwood-forested hills. Staying in a home at Sea Ranch includes use of three swimming pools, tennis courts, and ten miles of private blufftop trails.

The Sea Ranch Escape
(888) 732-7262 · (707) 785-2426
PO Box 238 · 60 Sea Walk Drive · The Sea Ranch, CA 95497
www.88searanch.com

The Sea Ranch Escape is located in The Sea Ranch Lodge. They offer a wide selection of fully furnished homes, from ocean-view homes to the forested hillside. Staying in a home at Sea Ranch includes use of three recreation centers with pools, saunas and tennis, plus access to 50 miles of maintained trails that are closed to the public.

Guerneville · Monte Rio

Village Inn & Restaurant
(707) 865-2304 · (800) 303-2303
20822 River Boulevard · Monte Rio, 95462
www.villageinn-ca.com · village@sonic.net

The Village Inn sits on the south bank of the Russian River in Monte Rio, just four miles west of Guerneville. Ancient redwoods back the historic inn, established in 1906. From most of the 11 guest rooms are close-up views of the river with a backdrop of mountains. The rooms have refrigerators, private balconies, and include a complimentary breakfast.

The inn also has an awesome restaurant that overlooks the river. They serve locally grown meats, produce, and dairy products. They have a full bar, an award-winning wine list, draft micro-brew beers, and an incredible dessert list.

Healdsburg

Camellia Inn
(800) 727-8182 · (707) 433-8182
211 North Street · Healdsburg, CA 95448
www.camelliainn.com

The Camillia Inn is a historic 1869 Italianate Victorian inn located on a quiet residential street only two blocks from the Healdsburg Plaza. The bed and breakfast inn has nine charming rooms, all with private baths. More than fifty varieties of camellias grow on the grounds. There is a pool and the breakfasts are fantastic!

Best Western Dry Creek Inn
(707) 433-0300 · (800) 222-5784
198 Dry Creek Road · Healdsburg, CA 95448
www.drycreekinn.com

The Dry Creek Inn is located between Alexander Valley and Dry Creek Valley. It is a mile north of Healdsburg's historic plaza and a mile from the Russian River. The inn has a pool, spa, fitness room, continental breakfast, and a complimentary bottle of wine. All of the rooms are equipped with refrigerators.

Kenwood

Kenwood Oaks Guesthouse
(707) 833-1221
Warm Springs Road · Kenwood, CA 95452
www.kenwoodoaksguesthouse.com
joan@kenwoodoaksguesthouse.com

Of all the places we stayed, the Kenwood Oaks Guesthouse is our favorite. This two-acre horse ranch has one guesthouse. It is situated adjacent to the horse barn and overlooks a pasture, backed by a wooded hillside with 300-year-old valley oaks. This charming house has a full kitchen and is very secluded. I could easily live there full time.

We stayed at the guesthouse a second time. From the moment we turned onto Warm Springs Road, Kofax, our labrador, was squealing with excitement. Upon arriving, he barreled out of the car to see Joan, the proprietor; her dogs, Ella and Honey; and sniff noses with her horses. (It is Kofax's favorite place also.) Joan offers boarding facilities for horses and the area is filled with equestrian trails, including trails at Annadel State Park, Sugarloaf Ridge State Park, Jack London State Historic Park, and Sonoma Valley Regional Park.

Petaluma

Best Western Petaluma Inn
(800) 297-3846 · (707) 763-0994
200 South McDowell Boulevard · Petaluma, CA 94952
bwpetalumainn@prodigy.net

The Petaluma Inn is close to the 101 Freeway and near Petaluma's historic downtown. The location is perfect for heading out in any direction. The Inn has a pool, guest laundry facilities, and a helpful staff.

Point Arena

Point Arena Lighthouse
(877)-725-4448 · (707) 882-2777
PO Box 11 · Point Arena, CA 95468
palight@mcn.org

The Point Arena Lighthouse has five vacation rentals. They are the former lighthouse keepers' houses on the peninsula. The cottages are completely furnished, with kitchens and ocean views. All of the proceeds from the rentals go to the preservation of the historic lighthouse.

Wharf Master's Inn
(800) 932-4031 · (707) 882-3171
PO Box 336 · 785 Port Road (by Arena Cove) · Point Arena, CA 95468
www.wharfmasters.com

Wharfmaster's Inn is located on the bluffs in Point Arena Cove overlooking the fishing pier and marina. The historic inn is built in the same style as the Wharf Master's House, dating back to 1865. The 23 rooms have private balconies, fireplaces, and whirlpool tubs.

Santa Rosa

Santa Rosa Hyatt Vineyard Creek
(707) 284-1234 · (800) 233-1234
170 Railroad Street · Santa Rosa, CA 95401
www.vineyardcreek.hyatt.com

The Hyatt Vineyard Creek Hotel and Spa is located in Santa Rosa's Historic Railroad Square alongside Santa Rosa Creek. The resort has an outdoor pool, sculpture garden, fitness center, and a spa. The garden area connects to the Santa Rosa Creek hiking trail on the Prince Greenway section of the trail.

Sonoma

Sonoma Valley Inn
(707) 938-9200
550 Second Street · Sonoma, CA 95476
www.sonomavalleyinn.com

The Sonoma Valley Inn is located just around the corner from the historic Sonoma Plaza. The inn has a heated pool, gazebo-covered spa, a fitness center with a steam room, and free guest laundry. The rooms have a private balcony, fireplace, refrigerator, a gift bottle of wine, and complimentary breakfast delivered to your room.

DAY HIKE BOOKS

Day Hikes On the California Central Coast ......978-1-57342-031-0 .....$14.95

Day Hikes On the California Southern Coast ....978-1-57342-045-7 ......14.95

Day Hikes Around Sonoma County ....978-1-57342-053-2 ......16.95

Day Hikes Around Monterey and Carmel..........978-1-57342-036-5......14.95

Day Hikes Around Big Sur ....978-1-57342-041-9......14.95

Day Hikes Around San Luis Obispo..............978-1-57342-051-8........16.95

Day Hikes Around Santa Barbara...............978-1-57342-042-6......14.95

Day Hikes Around Ventura County..............978-1-57342-043-3......14.95

Day Hikes Around Los Angeles..................978-1-57342-044-0......14.95

Day Hikes Around Orange County ....978-1-57342-047-1........15.95

Day Hikes In Yosemite National Park ....978-1-57342-037-2........11.95

Day Hikes In Sequoia and Kings Canyon N.P.....978-1-57342-030-3 ......12.95

Day Hikes Around Sedona, Arizona ....978-1-57342-049-5 ......14.95

Day Hikes On Oahu...........................978-1-57342-038-9........11.95

Day Hikes On Maui...........................978-1-57342-039-6 ....11.95

Day Hikes On Kauai..........................978-1-57342-040-2........11.95

Day Hikes In Hawaii.........................978-1-57342-050-1........16.95

Day Hikes In Yellowstone National Park.........978-1-57342-048-8 ......12.95

Day Hikes In Grand Teton National Park ....978-1-57342-046-4 ......11.95

Day Hikes In the Beartooth Mountains
Billings to Red Lodge to Yellowstone N.P. ....978-1-57342-052-5........13.95

Day Hikes Around Bozeman, Montana...........978-1-57342-054-9........13.95

Day Hikes Around Missoula, Montana ....978-1-57342-032-7 ....11.95

These books may be purchased at your local bookstore or
outdoor shop. Or, order them direct from the distributor:

The Globe Pequot Press

246 Goose Lane • P.O. Box 480 • Guilford, CT 06437-0480
on the web: www.globe-pequot.com

800-243-0495 DIRECT   **800-820-2329** FAX

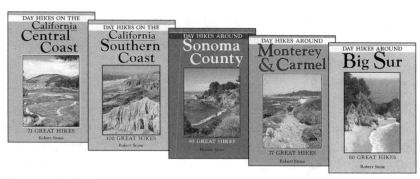

Laguna de Santa Rosa Foundation

50 Old Courthouse Square, Suite 609 · Santa Rosa, CA 95404
(707) 572-9277
www.lagunadesantarosa.org

This non-profit foundation is the only agency that focuses exclusively on the Laguna de Santa Rosa watershed. Their invaluable work aims to permanently preserve, protect, restore, and enhance the 10,000-acre watershed. To find out more about their organization and their learning center, or to get involved, be a volunteer, a docent, attend regularly scheduled docent-led hikes, or to make a tax-deductible donation, call or visit their website.

The Laguna de Santa Rosa Foundation is instrumental in the creation and maintenance of Hikes 43, 62, 63, 64 and 65.

Stewards of the Coast and Redwoods

P.O. Box 2 · Duncan Mills, CA 95430
(707) 869-9177
www.stewardsofthecoastandredwoods.org

This non-profit environmental organization works in partnership with the California Department of Parks and Recreation in the Russian River Sector. They provide the public with environmental stewardship programs, including educational and interpretive programs and resource management projects. They provide volunteers in the parks; sponsor interpretive talks; organize naturalist-led hikes, bike rides, and kayak trips; support land acquisition; and upgrade and build interpretive facilities. They have regularly scheduled docent-led hikes. Their focus is in Armstrong Redwoods State Reserve, Austin Creek State Recreation Area, Sonoma Coast State Beach, and the Willow Creek Watershed. To find our more or to be a volunteer, a docent, make a tax-deductible donation, or just enjoy one of their activities, call or visit their website.

Stewards of the Coast and Redwoods is connected with Hikes 30, 33, 38, 39, 40 and 41.

INDEX

Notes

About the Author

Since 1991, veteran hiker Robert Stone has been writer, photographer, and publisher of *Day Hike Books*. He is a Los Angeles Times Best Selling Author and an award-winning author of RMOWP (Rocky Mountain Outdoor Writers and Photographers). He is also an active member of OWAC (Outdoor Writers Association of California) and NOWA (Northwest Outdoor Writers' Association).

Robert has hiked every trail in the *Day Hike Book* series. With 22 hiking guides in the series, many in their third and fourth editions, he has hiked thousands of miles of trails throughout the western United States and Hawaii. When Robert is not hiking, he researches, writes and maps the hikes before returning to the trails. He spends summers in the Rocky Mountains of Montana and winters on the California Central Coast.